THE EVOLVED SELF

THE EVOLVED SELF
MAPPING AN UNDERSTANDING
OF WHO WE ARE

by Lloyd Hawkeye Robertson, PhD

University of Ottawa Press
2020

University of Ottawa Press
Les Presses de l'Université d'Ottawa

The University of Ottawa Press (UOP) is proud to be the oldest of the francophone university presses in Canada as well as the oldest bilingual university publisher in North America. Since 1936, UOP has been enriching intellectual and cultural discourse by producing peer-reviewed and award-winning books in the humanities and social sciences, in French and in English.

www.press.uOttawa.ca

Library and Archives Canada Cataloguing in Publication

Title: The evolved self : mapping an understanding of who we are / Lloyd Hawkeye Robertson, Ph.D.
Names: Robertson, Lloyd Hawkeye, 1950- author.
Description: Includes bibliographical references and index.
Identifiers: Canadiana (print) 20200206699 | Canadiana (ebook) 20200206710 | ISBN 9780776629308 (softcover) | ISBN 9780776629346 (hardcover) | ISBN 9780776629315 (PDF) | ISBN 9780776629322 (EPUB) | ISBN 9780776629339 (Kindle) Subjects: LCSH: Self. | LCSH: Culture. | LCSH: Memes. | LCSH: Counseling. | LCSH: Psychotherapy.
Classification: LCC BF697 .R57 2020 | DDC 155.2—dc23

Legal Deposit: Third Quarter 2020
Library and Archives Canada

Production Team

Copy editing   James Warren
Proofreading   Michael Waldin
Typesetting   John van der Woude, JVDW Designs
Cover design   Steve Kress

Cover image

Places to Stand by Jimy Sloan, 2016, 92 x 92 cm

The University of Ottawa Press gratefully acknowledges the support extended to its publishing list by the Government of Canada, the Canada Council for the Arts, the Ontario Arts Council, the Social Sciences and Humanities Research Council and the Canadian Federation for the Humanities and Social Sciences through the Awards to Scholarly Publications Program, and by the University of Ottawa.

ONTARIO ARTS COUNCIL
CONSEIL DES ARTS DE L'ONTARIO
an Ontario government agency
un organisme du gouvernement de l'Ontario

Canada Council   Conseil des arts
for the Arts   du Canada

Canadä

u Ottawa

Table of Contents

List of Figures

List of Tables

CHAPTER 1

Necessity and Invention
in Counselling

"Suzie" had experienced five suicide attempts.[1] Her previous therapist said the seventeen-year-old had been compliant with
treatment but remained "high risk." She obtained elevated scores
for low self-esteem, anger, suicide ideation, and depression on a
standardized measure of suicide probability administered during
our first session.

I attempted to normalize some of Suzie's experiences and
reframe others so as to place responsibility on the perpetrator of emotional and physical abuse (her father) and to help her see herself as a
competent actor and increasingly able problem solver over time. We
co-developed behavioural "homework" assignments that included
positive affirmations, meaningful and enjoyable activity, regular
physical activity, and reality testing to discover the accuracy (or inac-
curacy) of perceived slights from teachers, family, and peers. I had her
retell her "story" with suggested amendments to engender hope. Eye
Movement Desensitization and Reprocessing (EMDR) was used to
deal with specific instances of childhood trauma. Suzie participated
in all suggested activities, but her increasing levels of distress led me
to conclude the methods we were using were not being effective. A
re-referral at this point would have further accentuated the youth's
sense of hopelessness, so with an affected air of assurance, I suggested that we create a map of her self to find what was keeping her
from responding to treatment.

Mapping and Modifying the Self of a Client in Therapy

Viewing the self as a representational cultural construct (Blustein & Noumair, 1996; Dennett, 1995; Mead, 1912/1990; Shotter, 1997), I asked Suzie to prioritize four lists: 1) self-defining roles, 2) qualities she liked about herself, 3) changes she would make to herself if she could, and 4) things she believed to be true. Each unit of self-representation represented a small unit of culture. Following the lead of Dawkins (1976), I called these elemental units "memes." In the physical world, the existence of nuclear, electromagnetic, or gravitational forces leads to a structuring of matter, so I looked for analogous mental forces that could similarly result in mental structures. Shared affective, behavioural, and connotative characteristics present as forces of attraction. For example, a meme given the title "heart-shaped boxes" was associated, in the client's mind, with romantic love, and an "attractive force" was represented as a line connecting the two in figure 1.1. She experienced wistfulness coupled with feelings of emptiness and loss associated with these boxes, which she collected and displayed. I viewed this behaviour as a dramatic expression of her associated emotions, so the meme was linked to another labelled "dramatic person." By linking memes sharing connotative, affective, or behavioural dimensions with those prioritized by the client as more difficult to change closer to the centre, the self-structure pictured in figure 1.1 emerged.

Some readers will recall that grunge rock artist Kurt Cobain committed suicide in 1994 after recording a song titled "Heart-Shaped Box." Given Suzie's worldview, Goth-like appearance, and taste in music, it is likely she was influenced by this recording, but in adopting the meme, she necessarily gave it her own interpretation. Suzie also made a connection with popular culture in reporting that she compulsively rereads *The Bell Jar,* a book about a depressed and suicidal youth; the book title is represented in figure 1.1 as a self-identifying meme connected to memes labelled "suicidal" and "writer."

The meme labelled "depressed person" forms a hub or core connected to eight other memes, such as "ugly," "suicidal," and "father hater." Rumination may be predicted once consciousness is focused on this depressive cluster since the number of cognitive pathways to other parts of the self is limited. Figure 1.2 illustrates this ruminative cycle.

This client's cognitions could begin at any point along the paths reproduced in figure 1.2 and lead to suicidal thoughts. A feedback loop is illustrated leading from "dependent" to "insecure" to

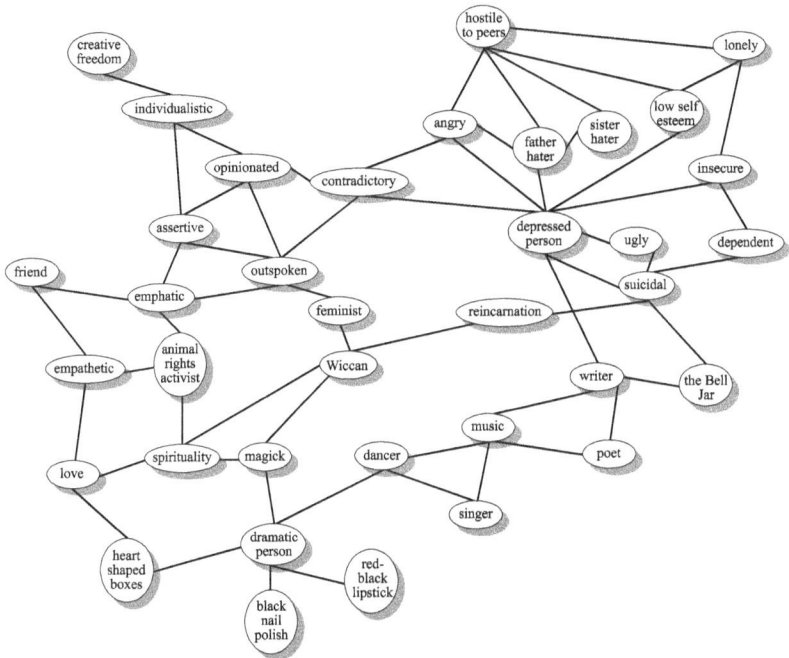

FIGURE 1.1. *Initial self-map of Suzie with edges between memes representing shared connotative, affective, or behavioural dimensions.*

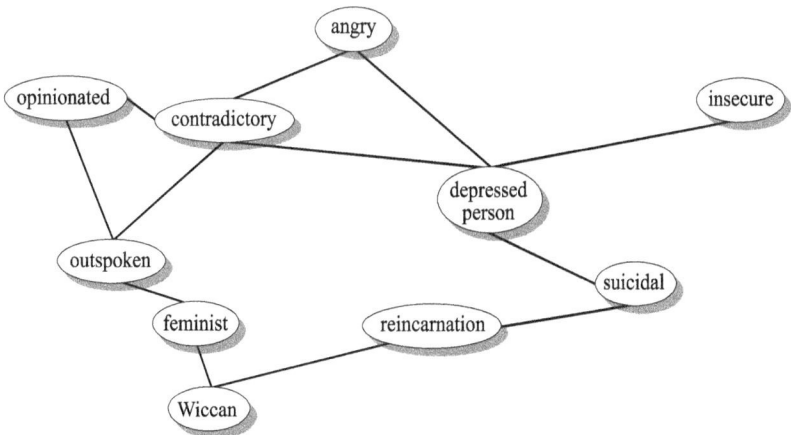

FIGURE 1.2. *An illustration of memetic self-map paths or routes leading to suicide ideation in the self of "Suzie."*

"depressed person" and returning to "suicidal." Rumination is thus circular, leading to increased client distress. While the most common pathway to suicidal thoughts is through depression, an alternate route leading from the client's beliefs in Wicca to reincarnation to suicide ideation is also illustrated.

Sequentially linked memes, as illustrated above, may be viewed as cognitive scripts leading to patterned behaviours within an overarching self-defining narrative. The self that is the protagonist in such narratives may be mapped so as to identify and graphically represent internal relationships and thematic possibilities. Returning to the total representation in figure 1.1, it can be seen that the removal of "depressed person," "suicidal," and "angry," without first preparing alternatives, would lead to fragmentation of the self as pictured. Operating on the assumption that most people, especially those who are depressed or suicidal seek self-stability (De Man & Gutierrez, 2002), I recommended that Suzie restructure her self in some ways before focusing on removing her depression and suicide ideation identifiers.

The meme "animal rights activist" in figure 1.1 was an earlier reframe of angry client behaviour associated with perceived cruelty to dogs and cats. Although animals are not human, we used this meme to inspire and inform a new thematic core, "human rights," in figure 1.3. That new meme included a behavioural injunction to fight for social justice.

The preparation of a new core meme involved examining, and in some cases reframing, those memes already present. Suzie had challenged teachers and other adults over the rights of children and youth, which resulted in her seeing herself as "outspoken." She believed that females generally suffered from sexism, and she embraced feminism. She believed that the Christianity of her parents was oppressive, and she embraced an alternative religious belief system (Wicca). She described herself as emphatic and empathetic.

Established memes were conscripted to support the new persona. For example, she had written prose and poetry focusing on her depression, and she read books that reinforced a negative and pessimistic view of life. With this new human rights shift, she began to read material that supported her views about animal, children's, and women's rights, and about her emerging views on spirituality. With encouragement, she began to write poetry and prose in support of her passionately held beliefs. She published some of her writings in a

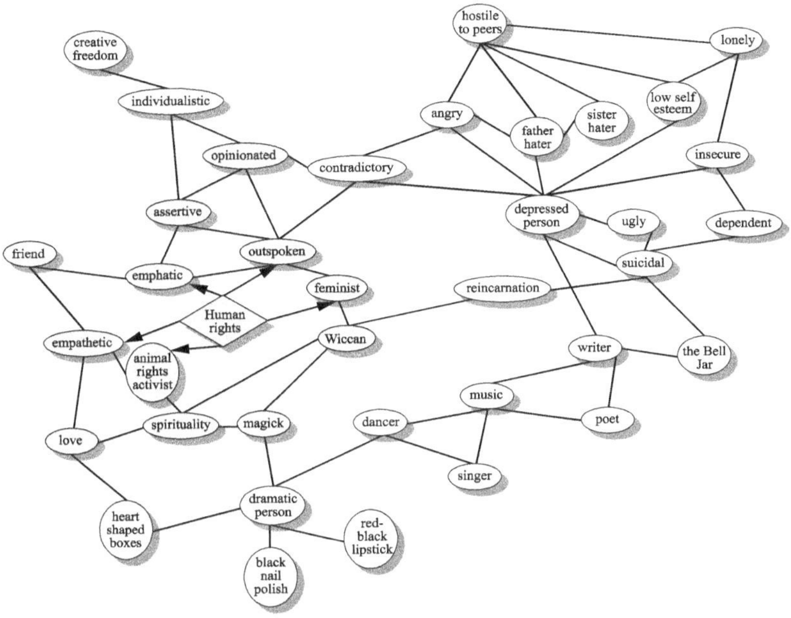

FIGURE 1.3. *A revised memetic self-map of a suicidal youth showing the location of a co-constructed new meme, "human rights," with supporting memes tinted in grey.*

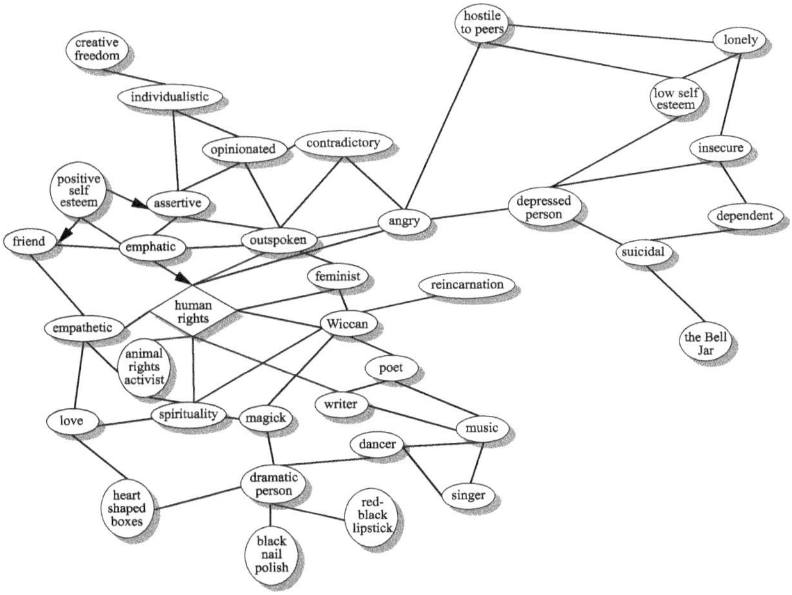

FIGURE 1.4. *Self-map illustrating changes in self-definition resulting from "homework assignments" designed to support the new core meme "human rights."*

student newspaper and was surprised by the positive regard she was given by peers. Her anger, which had been directed inwardly, reinforcing her depressive and suicidal self-representations, now became increasingly focused externally in the service of social interest. These changes are represented in figure 1.4.

Suzie developed a plan to move in with an aunt in a neighbouring community. She found that her writing, which still had an anti-establishment flavour, was accepted by a new group of friends with similar views. She began dressing differently and discovered that she was considered attractive. The meme "hostile to peers" withered and then disappeared. Suzie's mother and sister followed her in leaving her father, who at one time loomed quite large in her life, though now appeared as a pathetic derelict who could not take care of himself. Suzie lost much of her anger, but a level of disgust remained. She now saw herself as empowered to positively affect her future.

Over the course of about seven months, the new core we had developed became increasingly central to Suzie's self-definition, while those memes supporting her "depressed person" meme became fewer in number. We were then able to eliminate "depressed person" from her identity and reframe depression as an emotional state that we may sometimes experience without it defining who we are. She subsequently scored within the nonclinical range on a standardized test for suicide risk, and therapy was terminated. Suzie's mother called a year later to say that her daughter was doing very well socially and academically.

The method of preparing memetic self-maps described here may be understood using a branch of mathematics called Graph Theory (Robertson & McFadden, 2018). In GT the units represented in ovals (memes) would have been called "vertices" or "nodes." Connecting lines are called "edges" or "arcs." Proximity between memes gave the sense of greater attraction, and with GT it would be possible to quantify that attraction using edge line weight. In figure 1.1 we saw that the meme "depressed person" is connected to eight adjoining memes (in GT, degree = 8), supporting its designation as a core of the self-structure. As we saw in figure 1.2, sequential patterning can be observed between proximate memes with routes identified for habitual thoughts. Seen through the lens of GT, memetic self-mapping is a mathematical way of visualizing a naturally occurring phenomenon. As we shall see, it is also compatible with various heretofore competing lenses within the discipline of psychotherapy.

The Call of This Research

Notions of self-concept, self-esteem, self-actualization, and self-validation predominate in psychology, yet the core concept to which these constructs refer is less well understood. Eric Erikson wrote, "The ability to form intimate relationships depends largely on having a clear sense of self" (2003, p. 98). William Bridges (1980, 2001) tied his theory of adult transition to changes in this "self." The self was one of four pillars that Schlossberg, Waters, and Goodman (1995) used to understand how individuals cope with life transitions. According to Seigel (2005), the self "distinguishes you or me from others, draws the parts of our existence together, persists through changes, or opens the way to becoming who we might or should be (p. 3)."How do we come to have a particular understanding of our selves? What keeps selves sufficiently stable that they are recognizable to their "owners" and others? If it is a matter of belief, why is it difficult to change unwanted aspects of the self? To what degree did the mapping exercise contribute to the successful outcome in Suzie's case?

The idea of self as used here is intertwined with the notion of culture. We are defined according to information provided by our families, friends, communities, and society in conceptual units learned within our cultural milieu. Mapping the self is thus a relational activity concerned with both internal structure and external influences or determinants.

Readers will recall that Suzie was asked to prepare and prioritize four lists of self-descriptors. Memes were defined as having an affective dimension. Was this dimension sufficient to understand the emotional pain experienced by Suzie during initial stages of treatment? What mechanisms serve to maintain dysfunctional selves irrespective of the emotional pain involved?

Inter-meme attraction could serve to keep dysfunctional elements within the self in place. For example, "depressed person" was core to Suzie's initial self-representation. One can imagine that attempts to remove this meme from her self before an alternate core was prepared led to feelings of anxiety associated with structural instability that, in turn, served to draw depression back into her self. If a stable self feels better than no self at all, then one might unconsciously work to preserve those aspects of one's self that are familiar. We could understand this interaction as the individual unconsciously *choosing* to maintain dysfunctionality; however, at another level of abstraction, the dysfunctional meme is repelling more positive self-descriptors.

Dawkins (1976, 1982) was accused of inventing a tautology with respect to his presumption of memetic attraction and repulsion (Coyne, 1999; Gabora, 2004). It is not enough to suggest that the spread and persistence of specific memes in a given population are evidence of attractive forces. It is conceivable that units of culture spread due to survival value or due to conscious rational choice. If a mechanism can be demonstrated by which memetic attraction could occur, and if examples of such occurrences are found, then the tautological challenge would be answered.

Western philosophical thought has had an inordinate concern for matters of the self, and that is where we begin to answer some of these questions. Chapter 2 takes the reader through an exploration of that tradition and the schools of psychology concerned with such constructs as self-concept, self-esteem, and self-actualization. Flowing from the concerns of cross-cultural psychologists questioning of the relevance of "Western" therapies, chapter 3 explores some examples of self from outside the Euro-American tradition.

I return to Dawkins's meme in chapter 4. If the self can be construed as composed of elemental units of culture, as I argue it can, then it can be visualized and mapped. I argue that such an understanding of the self is compatible with Western[2] philosophical thought, cross-cultural evidence, and the practice of various schools of psychology. I also suggest an account of self as an evolved cultural construct that is compatible with existing knowledge.

The research method used, "Transcendental Realism" (Miles & Huberman, 1994), differs from the better known Grounded Theory in that qualitative data is used to elaborate, extend, or correct an existent theory. Miles and Huberman contend, "Qualitative research may determine causal relationships by 1) establishing temporal precedence, 2) constant conjunction, and 3) contiguity of influence" (p. 146). The theory of self elaborated in the first four chapters is tested using this method and the results are reported in chapter 5. Detailed self-maps of eleven individuals from both individualist and collectivist cultures were prepared and reviewed by the participants for accuracy and personal resonance. The power of qualitative research is enhanced by diversity, and this sample includes participants whose self-development has been enhanced through sports, primordial North American cultures, and secular humanism. In addition, the selves of two individuals from outside North America (Russia and China) are mapped.

Chapter 6 explores support for a cognitivist view and extends that view by applying the mathematical small-world network model to our theoretical understanding of self. Internal tension is noted between individualist and collectivist principles, and within this context, the evolution of religion is discussed.

The final chapter discusses the utility of memetic self-mapping to counselling practice. The case of the suicidal youth discussed in this chapter is reviewed along with a new case study. Cross-cultural implications of using self-mapping are reviewed. It is noted that memetic self-mapping has broad application across schools of therapeutic practice and may point to a uniting paradigm in psychology.

Notes

1 For the complete case study, see Robertson (2011c).
2 The term "western" is ordinarily used as an adjective designating a geographic relationship but where it is used as a proper noun designating a culture or a civilization it is capitalized in this document.

CHAPTER 2

The Self Within
Euro-American Thought

The self mapped in chapter 1 is a cognitive representation. Linked associated memes may be viewed as cognitive pathways forming narrative outlines, with the individual as protagonist. Suzie changed her self in ways to suggest increased self-actualization. If it is a possession as in the sentence "I have a self," then the owner who may then, presumably, acquire a better self, needs to be identified. If the self were to be viewed as a description of who we are, then that description must reference our material existence; however, a body as the owner of such a self would lack the consciousness necessary to realize its ownership and would not, therefore, have the capacity to make the statement "I have a self." Descartes (1643/1990) attempted to resolve this problem by picturing the self as a manifestation of an ethereal soul that can observe the world with detached disinterest because it was not of the world, it was of God. Thus, Cartesian dualism separated the mind from the world on both logical and religious grounds (Pickering & Skinner, 1990), but this dualism predates Christianity.

Both Aristotelian and Platonic schools in classical Greece also equated the self with the soul or mind, which was, in turn, seen as a spiritual force animating a physical being. The Aristotelian man had vegetative, sensitive, and intellectual souls, the combination of which explained behaviour. Platonic souls were multidimensional spiritual selves trapped in and animating bodies of matter. While carrying forward the assumption of primacy for the non-physical or spiritual, Christianity amended Plato by viewing the self as wilful individualism to be renounced so that the soul could be saved in submission to the will of a higher power (Cushman, 1995; Marx & Engels, 1892/1975; Pagels, 1989). This could not entirely remove the self from the picture since such an entity had to have a degree of self-consciousness to make that decision. By restoring the spirit of inquiry to the self as an activating part of mind, Descartes laid the groundwork for secular knowledge while at the same time limiting it:

> It was Descartes' philosophy that gave the incipient dualism of earlier times a sophisticated, logical base. In order to keep God in the picture of a material world then emerging from the findings of "natural philosophy," Descartes had offered the concept of a formal separation of mind and matter. This left scientists free to regard the physical world as subject to cause and effect while the mind remained the ever-mysterious seat of innate, spiritual essences, amenable to non-natural influences. It was a contribution that gave a huge spur to what became known as the physical sciences, for it freed them from the strictures of supernatural religion. But its effect on social science has been disastrous to this day. (Hutcheon 1996, 41)

Hobbes referred to Cartesian dualism as "the Error of Separated Essences." The state or "commonwealth" was all that protected the citizen from a state of nature where life was "nasty, brutish and short." Thus the citizen owed absolute allegiance to the sovereign whose duty it was to "lay down an authoritative interpretation of the Bible, and authoritative moral principles, for them" (Watkins 1964, 51). In this view, the uncontrolled rational mind was a danger to all.

David Hume (1739/2010) said reason evolved within a state of nature to serve more primal human desires: "Reason is, and ought only to be the slave of the passions, and can never pretend to any other office than to serve and obey them" (sec. 3, para. 4). The self is a bundle of perceptions and sensations served by an evolved form of reason based on certain unprovable premises, such as casual regularity.

With secularization, the self became understood as a psychological representation held within the mind. William James (1890) suggested a unity of mind and body: "The thought is the thinker ... for if my thinking is confused, I am confused: if my thought is blocked, I am blocked" (p. 401). Rom Harre (1991) despaired, "The self that manages and monitors its own actions and thoughts is never disclosed as such to the person whose Self it is. It is protected from even the possibility of being studied empirically by its very nature. Whenever it tries to catch a glimpse of itself it must become invisible to itself, since it is that very self which would have to catch that very glimpse. It is known only through reason" (pp. 52–53).

This chapter examines the use of reason, supplemented empirically where possible, to discern the self within psychological traditions emanating from post-Enlightenment Europe. It would be expected that a culture that once equated the self with an eternal independent soul would be predisposed to gifting it attributes of permanence, and it is with that perspective that we begin.

The Unitary Stable Self

The early twentieth-century triumvirate of Alfred Adler, Sigmund Freud, and Carl Jung agreed that individuals exhibited sufficient stability that a process of psychotherapy was required to effect change. Freud and Jung emphasized unconscious forces of phylogenetic origin with implications of determinism. Stability is achieved through a balance of genetic and cultural forces and not through the efforts of a self whose pretensions to free will are highly illusory. Adler, however, described psychological mechanisms for understanding a self that is both conscious and stable.

According to Adler (1967), the first task of therapy is to prove the "unity in each individual—in his thinking, feeling, acting; in his so-called conscious and unconscious—in every expression of his personality" (p. 69). Once this understanding is achieved then the client's underlying unitary belief system may be challenged. Adler (1927/1957) discovered that his adult patients had self-defining convictions consistent with a "secret goal" to compensate for felt inferiority in childhood. Such self-defeating goals must be revised if the client is to reach self-actualization. Resistance to change was countered by appealing to an innate drive he called "striving for perfection."

Does the implication that human beings are born with a teleological impulse for perfection imply a transcendent self? The Adlerian self does not come strapped to a pre-existent soul but is learned by children as they negotiate their way through family-of-origin structures. Having been born in an inferior position, the child's goal is to compensate for that weakness by establishing a role within the family. For example, an oldest child, reared in an authoritarian family that emphasizes educational achievement, may attempt to embody those values and will define himself accordingly. The second oldest will then be forced to find a niche not already occupied by the oldest. If, in the process, the child comes to believe that importance or self-worth is achieved through attention, power, revenge, or withdrawal, then those will become goals in adulthood. Such individuals would like to pursue socially useful goals such as cooperation, productivity, and creativity, but when discouraged return to their secret childhood goals. Adler's "striving for perfection" drive is thus defined subjectively. Self-actualization involves transcending one's insecurities within a framework of social interest. In a reflection of Hobbes, we are dependent on the collectivity to thrive; therefore it is in our interest to promote the collective well-being (Adler, 1967). Unlike Hobbes, Adler did not view it necessary to sublimate the self to a sovereign so that the collectivity could be preserved.

Research has supported Adler's theory of birth order with respect to the intergenerational transmission of values (Kulik, 2004), gender (Koch, 1956), and Myers-Briggs typology (Stansbury & Coll, 1998). Family life may be seen as preparation for the child to define themselves and their relationship to society. The felt experiences of the second-oldest child will necessarily be different from those of the oldest if for no other reason than the latter does not have an older sibling as part of the family matrix. It might be expected that transitional periods involving instability would create increased instability in children's self-descriptors, but this is not always the case. Kwiatkowska (1990) predicted that children beginning elementary school would face instability as compared to preschoolers because they were engaged in a transition to an unfamiliar environment (school); however, on measures of self-continuity and distinctiveness, older children scored higher for both change and stability of self-descriptors. While this finding supports the idea that self-stability is developmentally connected to maturation, other writers have suggested that the self as a stable entity occurs in late adolescence or early adulthood (Damon & Hart, 1988; Harter, 2012; Leahy & Shirk, 1985).

The notion that the adult self exhibits temporal stability has received considerable support (Blustein & Noumair, 1996; Corey & Corey, 2003; Jopling, 2000; Savickas, 2001), and much of what psychologists have called "client resistance" may be traced to the need to preserve it. As we saw with the case study in chapter 1, even a dysfunctional self may be preferable to instability, with change discounted as inauthentic.

Adlerian psychotherapy includes a review of childhood experiences to produce insight into the client's "secret goal," with the hope of overcoming the stability factor with respect to those aspects of the self requiring change. Sometimes a client's "secret goal," when it is consciously understood, can be incorporated into a socially useful plan. For example, a person whose belief is that personal significance is achieved only when one is noticed could become an entertainer. While the ultimate goal of therapy would be to ensure that self-significance is achieved whether the individual receives attention or not, conversion to a completely new self is not considered possible, or even desirable. Self-actualization involves developing potential flowing from an existing structure. To this end, Adler took the position that the client is the expert on his or her self and that therapy was a collaborative effort between experts.

In providing career and vocational counselling to adults, Savickas (2001) used Holland's (1997) six personality types (realistic, investigative, artistic, social, enterprising, and conventional) to demonstrate in each a "dispositional signature" linked to a set of adaptive strategies. Each Holland type represents a stable core to self-defining narratives used to interpret the world:

> These internalized narratives of the self usually include reflective descriptions about how the individual adapted to tasks and traumas. These narratives do more than explain where individuals have been and who they hope to become. By constructing a plot, the narratives address the question of "Who am I?" The plot explains how they are agentic and to whom they feel connected. These stories of competence and connection impose a narrative structure on lived experience, one that explains the purpose and meaning of life. (Savickas, 2001, pp. 309–310)

The self, then, consists of a stable core that includes personality traits around which a narrative is constructed. No attempt is made to change the core self, and in this example occupations are selected that are compatible with its demands.

Bridges (2001) saw the stability of the self as a problem. He suggested that painful adult transitions, as occur when grieving the death of a loved one, involve the feeling of being in limbo, in a "neutral zone," while "a new self is gradually being formed" (p. 3). Fear of change leads people to resist beneficial transitions. Reflecting on his own personal experience with his wife's infidelity and her subsequent death, he reported that the only way one obtains wisdom is by going through such "life transitions" at which point "you see the old world with new eyes and understand it in depth" (p. 183).

Bridges (2001) proposed a three-stage model of transition, beginning with an ending, living through a neutral zone, and then a new beginning. He postulated that transitions can be developmental, in the sense that the individual makes a conscious decision to change in some ways, or they may be reactive to an unforeseen crisis or events where the direction of self-change is imposed by circumstance. He predicted that in those reactive cases the individual will tend toward minimal change to maintain the stability of the self:

> I had always told my clients that if you let go of only the external (the person and the relationship itself), but didn't let go of the internal associations that had come to cluster around it, you would just find another person or relationship and attach the same hopes, fears, dreams, and beliefs to that one. That way, you would go through a change but not a transition—and you could count on ending up right back where you started. (p. 59)

Transitions take longer than change because the former involves the development of "a replacement reality and a new self" (Bridges 2001, p. 3). He predicted that once we have said goodbye to our old self, we will be in a neutral zone, a condition similar to grieving, while the new self is being constructed. The self-mapping exercise reviewed in chapter 1 demonstrated that self-change requires a reference to that which does not change at the transitional moment. We need aspects of identity, perhaps trait-based, upon which substantial change may be built. Savickas (2001) raised the intriguing possibility that a stable core may be masked by narratives. Later in this chapter, I will examine this possibility through the literature on constructivist and social constructionist selves. First, I will ground our understanding of the self through current neurological research.

Neurological Considerations in Understanding Self

While the self was once equated with an immaterial soul, it was also tied to the body in some ways. Descartes (1643/1990) thought he found the corporeal seat of the soul in the pineal gland. In 1911, Freud convinced

Jung of the importance of phylogenetic factors in the formulation of mind, and this concept continued to play an important role in subsequent theoretical formulations (P. T. Hoffer, 1992). Freud placed inherited drives present at birth in the unconscious id, but environmental and social constraints forced the development of an ego to temper its instinctual demands. It would be tempting to equate the conscious ego with the self; however, in discussing a patient who described himself as petty, egoistic, and dishonest, Freud (1917) wrote, "It would be fruitless from a scientific and a therapeutic point of view to contradict a patient who brings these accusations against his ego" (p. 246). That which accuses the ego must stand apart from it. Since the superego, as the seat of society's normative expectations, cannot be individually sentient Freud concluded, "We show in him one part of the ego sets itself over against the other, judges it critically, and, as it were, take it as its object" (p. 247). The self in this example included that part of the superego that set a standard or measure against which a volitional part of the ego made a critical judgment. An alternate interpretation would be that the entire triadic structure is the self which may then be divided into the "self-as-subject" and "self-as-object" for the purpose of linguistic analysis.

Following his split with Freud, Jung declared a collective unconscious to be part of a shared phylogenetic layer. By suggesting that archetypes are genetically encoded, instinctive, preconfigured patterns of action, Jung (1917/1972; 1981) reduced the importance of cultural transmission in understanding behaviour. The self is an archetype that encompasses both the conscious and the unconscious but is also the centre of the total personality. The notion that this centre moves from the ego to a point close to the unconscious during individuation recapitulates the early Christian belief that the self must be renounced so that it may merge with the divine.

Both Freud and Jung provide models of understanding human behaviour grounded in assumptions of determinism. The id is a repository of instinctual drives, and in managing its demands the overworked ego must also accommodate a culturally determined superego. For Jung even that culture is, in part, genetically determined through the medium of inherited archetypes held in the collective unconscious.

Freud posited the existence of unconscious psychological mechanisms that protected the psyche by repressing traumatic memories. He referred to conscious attempts at forgetting as suppression. In one experiment involving functional magnetic resonance imaging

(Anderson, et al., 2004) college students appeared to demonstrate the ability to suppress memories, thus supporting Freud's theory of the unconscious, but as Loftus and Garry (2004) noted, the instruction to suppress was only successful 10% of the time and did not involve trauma. Nonetheless, we need to consider that the self may consist of both conscious and unconscious elements, some of which may have been repressed.

Neurosurgeon Wilder Penfield (1975/1990) found that the stimulation specific areas of patients' neocortexes resulted in motor activity in some and sequential memories in others. He noted,

> When I have caused a conscious patient to move his hand by applying an electrode to the motor cortex of one hemisphere ..., invariably his response was: "I didn't do that. You did.".... When I caused the record of the stream of consciousness to run again and so presented to him the record of his past experience, he marvelled that he should be conscious of the past as well as the present ... He assumed at once that somehow the surgeon was responsible for the phenomenon. (p. 123)

Penfield failed to find any place in the cerebral cortex where stimulation caused a patient to believe or decide, and he concluded that "free will" must come from an external supernatural source. Greenfield (1995) observed that the memories stimulated in such a way had a dream-like quality, and the stimulation of the same cortical area sometimes produced different memories. She suggested that different parts of the brain needed to be stimulated concurrently to produce the sensation of will.

While working with patients who suffered from Alzheimer's, epilepsy, akinetic mutism, and anosognosia, Damasio (1999) observed, "Consciousness may be separated from wakefulness and low-level attention but it cannot be separated from emotion" (pp. 15–16). He concluded that there are two types of self: one autobiographical, necessary for reflective thinking, and another emotion-based proto-self, "a transient entity that is ceaselessly re-created for each and every object with which the brain interacts" (p. 17). He identified four neural centres, two limbic and two neocortical, by which the body unconsciously maps out its states and forms such a proto-self. Demonstrating unity between science and philosophy, Damasio's proto-self is a neurological analogue of Kant's "transcendental self"—that which must have prior existence so that self-recognition can occur—while his "autobiographical self" is similar to Kant's "empirical self."

Using neuroimaging, Arzy, Thut, Mohr, Michel, and Blanke (2006) investigated two distinct brain mechanisms, the temporoparietal junction and the extrastriate body area, by which the body situates itself. In the course of this investigation, they demonstrated how body position affects self-representations with respect to embodied and disembodied (as in imagined) self-location. They suggested that pathologies involving the disembodied self could be explained by the activities of brain structures responsible for spatially situating the embodied self.

In contrast to classical autism, "high-functioning" individuals with Asperger's Syndrome have a sense of self but are nonetheless unable to relate to others in socially expected ways. Using magnetic resonance imaging, Uddin et al. (2008) investigated brain responsiveness to images of the subjects' own faces and the faces of others in these "high-functioning" individuals and compared their responses with those of normally developing children. While both groups activated a right premotor/prefrontal system when identifying images of themselves, only the normally developing children used this system while processing the images of others. Deficits in neural activation may lead to an inability to recognize others as beings like ourselves with similar beliefs, desires, and perspectives. Bjorklund and Blasi (2005) noted that this "theory of mind" appears at about the same time and in the same sequence in most children around the world.

Gazzaniga (2000) reviewed a series of experiments with subjects whose corpus callosum had been severed. Experimenters were able to communicate visually with each hemisphere without the other hemisphere being aware of that communication. In one such experiment, conducted with fellow neurosurgeon Roger Sperry, a patient's left hemisphere was shown a chicken and his right hemisphere was shown a snow fall. Each hemisphere was asked to select a picture from a group of pictures that went with what they saw. The left hemisphere picked a claw and the right picked a snow shovel. When presented with both choices and asked why he made those choices patient P.S. stated, "Oh, that's simple. The claw goes with the chicken and you need a shovel to clean out the chicken shed" (2000, Studies on Consciousness, para. 5). Similar experiments with other patients showed a left hemispheric ability to narrate a plausible (but false) story from disconnected pieces of information.

Pinker (2002) concluded this research demonstrated that each hemisphere generates a "self," with the left weaving a coherent but false account of behaviour generated by the right. He described the unified self as an "illusion," and said that Gazzaniga and Sperry had "literally cut the self in two," with each hemisphere exercising "free will without the other one's advice or consent." He concluded, "The conscious mind—the self or soul—is a spin doctor, not the commander in chief" (p. 43). In fact, no selves were severed in this research because the self is a product of left hemispheric activity. Gazzaniga (2000) described the left hemisphere as "a device that begins by asking how one thing relates to another." He concluded that such a device "cannot help but give birth to the concept of self. Surely one question the device would ask is, Who is solving all these problems? Let's call it 'me'—and away it goes!" (p. 1320).

In a related experiment, Wolford, Miller, and Gazzaniga (2000) flashed pictures of red and green cards at the left and right hemispheres of two patients who had their corpora callosa severed in treatment for epilepsy. Patients were told that the cards would appear in random order and that 75% of them would be red. They were asked to predict the next card. In both cases, the right hemispheres tended to repeat the same answer (the red card), ensuring a 75% success rate. The left hemispheres adopted the less promising strategy of attempting to find a pattern.

Using positron emission tomography, Craik et. al. (1999) demonstrated how trait adjectives referenced under four separate positron emission tomography (PET) scan conditions resulted in a unique pattern of neocortical activation under self-referencing conditions. Also using a PET scan technology, Schwartz and Begley (2002) found that "thinking about moving produced brain changes comparable to those triggered by actually moving" (p. 217). They inferred that physical changes in the brain depend on attention focused on a particular activity and not necessarily the physical performance of that activity. They concluded, "The role of attention throws into stark relief the power of mind over brain, for it is a mental state (attention) that has the ability to direct neuroplasticity" (p. 339). Similarly, a person's conscious scripts have been shown to impact on emotional functioning presenting as distinctive patterns of brain activity in functional magnetic resonance imaging (fMRI) scans (Cerqueira, et al. 2010).

By measuring electromyogram changes in subjects, Libet (1985) found that readiness to act typically begins approximately

250 milliseconds before the decision to act. Libet opined, "There is no separate self jumping into the synapses and starting things off. My brain does not need me" (p. 226). He left room for free will, however, by suggesting that the self still has time (approximately 150 milliseconds) to veto an act once the process has started.

A conclusion that consciousness does not direct action (Blackmore, 2002; DiCarlo, 2010) is premature. As Radder and Meynen (2013) concluded, Libet's method was incapable of demonstrating that readiness to act was the cause, a necessary condition, a correlation, or even a regular succession to subsequent action. They apparently reached this conclusion without having read the earlier empirical study of Schurger, Sitt, and Dehaene (2012), who demonstrated that the neuronal activity of the resting brain ebbs and peaks and that voluntary self-initiated movements coincide with these peaks in activity. They described this peak activity as "readiness potential," with the decision to act made some milliseconds after, in accord with Libet's data.

The search for distinctive patterns of neural activity representing the self may be aided through an application of graph theory called "small-world networks." Such networks include a lattice of short path length connecting neighbouring nodes coupled with long-range connections between spatially distant parts of the network (D. J. Watts & Strogatz, 1998). Bassett and Bullmore (2006) described brain activity as a "small-world network" consisting of dense local clusters with short path lengths between nodes or vertices and with relatively few long-range connections linking those clusters. Using fMRI to examine the amplitude of brain activity in a group of subjects undertaking a visual awareness task, Godwin, Barry, and Marois (2015) demonstrated large-scale differences in functional neural connections, consistent with such a model.

While the neurological support for the idea that there is a self located somewhere in the brain is weak, the possibility that the self is an interpretation of a pattern of neural activity has not been discounted. Like most organisms, human animals have the capacity to subconsciously monitor their internal body states. In humans, this capacity has evolved to a capacity to recognize one's mirror image and to situate one's body in time and space. Using those same centres for self-monitoring, most of us have the twin capacity for recognizing others as being like ourselves. This development demands the construction of an autobiographical self whereby the being that is situated in time and space is similar to (but not identical with) others. This, in turn, permits the development of a theory of mind that allows us to predict the motivations of others as, if not identical to our own, at least understandable based on our own experience. Our autobiographical selves may be after-the-fact left hemispheric rationalizations, but they are grounded to the body by emotion that may be summarized as a "feeling of me." A scientific understanding of the cognitive or conscious self constructed under the aegis of such emotive priming needs to be consistent with the findings of neuroscience.

The Constructed Self: Variations on a Theme

We have seen that the self is normally sufficiently stable to allow for the development of continuing relationships and forward planning. We have looked at neurological evidence suggesting both a substratum below ordinary conscious thought that is concerned with self-awareness and a conscious self linked to left hemispheric brain activity. Such evidence is consistent with the constructivist claim that we interpretively construct our selves, but such an agentive constructer must exist outside of the self, at least until the initial self is constructed. Classical behaviourists resolve the issue by declaring the self to be the intersection of social, environmental, and genetic forces with retrospective delusions of agency.

Proponents of both schools would agree that our propensity to see patterns aids in the development of remembered grand narratives in which we play the role of the protagonist. The self then takes on the characteristics of the protagonist and we reinforce a feeling of constancy by playing archetypical roles. Constructivists take this to mean that we create our selves through the choice of roles. Therapy, within this paradigm, consists of building new memories and creating better interpretations of old ones so as to reinforce more satisfying roles. Constancy is maintained by framing these new understandings as "true selves" of which we were not previously aware.

Under this schema, the self is rarely, if ever, torn down like some condemned house to be replaced with a new edifice. We may take out portions of a crumbling structure, buttress the rest, renovate old rooms and add new ones seeking, if not an ideal self, at least one that is more fully functional. In his study of middle-class Madrid children, Torres (1990) attempted to gain insight into the simpler origins of the rambling structure of adulthood by observing sixty children between the ages of five and nine describing themselves during directed play. The older children included psychological characteristics in their self-descriptions without reducing the number of physical descriptors typically used by the younger children. They simply added more abstract conceptualizations to an existent base of concrete descriptors. The construction of the self is accumulative: the old rooms are not torn down; they are still used even as more elegant corridors are added.

While middle-class children may receive cultural supports in building positive identities, people with low status may face demeaning stereotypes. In an ethnographic study, Snow and Anderson (2003) found that US American[1] homeless assert positive individual identities by distancing themselves from other homeless, to whom negative societal descriptors were held to apply. Some engaged in obvious embellishments of their past histories while others emphasized internal moral principles or "street honour." The researchers concluded, "Many of the homeless are active agents in the construction and negotiation of identities as they interact with others. They do not passively accept the social identities their appearance sometimes exudes or into which they are cast" (p. 156). In a challenge to Maslow (1987), the daily struggle to meet basic physiological and safety needs did not preclude attendance to self-esteem and status needs.

Similarly, the chronically ill may have a self-definition at variance with that provided by their physical condition. Charmaz (1990) taught patients to use this "dialectical self" to monitor and externalize messages from the physical self, defining themselves as separate from their wasted and ravaged bodies. While young children begin developing their selves by describing physical characteristics, the terminally ill, in this example, were comforted by removing physicality from their selfhood.

At least some aspects of the self can be controlled by external agents. In 1965, Kenneth Gergen (1996) discovered he was able to easily manipulate the self-esteem of university students. Shocked by the implication the self has no voluntary agency, he ran from quantitative research describing it as a method that constrains results to support deterministic interpretations. His concern that the self is a mere repository of others' attitudes is based on at least two overgeneralizations: 1) that a measure of social effect on one aspect of self, self-concept, translates into a rule about the total self; and, 2) that the context of his research (university students in controlled conditions with a subject matter not necessarily seen by them as fundamental or "core" to themselves) did not impact on the results.

Classical behaviourists refuse to run from the deterministic view: "Every behaviour is considered to be completely determined by antecedent factors, leaving no room for cherished philosophical notions such as free will" (Chambless & Goldstein, 1979, p. 232). The self, then, is an illusion, like the protagonist in an archetypical story, flowing from a functionally unified system of responses. Are behaviourists then merely selfless entities conditioned to utter environmentally determined responses? Chambless and Goldstein sidestep this question by asserting that none of us will ever know what reality is, which if literally true (thus dismissing the notion of proximate objective reality) would mean that none of us has any basis for making any such propositions. B.F. Skinner recognized that self-descriptive behaviour was arranged by the community, but his suggestion that the resultant unified system of responses (the self) forgoes current reinforcers to avoid future aversive consequences or accepts current aversive consequences for the sake of a future reinforcement sounds dangerously close to recognizing that an organism is making decisions based on self-interest.

Smollar and Youniss (1985) used stem completion to assess contextually specific self-esteem. Eighty subjects divided equally into four age groups completed sentences like "When I am with my close friend of the same sex I am _____." Similar questions were asked in different contexts, for example, when with one's mother or father. Responses were coded using a system of content analysis that allowed new codes to emerge from the data. Preadolescents reported changes in self with regard to increases in sociability and cooperation, while late adolescents and young adults indicated increases in intimacy and sensitivity. The researchers concluded that the self was temporally and contextually specific.

It is not surprising that adolescents were more likely to describe themselves as more spontaneous and intimate with close friends than with parents. This result could be interpreted to suggest that self-concept, like Gergen's (1996) self-esteem, is manipulated by those around us. On the other hand, the structure of the stems chosen for completion suggests a definition of self-concept that will change with context. Had the stem structure assumed a unitary self, as in "In stressful situations I try to _____," the results could have been different. It may be the definitions of self-esteem and self-concept are sufficiently fluid that research into these concepts is invariably constrained by the paradigm from which the researcher operates.

The concept of self-efficacy implies an individual sense of empowerment over environmental constraints. Caprara et al. (1998) surveyed 324 adolescents (aged fourteen to eighteen), rating their self-regulatory efficacy, openness of communication with parents, and their involvement in delinquent conduct and substance abuse in an effort to correlate transgressive behaviour with self-efficacy. They concluded that self-efficacy serves to ward off negative peer influences and is accompanied by increased open communication with parents. They found a negative correlation between self-efficacy and delinquency, while a positive correlation was found between delinquency and substance abuse. Perceived self-efficacy had a correlation of -.68 (male) and -.48 (female) with the latent variable "antisocial."

The concepts of delinquency and self-efficacy are diffuse, fluid, and ultimately socially constructed. Had the subjects who scored higher on the delinquency measure operated from a conscious conceptualization of delinquency at variance from that of the dominant cultural society, then their sense of self-efficacy could be expected to be at least as high as those who measured low on the delinquency scale. This consideration lends support to the notion that within the context of the culture in which the study was framed, self-efficacy is linked to more open communication and pro-social behaviours. In any case, the Caprara study belies Gergen's fear that quantitative research necessarily implies a deterministic result.

Still, the determinists have had some impressive results. Classical and operant conditioning has been successfully used in the treatment of performance anxiety (Rodebaugh & Chambless, 2004), alcoholism (Trimpey, 1996), trauma (Devilly & Spence, 1999; Gerrity & Solomon, 2002), and conduct problems (Bloomquist & Schnell, 2002). Following their review of the literature, Warwar and Greenberg (2000) concluded that behavioural techniques by themselves may be as effective as combined cognitive-behavioural techniques. This interpretation would imply that a self, capable of higher order cognitive thought, is not needed, at least for those conditions for which a purely behavioural approach has shown efficacy. It would be expected that behavioural techniques should be effective for those conditions that are themselves a result of conditioning, but it may be that there is a more complex level of cognitive functioning for which purely behavioural solutions would be insufficient. Is it possible for a socially constructed being to transcend the determinants of his construction? Is a unified system of responses capable of achieving self-determined consciousness?

Social Constructionism and the Postmodern Alternative

That which does the self-constructing is assumed but undefined in constructivism. Concomitantly, the idea that the self is a naturally occurring but inert structure like a stalagmite is unsatisfying to those who believe they are "consciousness." Social constructionists seemingly attempt to have it "both ways" by suggesting we both create and are created by the social environment in which we find ourselves starting with the assumption of a mature culture capable of generating individual selves from a menu of possibilities. In explaining this self-construction, George Herbert Mead (1934/2003) proposed that the individual experiences himself "indirectly, from the particular standpoints of other individual members of the same social group, or from the generalized standpoint of the social group as a whole to which he belongs ... He must first become an object to himself only by taking the attitudes of other individuals toward himself within a social environment or context of experience and behaviour in which both he and they are involved" (p. 126).

While such an interdependent self would not be capable of exercising free will at the onset, it provides an explanation as to why some of us cling to negative self-definitions that bring emotional distress instead of simply constructing better selves—those persons we count as significant (or their memories) tend to hold a negotiated self in place. The concept of interdependence also provides an explanation as to why many humans subsume their selves to the will of religious or ideological collectivities. Eric Hoffer (1966) suggested the core of this tendency has to do with negative self-definition: "The frustrated follow a leader less because of their faith that he is leading them to a promised land than because of their immediate feeling that he is leading them away from their unwanted selves" (p. 110). Strong (2000) recognized this social constructionist "dark side," of "selves at the mercy of their social circumstances" (p. 82). The modicum of free will potentially generated by a negotiation between individual and culture is negated by the inequality between the two. Further, while self-efficacy may enhance self-esteem in some contexts (Bandura, 1999; Bandura, Barbaranelli, Caprara, & Pastorelli, 2001; Wiedenfeld, et al., 1990; Witkiewitz & Marlatt, 2004), there remains the suspicion that this self-efficacy is "a positive self-enhancing illusion" (S. E.

Taylor, 1989, p. 7). Gergen (1996) declared the issue to be ideological: he favoured an ideology of communalism, interdependence, and participatory decision-making. The assumption that declaring an issue to be "ideological" allows one to choose a preferred position, without reference to objective measures, has potentially dangerous consequences. Gergen's notion of participatory decision-making presupposes will sufficiently free to allow participants to engage in reflection, discussion, negotiation, and compromise. Stating, in effect, that one believes in free will because of a personal preference gives all competing ideological beliefs equal validity. A more secure grounding of the espoused ideal would be offered by a description of the self and free will compatible with existing evidence; however, if one chooses to question the very idea of objective inquiry, then any methodology will be perceived as inconclusive. The leading hermeneutic philosopher of the twentieth century challenged all science from this perspective:

> Basic concepts determine the way we get an understanding beforehand of the area of subject matter underlying all the objects a science takes as its theme, and all positive investigation is guided by this theme ... But since every such area is itself obtained from the domain of entities themselves, this preliminary research, from which the basic concepts are drawn, signifies nothing else than an interpretation of those entities with regard to their state of Being. (Heidegger, 1962, p. 30)

With this understanding there can never be any one correct interpretation (Patton, 2002), and the challenge is to "enlarge the scope of our interpretation"(Packer, 1989, p. 106). "One engages in a hermeneutic approach to data in order to derive a better understanding of the context that gives it meaning" (Rudestam & Newton, 2001, p. 40). The hermeneutic circle is a spiral of deepening understanding as one proceeds through repeated cycles of induction and deduction or, as Rennie (2000) suggests, induction and abduction. The self is understood in the context of the individual's history, culture, and pre-understandings. As an example of this hermeneutic approach, Wilcke (2006) sought a "a totality of meaning in all its relations" with respect to ten refugee women from the former Yugoslav province of Bosnia and Herzegovina. Subjects were asked open-ended questions such as "What is the experience of a woman refugee from the former

Yugoslavia?" and "What helped you survive the experience?" Responses were transcribed and reviewed by the research participants for elaboration.

While this research is true to the notion that the self is a narrative defined according to unique histories, little is offered that is generalizable. We are left with interesting stories of unknown utility. Rennie (2000) suggested that too much caution expressed as reluctance to give rein to researcher subjectivity can result in "missing" the life of the experience under study, while giving undue rein expresses the life of the analyst more than that of the respondents. From this perspective, research is about privileging competing subjectivities.

Narrative therapy applies this hermeneutic approach to psychotherapy. The self is considered to be an understanding based on our interactions with others and our subjective interpretations of our experiences. We are a set of beliefs, arranged in the form of a personal story that we hold to be true. Polkinghorn (1995) explained, "Plots function to compose or configure events into a story by: (a) delimiting a temporal range which marks the beginning and end of the story, (b) providing criteria for the selection of events to be included in the story, (c) temporally ordering events into an unfolding movement culminating in a conclusion, and (d) clarifying or making explicit the meaning events have as contributors to the story as a unified whole" (p. 7).

The materials from which personal stories are constructed are provided by culture. The individual operates within the constraints of social interactions, in effect negotiating their selves with others. Agency rests in the ability to choose a particular story that fits a given context. In narrative analysis, the researcher or therapist develops or discovers a plot that displays linkage between its elements while mindful of alternate interpretations. Events are configured to show how they advance a plot. Power, knowledge production, and institutional practice work together in social settings to produce multiple discourses with the resultant self in constant flux. Edwards (1998) explained, "Self categorizations, like categorizations of other people and of everything else, are discursive actions done in talk, and performative of talk's current business. So the best way to examine them is to find how they are used, and what kinds of discursive business they do, on and for the occasions when they are deployed" (p. 17).

Widdicombe (1998) stated that categories are inference-rich and as such must be evaluated within individual and group contexts.

"Social identities cannot simply be assumed; instead, we need to be sensitive to ways that group membership and non-membership are negotiated, rejected or achieved" (p. 70). Zimmerman (1998), in studying the role of social identities in communication, reproduced a transcript of an attempted conversation between a caller and a professional complaint-taker, where the caller refused to take on the role of client and the complaint-taker refused to give up the role of professional. When neither proved willing to move from the script associated with their chosen role, discourse proved impossible. He concluded that discourse identities are part of a negotiated interactional process providing focus for the type of discourse projected in a spate of talk.

By analyzing interviews with thirty recently divorced or separated individuals and after adding a longitudinal component, Hopper (2003) revealed how our perceptions conform to changing roles. Prior to the decision to divorce, roles were confused, with both parties frequently voicing similar concerns. When one person made the decision to divorce, the discourse changed: "Whatever the specifics of their situations, initiators generally articulated a vocabulary of individual needs and non-initiating partners invoked a vocabulary of familial commitment ... The two vocabularies emerged only after the decision to divorce was made" (pp. 258–59). Hopper's research illustrates how memories change with context and motivation. In a series of experiments spanning decades, Loftus and Ketchum (1994) were able to implant false "repressed" memories of abuse in subjects, which supported "shifting our view from the video recorder model, in which memories are interpreted as the literal truth, to a reconstructionist model, in which memories are understood as creative blendings of fact and fiction" (p. 5). If memories are malleable, then a social constructionist stance, whereby various "truths" are individualized and subjective, seems tenable. Heidegger (1962) extended his critique of science to include all intelligent thought: "Intelligent calculation is oriented towards objects and places them at man's disposal. Its levelling grasp brings all things down to one level: extension and number are its predominant dimensions ... The degeneration of thinking to intelligence can only be overcome by thinking that is more primordial" (quoted in Habermas, 2005, para 4).

Since intelligent thought is degenerate and what passes for truth is dependent on contextual interpretation, how can knowledge claims be made? Heidegger (1962) explained, "Dasein possesses—as constitutive for its understanding of existence—an understanding of the Being of all entities of a character other than its own" (p. 34), concluding, "Dasien is an understanding potentiality-in-Being, which in its Being, makes an issue of Being itself. In every case, I myself am the entity which is in such a manner" (p. 274).

Dasein is a true ontological being or understanding contrasted with the self of modernity, and its existence in him allows Heidegger to transcend both science and relativism. Since only a few are capable of Dasein, the masses must be led. In 1933, he declared a new reality, with the German people "finally coming into their historical destiny, totally inside of and guided by the state" (quoted in Joris, 1989 II, para. 18). German fascism, he believed, would address the "spiritual crisis of the times" (P. A. Johnson, 2000, p. 7) and with its fall at the conclusion of World War II, he concluded that mankind was doomed (Heidegger, 2017).

While it might be tempting to divorce Heidegger's philosophy from his politics, such a view ignores the hermeneutic belief that who we are (and what is accepted as truth) is dependent on historical and social context. Since Heidegger's antecedents are the same for both his philosophy and his political beliefs, we have to assume a relationship. The submission of the ordinary self to the will of a pro-Nazi Dasein reminds us of Heidegger's teaching, as a pre-Jesuit initiate, of the need to renounce the self to submit to a higher power.

Without Dasien, hermeneutics becomes an exercise in relativism. As we have seen, Gergen (1996) viewed ideology to be a matter of personal preference, and he disparaged quantitative research for failing to support that preference. Voicing a concern about this inherent relativism, Doen (1998) wrote, "The great systems of thought like religions, ideologies and philosophies, come to be regarded as 'social constructions of reality.' These systems may be useful, even respected as profoundly true, but true in a new, provisional, postmodern way" (p. 381). He warned that with such relativism accounts of twenty-eight million Amerindian people killed in the Americas as a result of colonial expansion can no longer be taken as objective truth, thus aiding the colonizers. Similarly, the holocaust, global warming, antiviral vaccinations, and racial equality become interpretations subject to individual preference.

With postmodern relativism, each self potentially becomes its own Dasien. Wortham (2001) suggested a self emerges as a person adopts characteristic positions with respect to others. Using textual transcriptions of discussions, interviews, and newscasts, he analyzed a class in Spartan history, the autobiographical story of a woman named Jane, and the news coverage reporter Dan Rather gave then US president George W. Bush. Wortham said a teacher in the Spartan history class "spoke with the voice of a (modern) welfare critic" (p. 38) in defending the custom of leaving sickly babies to die outside Sparta. Jane was described as having two selves—one passive and vulnerable, the other active and assertive. Rather was said to have made Bush speak with the voice of a criminal defendant with respect to alleged inconsistencies in his reasons for invading Iraq.

From a realist perspective, these interpretations might be objectively true (or not), but the researcher, operating from a different perspective, failed to consider and evaluate alternate possible interpretations. The class transcript indicates that the teacher was attempting to speak with the voice of an ancient Spartan leader in a role play. No evidence was presented as to how an actual Spartan leader would have talked differently. Jane, from her teenage years to midlife, consistently presented herself first as a victim and then as an assertive individual in stressful situations. An Adlerian interpretation that she had one self that exercised two favoured coping strategies is also plausible. Finally, if in fact Bush was less than forthright about his adventures in Iraq, then his defensiveness when questioned was to some degree his own voice. The failure to acknowledge and examine evidence for alternative explanations privileges the ideological worldview of the researcher. Dasien inevitably reappears.

Richardson and Fowers (1997) seem to be speaking of this when they suggest that postmodernism sets forth the "ultimately implausible view" that the self is "determined by historical influences," yet is "radically free to reinterpret both itself and social reality, for its own self-invented purposes" (p. 280). To engage in forward planning, any sentient being must begin by accepting, even tentatively, a hypothesis. If human reason and science are discounted as a means for choosing between competing knowledge claims, then this choice will necessarily be made from appeals to authority, intuition, tradition, or various bias-prone heuristics. While such means restrict the selection of effective alternatives by the individual, they are potentially disastrous for any democratic society. Not only do science and reason provide a mechanism to resolve differences, they create an orientation whereby even strongly held beliefs may be deemed to be tentative pending further evidence, allowing people of different worldviews to coexist, with minority opinion respected. This legacy of humanistic tolerance flowing from Enlightenment thought has been undermined by attacks on "modernity" and so-called Western science by detractors who claim "other ways of knowing" have equal or greater validity. Strong (2002) declared science to be a "White, male way of knowing" and that "truth" is something arrived at through the "discourse of knowledgeable people" (p. 3). In premodern societies, these "knowledgeable people" were often religious leaders who formed their own hierarchies of authority based on "knowledge" that was divinely revealed.

In a postmodern world, those who are counted as knowledgeable are opinion leaders who are recognized by those sharing a particular worldview. In effect, this leads to a kind of tribalism between competing Dasiens who fail to recognize others as such. Fundamentalist Christians and Muslims who take a literalist interpretation of their respective holy works would view those religious leaders who support their views as "knowledgeable people" and dismiss scientific evidence that would challenge such beliefs as, at best, misguided and at worst as the work of Satan. Similarly, people who believe that vaccinations cause autism in children would be expected to dismiss "the conspiracy" of scientists who suggest otherwise. Feminists might dismiss evidence that the gender "wage gap" in Euro-American countries is linked to female choice, not discrimination, as a product of "patriarchal backlash." People who wish to dismiss evidence of human contribution to global warming may believe they are "knowledgeable people" and that those promoting this "hoax" are motivated to gain government funding dollars, or perhaps, destroy capitalism. One recent study (Hawkins, Yudkin, Juan-Torres, & Dixon, 2018) found that holders of various belief systems in the United States had coalesced into various large "tribes," each with their own news media, political stance, and recognized knowledge leaders. Not only do these tribes disparage each other, they do not talk to each other.

In a postmodern world orthodoxy cannot be tentative and must be enforced. Mueller (2004) suggested that university Research Ethics Boards in the social and behavioural sciences had shifted focus "away from 'public safety' to such nebulous goals as 'worthwhile topics' and 'socially desirable outcomes'," with such concerns leading to "censorship rather than efforts to protect public safety" (p. 299). He further described a series of "mobbings" by students and staff of academics accused of not following orthodoxy. Since Mueller issued his warning, tenured professors have been dismissed for expressing politically incorrect views; and speakers with views that diverge from accepted orthodoxy have been "deplatformed," that is, disinvited from speaking on campuses. While it is impossible to know how many papers have been refused publication because they challenge accepted orthodoxy, we know of one case of a paper being "de-published" from a reputable journal following sustained political pressure, including death threats. The author had challenged ortho-doxy by listing perceived benefits of colonialism, and it was of sufficient academic merit to have passed a peer review (Gilley, 2017). Conversely, Pluckrose, Lindsay, and Boghossian (2018) tested whether bogus articles would be published in leading "grievance studies" journals if they used the language and promoted the perceived biases of those journals. The answer appears to be "yes, sometimes." For example, articles suggesting that men should be trained like dogs, and that white male students be chained and not allowed to speak in some university classes, were accepted for publication in feminist journals along with a rewrite of a chapter of *Mein Kampf*.

While the relativism that is core to narrative and other current psychotherapies encourages each therapist to be accepting of their cli-ent's interpretive worldview, this is difficult to sustain at the level of the collectivity. By reducing science to "one way of knowing," in effect giving it the same status as a religion, postmodernism removes a non-repressive means for resolving public debate. Competing orthodoxies must then resort to methods of social control to extend and enforce their particular worldviews.

What would social constructionism grounded in realism look like? A realist position is that there is an objective reality outside our-selves that we can discern using rational processes. In such a view, the self is partly determined by genetic and environmental forces but is also partly dependent on culture, which we help to create. There are possible problems. Seigel (2005) suggested, with more than a hint of irony, that constructionists are inferring a Cartesian-like dualism: "Anyone who pictures the self as tightly wrapped up in the cocoon of its social or cultural relations necessarily locates the consciousness that can theorize such containment outside it, thus simultaneously calling forth a different kind of self, ready to take free light on wings whose anatomy descends from pure reflectivity, however much it has been pre-configured as life or some mysterious absent presence" (pp. 649–650). Acknowledging the influence of culture while assuming, in constructionist fashion, agency within that culture has led to an apparent contradiction. This book attempts to answer that contradiction.

Considerations of the Objective and Subjective

The perspectives of the self examined in this chapter are not necessarily mutually exclusive. Neurological research was reviewed demonstrating a built-in mechanism whereby cognitive representations of the self could occur, but the account is further complicated by consideration of inherited predispositions and drives. There are apparent differences between those who contend the self is stable and those who contend it is multiple, but it is possible to conceive of a stable core self cloaked in various facades or presentations that are triggered by context. What is the facade and what is real? Are we free to create our own realities?

Before there were behaviourists, constructivists, or constructionists, James (1892/1999) described the self as a unity consisting of both subject and object, partly known and partly knower. The subjective "I" consists of that which observes while the objective "me" consists of those qualities that are observed. The objective self includes our material possessions including our bodies and the social roles we play which change with context:

> Properly speaking, a man has as many social selves as there are individuals who recognize him and carry an image of him in their mind. To wound any one of these images is to wound him. But as the individuals who carry the images fall naturally into classes, we may practically say that he has as many different social selves as there are distinct groups of persons about whose opinion he cares. He generally shows a different side of himself to each of these different groups. (James, 1892/2003, p. 122)

The subjective "I" includes elements of continuity, distinctness, and volition, which may be thought of as inference built on the "feeling of me" described by Damasio (1999). Mead (1934) suggested a way that the "I" could evolve from the objective "me." The individual develops a cognitive self-structure based on the child's early social precepts as "partial selves—or 'me's'—which are quite analogous to the child's perceptions of his hands and feet, which precede his perception of himself as a whole" (Mead, 1912/1990, p. 198). A unitary self results when these social selves are combined into a "generalized other," which may be viewed as internalized social control. The individual then reacts to this generalized other as though it had the Jamesian subjective elements.

The model of the self developed by James and Mead was based on their own reflective thinking and it fell to others to conduct related empirical research. Damon and Hart (1988) used both quantitative and qualitative methods to study the development of the self in youth ages six to fifteen. Rejecting existing standardized scales, they used open-ended questions like "What are you like?"; "Why is that important?"; "What are you not like?"; "What kind of person are you?"; and "What are you especially proud of about yourself?" to measure the Jamesian objective self. The answers to these questions were then coded for physical, active, social, and psychological responses. The authors also posited a complementary hierarchy of age-related complexity for each categorization: categorical identifications, comparative assessments, interpersonal interpretations, and systematic beliefs and plans. The researchers found a positive correlation between age and modal level, with a tendency toward increasing complexity with age.

Damon and Hart then turned their efforts to measuring the subjective self, which was assessed with questions like "How did you get to be the way you are?" Continuity of self was assessed with questions like "If you change from year to year, how do you know it's the same you?" Questions like "What makes you special?" and "What makes you different from everyone else you know?" were asked to measure the quality of distinctness. Again, interpretive levels were assigned responses. For example, level one of the Agency component was described as "Supernatural, biological or social forces determine the existence or formulation of self" (p. 70). By this categorization, the behaviourists described earlier were operating from the lowest level of Agency! Level 4 of Agency was described as "Personal or moral evaluations of life possibilities influence the existence or formation of the self." An example of a Level 4 response to the question "How did you get to be the way you are?" was, "Well, I decided to be kind to people because I've seen lots of kids hurt other kids' feelings for no reason, and it's not right or fair. Nobody should try to hurt another person's feelings or be mean to them" (p. 71).

With this interpretative template, Damon and Hart (1988) found that a sense of continuity and distinctness develops in an ordered sequence that is preceded by parallel understandings of the objective self. They noted, "During childhood, the sense of identity—continuity and distinctness—is attributed to unchanging self-characteristics. … However, the rapid cognitive, social and physical changes that accompany adolescence makes [sic] this belief in the absolute stability of self-characteristics untenable" (p. 129).

Agency did not correlate significantly with the development of continuity. They concluded that a sense of agency develops through four progressive levels: 1) self-development is seen as nonvolitional, 2) the self's own wishes and desires are considered sufficient to control the evolution of self, 3) self-formation is conceived as a process that occurs within a social matrix, and 4) volitional control of self-formation is derived from deeply held personal values. In an attempt to pre-empt possible criticism that their findings could be culture-bound, they replicated their study in a Puerto Rican fishing village with similar general findings, although the Puerto Rican children were more concerned about relational effects and less concerned about the relative superiority of their actions.

This research forced subject responses into pre-existing categories, and the statistical analysis used to demonstrate longitudinal change was constrained by this categorization. Specifically, the researchers took seven elements representing two characterizations of the self (objective and subjective), and coded responses to those very same elements, thus ignoring the possibility that other elements could have more accurately reflected an individual's self or that there may be an interpretive relationship between elements. Further, given Hart and Damon's (1985) earlier recommendation that reflectivity be added to the Jamesian subjective self, it is surprising they did not attempt to assess it.

In Jamesian fashion, Harre (1991) attempted to resolve the apparent dichotomy between the stable self and the social constructionist position by positing a singular "Self-1" accompanied by "Selves-2" within the person. The idea of agency along with the sense of continuity is embedded in "Self-1.""Selves-2" are based on observed behaviour and accompany the different roles individuals play in the course of their lives. Later, Harre (1998) extended the self into social discourse by adding the idea of "Selves-3," which is how others perceive us. Harre (1984) embedded the Self-1 in the language of indexical pronouns: "I,' the first person pronoun, does have a referential force to a hypothetical entity 'the self,' in much the same way that the gravitational term g refers to a hypothetical entity, the gravitational field" (p. 82). Similar to how the Freudian ego develops from the inter-action of the id and the superego, the "I" then develops a theory about who it is. Like theories in the natural sciences, these theories of self can be amended with further evidence, but unlike natural science theories, we tend to become our self-definition.

Missing from these accounts of a composite self is an under-standing of how cultural and genetic factors interact to produce a self that is at once determined and self-determined. Agency implies free will. The assumption of Plato, Descartes, and Kant that this will was divinely given ignores the fact that any such will must be subject to the parameters of the giver and thus cannot be truly free. The default position for monists has been that the notion of free will is an unnec-essary and distracting abstraction, but attempts to adopt an integrative bio-psychosocial model have met with limited success among those who practise psychotherapy. A study of 136 psychiatrists and psy-chologists in Montréal, Canada, (Miresco & Kirmayer, 2006) found that clinicians continue to make "the same intuitive cognitive sche-mas that people use to make judgments of responsibility leading to dualistic reasoning … The mind-brain dichotomy may persist among mental health professionals because it reflects a basic cognitive schema that is used intuitively to understand human behaviour" (p. 913). In a previous work (Robertson, 2017), I noted that most schools of practice in psychotherapy have emphasized individual choice and empowerment within the therapeutic relationship, and that the rejec-tion of the classical behaviourism paradigm flowed from deeply held cultural assumptions about volition and free will. Free will and its perceived opposite, determinism, may not be mutually exclusive, but the psychological mechanisms by each could be accommodated need exploration. In chapter 4, I propose an evolutionary process that could provide such an explanation. Related to this, the discussion of the self thus far has been within the Euro-American traditions of psychology and philosophy. Does the self have applicability outside that tradi-tion? An examination of the concept in traditional collectivist cultures may help us to answer that question.

Notes

1 It has been a convention to refer to the citizens of the United States of America as "Americans;" however, in this work all people from the Americas are included in that term.

CHAPTER 3

The Self in Collectivist Cultures

Chapter 2 examined perspectives of the self falling within the tradition of post-Enlightenment Euro-American thought. The extent to which we are the product of social learning influences the amount of variability available for self-construction. If our minds were "blank slates" at birth, then from a postmodernist position, there should be an infinite variety of human cultures with a concomitant variety in human selves. If there exists an objective reality, then cultures that best conform to that reality will, in the long run, be more successful with this dynamic constraining variation in both culture and self-construction. Of course, the existence of commonly inherited genetic traits that governed or otherwise influenced behaviour, emotions, and thinking would further constrain cross-cultural variation.

The assumption that newly born children are "blank slates" upon which attitudes, behaviours, and gender mandated by a given society are imprinted has been debunked (Connellan, Baron-Cohen, Wheelwright, Batki, & Ahluwalia, 2000; Pinker, 2002). We now know that humans are born with temperaments, cognitive structures, learning capacities, and sex-linked behaviours that appear developmentally or are latent, triggered by environmental stimuli. Behaviour that is normative across human cultures is either suggestive of genetic heritability, or a verifiable "good idea," universally adopted for survival value—for example, making fire.

There is room for cultural divergence in expression and interpretation of genetically heritable traits. For example, while vocalizations of happiness and sadness are universal, Japanese listeners rated the emotional level of actors portraying sounds of anger, disgust, fear, and pleasure as being less intense than did Canadians listening to the same sounds (Koeda, et al., 2013). Similarly, it is possible to envision a genetically transmitted core basis of the self embedded within cultural diversity.

If the self of conscious awareness is a cultural construct, and if it is found across human cultures, then its survival benefits must outweigh its significant costs. If, however, we were to find functioning human societies where people did not have selves, then we could conclude that the self is a nonessential idiosyncratic artifact. The suggestion that the self is a modern or Western invention (Foucault, 1982/1997; Holstein & Gubrium, 2000; C. Taylor, 1989) implies that many selfless individuals are functioning or have functioned until relatively recently in our history.

In this chapter, I examine the self from various cultural perspectives. As we saw in chapter 2, the self can be viewed as the personal definition for the pronoun "I." Once the notion of an "I" has been taught, it begs further definition. Such a self must be contextual and learned in the second person from the perspective of those with whom one interacts. Thus, the self at this level of abstraction is most efficiently learned through the medium of language.

The use of language couples the ability to communicate with large numbers of speakers with an increased ability to store remembered responses into one's repertoire of possible behaviours. Vicarious learning of the responses of others through storytelling and mentoring further increases the potential range of response to changing conditions. Human children now learn language so easily that Chomsky (2014) hypothesized a "universal grammar" that is genetically transmitted and unique to our species. Richerson and Boyd (2005) reasoned that such a language instinct would have co-evolved with those social instincts that permit us to work together collectively. Since culture is encoded in language, and the self consists of units of culture, it is through language that self possibilities are both constrained and expressed. Thus, differences in language use would be expected to result in differences in self-construction.

Grammar and Cultural Appropriation in Selected Amerindian Cultures

Languages vary in the construction of grammatical gender. The European use of sex to designate gender is most pronounced in the Romance languages, where all nouns are designated as male or female. In contrast, languages that are aboriginal[1] to North America typically distinguish animate and inanimate gender with verb forms agreeing with the designation of the noun.[2] Prototypically, the Amerindian language Cree has no pronoun designating a person's sex as in "him" or "her" but does have third-person pronouns for animate beings, for example, *wiya* means "him/her" in the Plains Cree dialect. These pronouns, and others referencing inanimate objects, are often not needed because sentences are conjugated according to the designated gender form. Thus "she/he is big" is translated *misikitiw*, but "it is big" is *misaw*. The Cree language uses these gender differentiations to reflect a cultural worldview; for example, drums and stones are considered animate, but the earth is not.

It would be expected that selves in cultures using sexual gender in language construction would, to some extent, reflect embedded associations with masculinity or femininity built into the language in which thought occurs. The selves of such individuals would be defined by attributed male and female characteristics to an extent not observed in those adults aboriginal to North America who were raised in a cultural and linguistic structure that defined gender differently. We would also expect that people in those cultures that define gender in terms of animation might be more predisposed to incorporate relatedness to all things considered animate into their sense of self. Sex differences that are genetically heritable would be exhibited in all cultures irrespective of the grammatical gender system used.

Since sexually referenced gender reinforces notions of male-female dichotomization, we could predict that many people from such cultures would be predisposed to find various forms of transsexualization as unnatural, even perverted. Similarly, we would predict that selves constructed within cultures whose grammatical structure promotes a dichotomization between the animate and inanimate would be less likely to incorporate the inanimate into their self-structure. It should not typically occur to the mind of the one raised Ojibway, Siouan, or Navajo to join animate with inanimate. At first blush, the aboriginal Mother Earth appears to disprove this hypothesis.

There is no exact translation for the animate word "mother" in Cree. *Kikawiy* literally means "your mother" in the plains dialect. "My mother" is *nikawiy*, and his/her mother is *okawiya*. As can be seen from this conjugation, all things animate are related and cannot stand outside of their relationships. Conversely, "Earth" in Cree is governed by the language rules given inanimate objects. While it is possible to speak of my earth as in *nitaskiy*, it is also possible to speak of the Earth (*askiy*) without possession or directionality. Since the prefixes and suffixes used to generate sentence meaning in Cree are different for the animate and inanimate, the joining of mother and earth in one phrase becomes problematic. Either "mother" must be turned into a thing or earth must be animated, which breaks the linguistic rules. This melding should not occur, yet "Mother Earth" is, in the modern era, widely accepted as an aboriginal concept flowing from an ancient feminine deity.

In his examination of Hopi, Navajo, and Yaqui legends, Gill (1991) found no evidence of such an earth mother deity nor any direct reference to the concept. My own research into Cree, Dene, and Saulteaux (Plains Ojibway) cultures has similarly revealed no such concept. The most ancient legend I found common to these three cultures aboriginal to Canada reveals a relationship between people and the earth in keeping with the language structures common to all three. In brief, the story of Muskrat begins with Earth covered by ice. The ice melts, leaving nothing but water covering the land. Two boys survive by floating on a log. They call on various animal relatives for assistance (the actual animals vary according to the culture in which the legend is told), but none are able to help. Finally, they call upon small, weak Muskrat. Upon hearing their plea, Muskrat dives below, deeper than s/he had ever done before. Finally, lungs bursting, s/he reaches the bottom and grasps some soil. Nearly dead, clinging to his small portion of earth, muskrat reaches the surface. The boys take this small amount of earth from his/her failing hands and sing their song. With the song, the soil expands to include hills and valleys with all kinds of plants upon which the people and other animals may thrive. The lakes remain as a reminder of what once was.

The legend of Muskrat reveals a relationship between animate beings acting on an inanimate Earth to create a habitation suitable for survival, thus displaying qualities of competence (knowing what to do), autonomy (taking individual action), and relatedness (in this case, connecting all life). The European experience flowing from sexual gender is quite different. In Spanish, as in other Romance languages, Earth is expressed as "the earth" (*la tierra*), and cannot be expressed in any way other than in its feminine form. One of the earliest Greek legends has Mother Earth, in the name of Gaia, mating with both Uranus (the sky or heaven) and their son Pontus to produce the titans, who in turn mated and produced the gods. Gaia practised early birth control by having her son Cronus castrate his father while he slept.

Gaia then helped her grandchild Zeus defeat Cronus and the rest of the Titans. This allowed the gods (her grandchildren) to establish personal relationships with humans, whom they advised, directed, and with whom they sometimes mated. The European legend is infused with sexual creation and violence. The evolution of the more recent Amerindian appropriation reflects a different worldview.

Gill (1987) traced all published references of an Amerindian notion of mother earth to just two nineteenth-century sources. The earliest such reference was attributed to the Shawnee chief Tecumseh, who forged an alliance of Amerindian nations resisting US expansion into the lands south of the Great Lakes. In 1810, he met with US General W. H. Harrison to negotiate a possible peace. An aid to the general is reported to have offered Tecumseh a chair with the words "Your father (General Harrison) offers you a seat," to which the chief is said to have replied, "The sun is my father and the earth is my mother and I will repose upon her bosom" (p. 14). There were no official transcripts of these proceedings and Harrison's private notes make no reference to the incident. The first known record of this conversation was published in *The National Recorder* about eleven years after the reported conversation! Tecumseh had been killed fighting with the British in the War of 1812 and the newspaper was paying a tribute to his legend. The quote was subsequently repeated in other media and appeared in a fictional New York play where the words were attributed not to Tecumseh but to the eighteenth-century Ottawa chief Pontiac.

More than seventy years after the death of Tecumseh, on the opposite side of the American continent, Wanapum[3] tribal leader Smohalla is reported to have said to US Indian Affairs (IAB) officials, "You ask me to plough the ground. Should I take a knife and cut my mother's bosom?" (Memoirs of Major J.W. MacMurray as quoted in Gill, 1991, p. 131). Smohalla had led a campaign resisting enforced settlement on Indian reserves, and he was reacting against an IAB plan to teach the Wanapum settler's ways of farming and mining. As a religious leader and prophet, he presented Earth as a maternal being. He described the farming practice of haying as cutting mother earth's hair, a practice he maintained showed disrespect. He described mining as digging into Mother Earth's body and chipping away at her bones. But these were not traditional sentiments.

Smohalla was voicing new teachings flowing from visions he had during a spiritual pilgrimage to a mountain top. The subsequent creation story he told the IAB officials involved a male creator-god with human emotions who made humans on a feminine earth as a way of dealing with his loneliness. This god became angry because the humans of his creation could not share and live in harmony. Some humans had become greedy and oppressive, and these "whites" would be removed from America. He predicted that at the time of their removal the spirits of deceased aboriginal people would return to their bodies in a great resurrection. In the meantime, aboriginal people needed to maintain their sacred way of life to hasten that day of reckoning and their place in it. Another new teaching was that no work was to be done on the Sabbath, a day reserved for celebrating sacred traditions. As can be seen, this new "Dreamer Religion" as it came to be known, parallels Christianity in some ways, and within this frame we can understand the concept of mother earth as grafted onto a movement whose impetus was cultural preservation. The aboriginal actors in this narrative are presented as wronged but righteous people with a special relationship to Mother Earth who, by remaining faithful to a set of beliefs, would reap benefits to which they are entitled. This narrative resonated with Aboriginals across the continent.

It is probably no accident that the grafting of Earth to mother happened first among one of the few aboriginal peoples whose language group, Sahaptin, lacks grammatical gender. But lack of grammatical resistance to a particular conceptual change does not necessarily equate with movement to do so. The driving force for this new religion, and thus the appropriated and aboriginalized concept of mother earth, was the political goal of resisting assimilation. Smohalla may have been consciously creating a modern myth or parable for that purpose. In 1871, prior to his mountain top vision, he had given a different and more traditional view, recorded at a tribal council meeting:

> It is good for man and woman to be together on the earth; a home is given and they are placed in it. We do not know how the earth was made, nor do we say who made it. The earth was peopled and their hearts are good, and my mind is that it is as it ought to be. The world was peopled by whites and Indians and they should all grow as one flesh. (Bell, 2011, para. 8)

The selves within cultures will vary according to cultural predispositions, conceptual associations, and available archetypes. The aboriginalized concept of Mother Earth offered a new archetype whereby the spiritual man may define his relationship with the land

and his oppressors with a sense of dignity, righteousness, and confidence in the future. This narrative proved to have sufficient appeal that once it developed in a genderless linguistic environment, it overcame barriers of grammatical gender elsewhere. This account illustrates that language constraints are not absolute—as cultures evolve in response to political, economic, and social pressures, languages co-evolve to adapt. For example, some modern Cree speakers now treat *askiy* or "earth" as an animate noun in their sentence construction.

The earlier account of Tecumseh was not really about cultural change among the Shawnee but about cultural change among US Americans. The United States had successfully colonized the land south of the Great Lakes. The "pagan savage" myth that allowed them to implement a ruthless campaign of violent oppression was gradually replaced with a "noble savage" myth that would allow for a kind of accommodation with the survivors. The mother earth concept allowed the English speakers to see the conquered people as related in some way to their own noble but distant past. From this perspective, the early nineteenth-century concept of mother earth was part of a dialogue between English speakers seeking a different understanding of their colonized subjects.

Given the distress of colonization, it would have been surprising if aspects of European culture had not been assimilated into Amerindian cultures. As a further example, the Ghost Dance movement of the late nineteenth century combined the aboriginal "round dance" with the messianic Christian tradition of Paiute Medicine Man Wovoka's (Jack Wilson's) upbringing. Like Smohalla and adherents to his Dreamer Religion, the Ghost Dancers believed those of European ancestry would be eliminated and the American continents restored to their original inhabitants in the messianic tradition. Other concepts thought of as Aboriginal also show this form of cultural appropriation. The modern Medicine Wheel usually contains the quadrant "mental," a European concept not found in Algonquian languages; indeed, the concept of the wheel is not traditional to Amerindian or Inuit cultures. Sweat lodges have commonly become "mixed," in that both men and women participate, but the earlier tradition was male only. Prayer too has changed. Prayers are no longer commonly offered to intermediary spirits with intercessions now directed toward the Great Spirit, renamed "the Creator." In Canada, the term "First Nation" is often used in reference to Amerindian peoples, but the concept of "nation" is a relatively recent European development with no analogue in traditional aboriginal American cultures. While all cultures evolve, often by borrowing from others, vestiges of the collectivism necessary for survival in hunter-gatherer societies remain. Berry (1999) found that hunting, trapping, and fishing were mentioned as traditional activities in aboriginal focus groups held across Canada lending support to the notion that a relationship with the land remains an important component culturally.

In one view, culture is comprised of the sum total of a group of peoples' worldviews, customs, beliefs, and behaviours, with individual persons interpretively choosing their beliefs and practices. In a second view, culture consists of a worldview that comprises customs, beliefs, and behaviours that people learn. In this second, essentialist view of culture, peoples' personal happiness is secondary to cultural propagation. In this frame, cultural appropriation, sometimes framed as "assimilation," is seen as a threat potentially reducing the culture's distinctiveness and reach. People who do not live in a prescribed way are thought of as having "lost" their culture, and the adoption of children to people of other cultures may be thought of as "theft."

The modern "Historic Trauma" movement falls within the tradition of Smohalla and Wovoka in its attempt to maintain an essentialized version of aboriginality. Superficially, Historic Trauma medicalizes the historical experience of being colonized. Such experience is said to have created trauma in the survivors who experience depression, self-destructive behaviour, anxiety, low self-esteem, anger, difficulty recognizing and expressing emotions, addictions, and suicide ideation (Brave Heart, 2003). It is not clear how many people have all, or even a majority, of these symptoms, and the separate histories of the colonized are not considered. For example, no distinction is made between the nineteenth-century northern plains Blackfeet, who were given smallpox-infected blankets by the United States military (Ewers, 1958), and the neighbouring nineteenth-century Cree, who were vaccinated against smallpox by Britain's Hudson Bay Company (Denig, 1856/1961).

In treating this Historic Trauma, Brave Heart (2003) induces historically traumatic memories using audiovisual materials through which participants "relive" genocidal massacres. She then treats this trauma using Lakota prayer and purification ceremonies, explaining, "This is done in order to provide opportunities for cognitive integration of the traumas well as the affective cathartic working-through necessary for healing" (p. 11). Another interpretation is that she teaches people to have a trauma reaction to events of which they were not previously aware, and then uses the resultant trauma reaction to induce changes to the self. Unfortunately, we cannot know with certainty what a pre-contact aboriginal self would look like.

If the self is a European construct with Europeans ethnocentrically assuming that all others have selves, then the first alternative, that culture is the current aggregate of individuals who have chosen particular identities, would not apply. The quality of self-awareness or self-consciousness that comes with selfhood necessarily introduces the notion of individuality—we must locate our own consciousness as distinct in some ways from a collective consciousness in the process of becoming self-aware. This would result in tension between collective cultures and the individuals who comprise those cultures, sometimes with religious or militarist injunctions to renounce the self in the service of the collectivity (Foucault, 1982/1997; Foucault, Rabinow, & Dreyfus, 1983/1997).

Since it is necessary to situate oneself temporally and contextually in order to exercise personal volition and reflective reason, the notion that non-occidental people lack selves is to deny them these capacities. A less controversial position would be that people in all societies have selves but that some cultures support the primacy of the individual while others support the primacy of the collectivity. In support of such a dichotomy, Blustein and Noumair (1996) suggested that while occidental societies view the self as unitary and stable, non-western societies view it as flexible and varied. In this formulation, the personal self in collectivist societies blends with others and differs according to context. The collectivist self is viewed as dependent on social relations in contrast to the contextually independent Euro-American self. While this view sounds elegant, it is hardly complete. None of the German, French, and British philosophers in Seigel's (2005) review of post-Cartesian European thought regarded the self as independent of social relations. Differences between individualist and collectivist selves may be more of emphasis and expression, evolving in response to economic and social pressures while maintaining fundamental characteristics essential to selfhood.

The Euro-American or "Western" self has been evolving rapidly since the time of Smohalla and Tecumseh. Cushman (1995) described the nineteenth-century US American bourgeois self as "individualistic, hardworking, moralistic, frugal and emotionally restricted" (p. 62). As capitalism changed to a consumer economy, personality replaced character as an essential component of self, he argued. The need to attend to the details of one's public performance, implied in the development of personality, created the ideal consumer as people became commodities. Such an empty self "experiences a significant absence of community, tradition and shared meaning" and interprets "the absences, loneliness and disappointments of life as a chronic, undifferentiated hunger" (p. 79). He argued that psychology is ahistorical in attempting to heal this self so as to perpetuate the consumer economy, forgetting that Adler (1927/1957, 1967) and Fromm (1969) had previously integrated history and social forces into their psychological formulations.

The rapid evolution of Euro-American cultures in response to economic and technological change meant that people aboriginal to the Americas encountered European colonizers at different stages of the latter's cultural evolution. Aboriginal cultures themselves were experiencing extensive change as a result of this contact, and the values and beliefs of some colonizers, such as missionaries, sometimes were at variance with the values and beliefs of those colonizers representing industrial and commercial interests. Thus, cultural systems with different historical bases co-evolved in different ways dependent on time and location. Since we cannot say with certainty what a precontact aboriginal self would have looked like or the extent to which such selves existed, an argument against the notion that the self was a modern European invention needs to reference cultures that were not so influenced by the European experience.

The Buddhist Experience of Self

The founder of Buddhism is said to have examined each of the fundamental building blocks of reality (the dharmas) approximately 2,500 years ago, and he reported finding no self therein. Given our understanding of the self as a complex of cultural units, this would be like examining a pile of bricks and finding no wall in any of the bricks (or, as we saw in chapter 2, finding no self in the brain). Of course, the definition of the self as a cognitive, culturally based structure may not have been available to Gotama Siddhattha (Gautama Siddhartha in the Vedic translations). Drawing on the work of Rhys Davids, who translated the writings of Siddhattha from the original Pali text, Hutcheon (2001) quotes the original Buddha: "Since neither soul nor aught belonging to soul can really and truly exist, the view which holds that this I who am 'world,' who am 'soul' shall hereafter live permanent, persisting, unchanging, yea abide eternally: is not this utterly and entirely a foolish doctrine?" (p. 5).

In this text, Siddhattha appears to be debunking the idea of self already present in South Asian culture in the fourth century BCE. Since Brahman (ultimate reality) and Atman (self) are ultimately the same, there is an assumption in traditional Hindu teaching of an immortal soul associated with the indexical first-person pronoun that it is both eternal and unchanging. The Buddha's concept of no-self thus may be considered a critique of the posited existence of an eternal ensouled self. Would the Buddha have been comfortable with the modern definition of the self as a cognitive structure? While Theravatan Buddhists follow the Pali texts, the Mahayana tradition accepts, as inspired, Vedic translations. From this tradition, Tibetan monk Sogyal Rinpoche (1993) writes, "Two people have been living in you all your life. One is the ego, garrulous demanding, hysterical, calculating, the other is the hidden spiritual being, whose still voice of wisdom you have only heard or attended to" (p. 120).

Sogyal Rinpoche (1993) is clearly not using the term "ego" in the Freudian sense, as the source of reason balancing the conflicting demands of the superego and id. Instead, he assumes the presence of two selves in the individual: one false and one true. From whence does the hidden true being come? It cannot be a changing cognitive structure, otherwise we would be left with a multitude of possible true beings in opposition to each other. Since this one true self can exist without being in the consciousness of the person in whom it dwells, we must presume it was present from some source outside the body and is eternal and unchanging: something like the Hindu notion of Atman. It appears as though this Tibetan strain of Buddhism relies on an essentialist and possibly eternalist definition of self of the kind debunked by the Master!

Buddhism evolved further as it crossed the Sea of Japan. Kabat-Zinn (1994) offered the following explanation of the Zen Buddhist doctrine of "no-self": "No-self does not mean being a nobody. What it means is that everything is interdependent and that there is no isolated, independent core you" (p. 238). As we shall see in the following section, this understanding is in keeping with the Japanese language, which defines self as a fraction of some other collective unit. The self that does not exist in this paradigm is a hypothesized individualist Western version of the concept, but this could not have been the self

Siddhattha was debunking in the fourth century BCE! In arguing for the ultimate dissolution of self into oneness with the universe, early Buddhism appears to have been counselling against both the concepts of an individual and eternal self. A self must be present in a culture to necessitate its negation. Individualism must have been an aspect of South Asian selves at the time of Siddhattha.

Kabat-Zinn's understanding leaves open the possibility of a relational self constructed in language. Another practitioner of Zen, Alan W. Watts (1963), suggested that the concept of self was never totally eliminated from Buddhism:

> The Supreme Self, is always just beyond its own control of itself. In the words of the philosopher Shankara: 'The Knower can know other things, but cannot make Itself the object of Its own knowledge, in the same way that fire can burn other things but cannot burn itself'. ... This, then, is why the way of the Buddha is, at one moment in history, a way of complete withdrawal from *maya*, the cosmic game, and at another, the way of the Bodhisattva who lays aside the endless peace of *nirvana* to return into the cycle of birth-and-death. ... (pp. 88–89)

In Watts we are seeing an example of Buddhism as expressed by a university-trained US American. A Western influence on Buddhism can be seen in the Kyoto School that incorporated both Western philosophical thought and Christianity into Zen. Its leading philosopher, Kitaro Nishida (1921/1990) talked about the necessity of sin and repentance in advocating god-belief with a pantheistic approach that nonetheless included a personal god to which prayers are offered. Both the self and things are experienced equally in pure experience. The existence of a singular "true self" is assumed, existing as the unifier of subject and object. God is defined as the ultimate basis of this unity. Nishida advocates feeling pure experience without interpretation. Similar to the German philosopher Heidegger, he asserts that it is thinking that creates imperfection.

Psychologist and Zen Buddhist Susan Blackmore (1999, 2002) declared the self to be an illusion because it is constructed of memes. She challenged the notion of a Jamesean stream of consciousness consisting of temporally ordered mental representations by referring to neurological research into the colour phi phenomenon. In this experiment a red light is flashed at one point followed by a green light a short distance away. Subjects experience the red light as travelling toward the green light and changing colour from red to green at the mid-point. If there exists a stream of consciousness, how did the travelling light know to change colour at the mid-point before the green light flashed? Blackmore concluded that consciousness is constructed backward from focusing loci. We only think we see things as they happen, but in fact there must be a time delay in which our brains construct an interpretive narrative as to what is happening "out there." An implication of this position is that the temporality assumed in the Jamesian, 'I' might be a variable cultural construct. We learn to interpret reality in certain ways and those interpretations govern our perceptions.

If there is no stream of consciousness, and if the self is constructed of units of culture that create, in Blackmore's metaphor "a meme machine," then we are left with an illusory self dependent on social convention with no room for a "true self" to which we can aspire. Such an interpretation of the Buddhist concept of no-self is compatible with behaviourism and social constructionism. Kwee (2012) made this connection in stating, "The New Buddhist Psychology's love affair with social constructionism is centred around relational interbeing" (p. 262). This "Relational Buddhism" is an attempt to unite Theravatan and Mahayanan forms of the religion within a scientific paradigm that eschews god belief and metaphysical explanations in favour of free and critical thinking based on evidence and assumptions of natural causation. The self is thought of as a focus of numerous interrelational transactions, with the "no-self" doctrine interpreted as meaning that no self is independent of social and relational bonds and that it may be viewed as a product of those relational forces. Paradoxically, Relational Buddhism also values individual volition: "For the mature who have the capacity to freely think, pick, and choose, who wishes to decide for themselves in joint collaboration, and who does not want to blindly follow holy dead men and their rules, there is a psychological roadmap that might generate sustainable happiness for all in interrelatedness" (Kwee 2012, p. 270).

To summarize, Siddhattha espoused a no-self doctrine in reaction to an earlier Hindu concept of self that was thought to exist independently of the bodies it inhabited, but various interpretations of that doctrine exist. Tibetan Buddhists allowed for an essentialist "true self." Zen allowed for a self that was said to not exist independently of social relations. Forms of Buddhism have also displayed compatibility with modern scientific thought. In one case, the no-self doctrine was affirmed through the assumption that a memetic self is necessarily illusory, and, in a second example, the self was viewed as a construct that results from interrelatedness. In Relational Buddhism, we see a movement that more closely resembles a school of psychology than a religion. In conclusion, the suggestion that the self is a purely European construct is mistaken. Buddhism encountered the concept of self in all of the cultures with which it came into contact, and it responded with its own adaptations and interpretations.

Examinations of the Self in Selected Collectivist Cultures

When the Roman Catholic Church could still call itself "universal," at least in the European context, self-denial was used to maintain a collectivist culture in which even the roles of kings and queens were prescribed and sanctified (Foucault, et al., 1983/1997). Taylor (1989) lamented that, with the influence of Descartes and Rousseau, "The source of unity and wholeness which Augustine found only in God is now to be discovered within the self" (p. 362). He complained that the resultant modern self of instrumental reason "lacks the force, the depth, the vibrancy, the joy, the élan of nature. But there is worse ... the instrumental stance toward nature constitutes a bar to ever attaining it" (p. 383).

In examining the presumed dichotomy between the individualist and collectivist self, it is easy to forget that the so-called "individualist" Euro-American self emerged from a collectivist culture. Some Euro-Americans continue to seek meaning and purpose through a denial of this modern individualist self by merging with a "universalizing" religious or ideological movement. The notion that the self is ill-equipped to find such meaning and by its very existence negates the unity and wholeness provided by religious faith resonates with their experience. Like Charles Taylor, they view the Euro-American self as a soulless machine, calculating and self-absorbed. They look to a higher authority to differentiate good from bad and what is worth doing from what is not worth doing. By connecting with an ultimate authority, they seek to regain the vibrancy and joy they imagine was lost.

The logic supporting a dichotomization of cultures between individualist and collectivist seems compelling. The ideology of capitalism that evolved to justify the prevailing Western economic system stresses personal acquisition of material wealth. The religions of the Euro-American peoples evolved to incorporate a "Protestant work ethic," sanctifying those habits of thrift and hard work that are thought to have made capitalism successful. In contrast, collectivist cultures are understood as de-emphasizing the individual in the interests of religion, society, and/or family. The word for self in Japanese, *jibun*, is linguistically a fraction—becoming whole only when occupying one's place in a social unit (Rosenberger, 1992). The Japanese language reflects and promotes the idea that the person is understood in terms of meaningful contexts and relationships with comparatively less use of indexical pronouns than is found in European languages.

Korean mothers spend a third of the time talking to their children about their past as compared to US American mothers (Cross & Gore, 2003). It is likely that people with a more acute understanding of their personal past, including significant transitions, will more likely define themselves as unique individuals with a self-determined future. East Asian women are more likely to define themselves in terms of group membership as compared to US women, who are more likely to define themselves in terms of close relationships (mother, wife, best friend). While both orientations contribute to a sense of community, those personal communities built around family and friendship ties are likely more individualized than self-definition based on membership in larger amorphous communities. Lent (2004) suggested that self-esteem, measured as self-satisfaction, was found to relate more highly to global life satisfaction in individualist than in collectivist nations, while relationship harmony was found to be a better predictor of life satisfaction in a collectivist context. With less emphasis on a personal past, more emphasis on group membership, and more satisfaction from relationship harmony, one might expect that Asians and other peoples from collectivist cultures exhibit a diminished sense of being unique individuals as compared to those from European-based cultures. If we evolved as social animals, then we would expect to find a human genetic predisposition for collectivism. Given that Euro-American cultures are primarily populated by Caucasian peoples, might such people be less predisposed genetically to collectivism than other humans?

One allele of the oxytocin receptor polymorphism rs53576 is associated with more sensitive parenting behaviour, increased empathy and greater separation anxiety as compared to those without the allele, but the incidence of this "social sensitivity" allele is lower in

Asian than North American populations (Kim, et al., 2010). From the distribution of this allele, one would expect American cultures to be more collectivist than Asian. Of course, it is possible to argue that nature sets the parameters within which nurture may operate, and if all humans are a combination of collectivist and individualist tendencies, then cultural variation within a range of possibilities would be dependent on historical, social, and economic forces.

Religion might serve to enshrine various combinations of individualism and collectivism in a given culture. Since religion may also be related to well-being, Sasaki, Kim, and Xu (2011) sought to examine the relationship between gene polymorphism rs53576, religiosity, and psychological well-being. It was hypothesized that people with this allele have a greater genetic predisposition to identification with a collectivity. Since religion is one structured form of collectivity, it was expected that people with this allele who are religious would demonstrate greater psychological well-being than those with the allele who are not religious. Their comparison of a sample of 134 South Korean and 108 US American Christians gave conflicting results. As expected, religiosity did not predict psychological well-being for those without the allele in either culture. For those genetically predisposed to social sensitivity in South Korea, religiosity was associated with increased well-being, but in the United States this effect was reversed. The dogmas taught within the Christian communities in each country are similar; indeed, Christianity in Korea resulted from intensive missionary activity from the United States following the Korean War. The study's authors suggested that religions set in a North American cultural context emphasize individual choice and responsibility more and social affiliation less than those in the East Asian cultural context; that is, underlying cultural differences influenced the application or interpretation of otherwise identical dogma. Since US culture reflects greater emphasis on individualism, religions in that country relate to their membership in ways that conform to this norm while in South Korea the same religions place more emphasis on the social aspects of their dogma. People with the social sensitivity allele find religious participation in the US context less conducive to their sense of mental well-being; however, this does not explain why those with this allele who were nonreligious fared better than their religious peers in the United States. It could be that those with the social sensitivity allele who sought encompassing and directive religious communities in the United States experienced disappointment if their religion of choice had assimilated more individualist values, while the nonreligious with this allele were more activist in seeking and developing alternate communities that support this personality trait.

In summation, Christians in the United States find themselves in a culture emphasizing individualism, and their religion is less satisfying for those carrying the social sensitivity allele as compared to their Korean counterparts. In keeping with the concern of Taylor (1989), Christianity failed to preserve a level of collectivism that would have been satisfying to those carrying the social sensitivity allele in European and US American societies. Instead of acting to transmit a foreign individualist culture, Christianity was able to accommodate collectivist cultural norms in the South Korean context. That country has also developed a vibrant capitalist economy. If capitalism was the driver for Christianity's evolution away from its earlier collectivism, then we could predict that either the level of individualism in South Korean culture should increase or the nature of capitalism in that country will change.

In comparison with South Korea, Japan has not been amenable to Euro-American religious influence. While approximately a third of the South Korean population has converted to Christianity, only 1% of Japanese have done so. Of course, using formal membership in religion as a marker for the export of culture is an imperfect method of measuring cultural attrition. As we have seen in our examination of Buddhism, Christianity has had an influence on the evolution of at least one Buddhist sect in Japan. Further, religion is not the only vehicle by which the values, practices, and traditions of a dominant culture can be exported to a colonized people. Although Japan became a capitalist state subsequent to its defeat in the Second World War, its capitalism has been modified to reflect some aspects of collectivism. More than two-thirds of the shares traded on the Tokyo Stock Exchange, for example, are owned by large collections of industrial groups with the resultant network of cross-shareholdings dictating that the well-being of one company is enhanced by the well-being of others. While it is tempting to suggest that the Japanese have curtailed market forces enhancing competition while increasing rewards for intercorporate cooperation, it is important to note that competition between corporations within North American capitalism is also to some extent illusory. Interlocking directorships in North American publicly traded companies are common, and significant competition in price is so rare that when it happens it is commonly referred to as a "price war." With this caveat, it is reasonable to assume that collectivism would result in more examples of systemic cooperation than would be the case in individualist cultures.

Evidence of collectivism is seen in Japanese –corporate-worker relations. The adversarial system in North America, which resulted in the creation of unions to protect workers, is replaced in Japan with a system of mutual loyalty. Workers are expected to be loyal to the company, and in return receive job security—often for life—with retraining, pensions, and social protection available as needed.[4] The collectivist modifications seen in Japanese capitalism may be understood in relation to Japanese grammar. If the individual does not exist except within social relations, then the importance of corporate identification and loyalty are magnified: the workplace provides a social context in which self-identification is made possible. On the other hand, it is important to note that the protections afforded the Japanese workers by their employers are often provided by elected governments in Western societies, with those in western Europe providing a greater "social safety net" for their citizens than those in North America. While such governmental intervention reflects a collective societal responsibility sometimes referred to as socialism, the corporate-worker relationship in Japan suggests a different cultural adaptation.

That adaptation may not be related to any latent dispositions of the Japanese. Chiao et al. (2009) used magnetic resonance imaging to compare the mental self-representations of university students from Chicago, USA, with university students from Nagoya, Japan. As predicted, students who defined themselves through their social contexts and relationships used a different part of the neocortex as compared to those who used general (individualist) self-referencing self-definitions; however, the participants' cultural values with respect to individualism or collectivism had no relationship to their cultural affiliation. In other words, the students from Chicago were as likely to define themselves through their social contexts as were the students from Nagoya! It appears as though even language is limited in its capacity to create individualist or collectivist self-definitions.

In a study that helps put the presumed dichotomy between the individualist and collectivist into perspective Shi, Frederiksen, and Muis (2013) counted verbal exchanges indicating individualist or social orientations in self-regulated learning in separate Chinese and Canadian learning dyads. As predicted, the Canadian dyads exhibited a predominant number of comments (70%) indicting an individualist orientation in their exchanges with fellow dyad members. Even so, half the verbal exchanges in the Chinese dyads were individualist in nature. Further, when the dyads were mixed between Chinese and Canadian the cross-cultural learning couplets exhibited the same individualist response pattern as the Canadian-only dyads. While the Chinese participants in the study had a preference for an increased use of statements suggesting a collectivist orientation when interacting with fellow Chinese, they exhibited no difficulty in switching to a more individualist response pattern when partnered with a more individualist student, and they did so at a level equal to that of their Canadian counterparts.

In another study involving university students, letters seeking advice on a spectrum of personal issues were translated into English and Farsi and distributed to a sample of students at Carleton University, Canada, and the University of Tehran, Iran (Tavakoli, 2013). The advice given by these students was then coded into four categories: changing the self, tolerating the condition, changing the situation, and compromising. As predicted, the Iranians were more likely to give advice recommending that the individual change themselves to fit the situation (37.2% of responses for the Iranians as compared to 13.7% for the Canadians) and were more likely to advise counselees to tolerate the situation (18.5% as compared to 2.7%). The Canadians, on the other hand, were more likely to give advice involving changing the situation to suit the self (72.6% to 39.9%) and seek a compromise (2.1% to 0.5%). While statistically these results indicate a cultural difference, all four categories were represented in both nationalities with an individualist response (changing the situation to suit the self) being the leading type of advice given by both subgroups. Thus, the differences are more of degree than kind and may be explained by other variables including political contexts of authoritarianism verses democracy.

University students who participate in international studies may be predisposed to a cross-cultural flexibility not present to the same degree in their countries of origin. Further, these studies involving Canadian-Chinese, US American–Japanese, and Canadian-Iranian comparisons did not involve the element of cultural dislocation. After working with largely East Asian immigrants and foreign students in Vancouver, Canada, Ishiama (1995) suggested that the subjective impact of cultural relocation involves a threat to one's validation system, with a resultant undervalidation of self. The cultural milieu is necessary for both self-construction and maintenance, and it begins to deteriorate when not reinforced by familiar cultural interactions or when confronted by unfamiliar cross-cultural interactions that challenge assumptions upon which the originating self was developed. The resultant undervalidation or invalidation of self may lead to feelings of insecurity, discomfort, abandonment, self-depreciation, incompetence, helplessness, alienation, and/or meaninglessness. Ishiama (1995) used a process similar to grief work to assist individuals facing cultural dislocation. In grieving, the individual confronts a loss and a new reality and redefines him or herself in the context of this new reality.

In a study of 615 South African undergraduate students, Heaven, Simbayi, Stones, and Roux (2000) concluded that the identities for self-identified (Caucasian) Afrikaners were mainly linked with ethnic language (Afrikaans) and religion. Among self-identified black South Africans, however, social identities were more encompassing, including the notions of being a global citizen and South African. The researchers concluded that the values measured implied different identities founded on different ideological objectives. In this example, ideology is a basis for differing learned worldviews. Economic forms and ways of social integration may be viewed as ideologies superimposed on an underlying self containing both individualist and collectivist elements. A prevailing ideology may accentuate individuality or collectivism, and that ideological perspective may be reinforced by the language used; however, the self continues to generate a sense of uniqueness that is paradoxically dependent on social relations. That is not to say the ideology is without effect.

The overarching individualist world view of modern capitalism in the United States may contribute to self-serving attributional bias. Persons demonstrating this bias make more internal, stable, and global attributions for positive, compared to negative, personal outcomes. Put simply, US Americans may be expected to attribute positive results to their own individual efforts as compared to Asians with the self obtaining those results viewed as relatively stable. In a study of individualism in the United States, Harter (2012) found that blacks demonstrated the greatest levels of such individualism followed by whites, Asians, and Hispanics. People from individualist cultures reported higher levels of narcissism than those from collectivist cultures.

It is interesting that blacks in the United States demonstrate greater levels of individualism that either whites in the same country or blacks from South Africa. Blacks in the United States appear to have internalized an ideology of individualism while simultaneously maintaining an identity as a black person. In contrast to the global citizen identity assumed by university educated blacks in South Africa, whites in that country appear quite provincial—in keeping with their recent segregationist past and a co-occurring sense of political isolation. The finding that Asians in the United States exhibit lower levels of individualism than whites is not surprising given the collectivist cultures from which most Asians (or their recent ancestors) immigrated. The finding that Hispanics exhibited similar characteristics as Asians is surprising since Hispanics are mainly of European descent. This result suggests that cultures may become increasingly collectivist dependent on their social and historical circumstance. The forces in the United States contributing to a collective Hispanic identity need study. Additionally, it would be instructive to know if a pan-Hispanic collective identity is exhibited in other American countries.

While considerable variation is noted in the expression of the self between cultures, it is worth noting that the self was a viable construct in all. It is reasonable to assume that people with higher social identities would be more collectivist than those who score higher for personal identity. Using this dichotomy, Seta, Schmidt, &Bookhout (2006) divided a sample of 165 US American introductory psychology students into two groups: those with higher personal identity and those with higher social identity using Cheek's Aspects of Identity Questionnaire. Participants were shown a videotape of a discussion between actors identified as Greek and non-Greek, and they were asked to give an opinion as to why a targeted Greek expressed the opinions he had in settings involving conflict and consensus. As predicted, those who scored higher on the social identity scale tended to cite group membership (Greek) as the source of the targeted male's opinions while those who scored higher for personal identity tended to cite individual personal characteristics. Since all of the participants in the study were native-born from a US university, an implication of this finding is that there is considerable variation within this culture with respect to individualism and collectivism.

The view that an individual-collectivist dichotomy is too simplistic received support in a study of distress experienced by 727 university students drawn from campuses in the United States and

Thailand (M. S. Christopher, D'Souza, Peraza, & Dhaliwal, 2010). The researchers generated three hypotheses: 1) US students would report stronger independent self-construal than Thais, and Thais would report stronger interdependent self-construal than US Americans; 2) Distress would be positively related to interdependent self-construal and negatively related to independent self-construal among US Americans; and, 3) Distress would be negatively related to interdependent self-construal and positively related to independent self-construal among Thais. As predicted, the US students exhibited a more salient independent self-construal relative to Thais, whereas Thais construed a stronger interdependent self. Surprisingly, independent self-construal associated with individualism and volition negatively predicted distress for both groups.

The implication that the quality of individual volition associated with free will has cross-cultural mental health benefits was examined in China (Li, Wang, Zhao, Kong, & Li, 2016). Two cohorts of Chinese high school students (N = 2,299) correlated a belief in free will with subjective well-being, consisting of life satisfaction and positive affect. The researchers reported that belief in free will correlated with subjective well-being. Unexpectedly for a collectivist culture, 85% of the sample reported a belief in their own free will!

All cultures examined thus far combined individualism with collectivism within the self, although that accommodation may have been masked by an official ideology. Although there must be commonalities that allow us to recognize a group of people as a culture, we need to make allowance for the range of possibilities within those cultures and the individualization of acculturative effects if we are to build a culturally inclusive psychology of the self.

Counselling Outside of the "Western" Tradition

The legacy of European colonization may, in part, explain the under-utilization of North American counsellors, usually Caucasian, by international students (Arthur, 2004; Jacob, 2001; Robertson, Holleran, & Samuels, 2015), Asian-Americans (Tang, Fouad, & Smith, 1999), and people aboriginal to the Americas (Dolan, 1995; Mitchum, 1989; Poonwassie & Charter, 2001). The practice of psychology has been pictured as a Western invention promoting a particular ethnocentric characterization of self (Blustein & Noumair, 1996; Cushman, 1995; Moody, 1999). If the profession were to promote markers of occidental civilization, such as capitalism or Christianity, as essential to a healthy self, then the charge of ethnocentrism in counselling would hold. Additionally, if the self is fundamentally different in non-Western cultures, then the psychotherapies developed within the Euro-American traditions would be expected to be ineffective irrespective of considerations of cultural imperialism. I began this chapter by postulating that fundamental differences in grammar could demonstrate differences in worldview, involving a possible diminution or negation of the self. I found that the self has been present across cultures with all exhibiting a mixture of individualism and collectivism. Since the self as a construct is central to the practice of counselling, differences in self-construction should lead to fundamental differences with respect to counselling. In this section, I examine evidence to support such a hypothesis by examining cross-cultural applications of Positive Psychology and by examining the accepted counselling practices of Inuit (in the United States "Eskimo") Elders.[5]

Positive Psychology falls within the cognitivist tradition that assumes a unitary and stable self. It critiques older schools of psychotherapy on their perceived focus on negative attributes including distress, weakness, and the diagnosis of mental illness. Positive psychologists recommend increased attention to positive affect, relationship flourishing, and personal strengths (Fincham & Beach, 2010). Davis and Asliturk (2011) describe Positive Psychology as "realistic," orienting clients in a way that is not overly positive or negative. Meaning and purpose, characterized by virtuous living and a quest for authenticity, is achieved even with people in harsh and unavoidable circumstances (K. E. Hart & Sasso, 2011).

Most psychotherapies involve learning about the client as a unique individual, building awareness of potential counsellor bias, respecting social context, using community and client resources, and building a supportive client-counsellor relationship. Positive Psychologists attempt to use this approach to understand clients cross-culturally with Seligman, Steen, Park, and Peterson (2005) noting, "The most commonly endorsed ('most like me') strengths, in 40 different countries, from Azerbaijan to Venezuela, are kindness, fairness, authenticity, gratitude, and open-mindedness, and the lesser strengths consistently include prudence, modesty, and self-regulation" (p. 411).

In their study of eight philosophical and religious traditions from China, South Asia, and the West, Positive Psychologists Dahlsgaard, Peterson, and Seligman (2005) identified five universal virtues: justice, humanity, temperance, wisdom, and transcendence. A sixth virtue, courage, was found in five of the eight traditions. Positive Psychology is not without its detractors. Christopher and Hickinbottom (2008) criticized the cross-cultural application of Positive Psychology as "the disguised ideology of individualism" for promoting "a moral outlook in which it is presumed that because meanings and values are subjective, persons should be free to determine both the meaning of and the means to pursue the good life, or 'happiness,' in whatever manner they choose so long as they do not interfere with the ability of others to do the same" (p. 566).

In this view, persons assigned to collectivist cultures should not be individually free to determine the means to pursue what they perceive as an ideal life if that pursuit strengthens or reinforces dominant or Western cultures. Such a view is reflected in the position that people with indigenous ancestry who have adopted "western" values are said to have lost their cultures and are deemed to be unhealthy (Brave Heart, 2003; Mehl-Madrona, 2003; Sanderson, 2010). Aboriginal cultural values are then defined as dichotomized opposites to European values. If occidental culture is individualist, competitive, materialistic, and time centred, then aboriginal cultures must be collectivist, cooperative, spiritual, and timeless. From this premise it is deduced that modern psychological methods must be antithetical to aboriginal counselling values and needs (Dolan, 1995; Poonwassie & Charter, 2001; van Uchelen, Davidson, Quressette, Brasfield, & Demarais, 1997). I found only one study that actually tested for cultural differences in values underlying counselling methodology.

The Inuit in Canada's Arctic were effectively the last peoples colonized in North America. At the time of this study (2002) some elders would have been children when first contact was made between their communities and Europeans. With the understanding that the Inuit had comparatively less time for cultural assimilation than aboriginal peoples elsewhere in America, Korhonen (2002) used grounded theory to compare their counselling practices with those of modern schools of psychotherapy. She segmented and coded the transcriptions of open-ended interviews with seventeen Inuit Elders[6] and five younger Inuit involved in counselling; and she used the same coding procedure on seventeen counselling textbooks referencing Adler, Bandura, Beck, Berne, Ellis, Glasser, Harris, Lazarus, May, Perls, Rogers and Wolpe. She reported that axial coding of the texts produced the following broad categories: "building a relationship," "information-gathering," "counsellor characteristics," "goal-setting," and "choosing interventions." The transcripts of the Inuit Elders and helpers produced the following broad categories: "values," "counselling relationship," and "'strategies." The coding produced unexpected agreement between theorists: "The unanimity of the holistic view of the client, and emphasis on acceptance of client perceptions and decisions in all aspects of the process—problem-definition, goal-setting, choice of interventions, etc.—was unexpected. Multicultural counselling seems to be a holistic, integrative, client-centered process identical to conventional counselling" (p. 277).

Even more surprising was the level of agreement she found between so-called Western and Inuit methods: "Effective counselling in both a traditional Inuit framework and with younger Inuit seems also to be a client-centered approach based on trust, understanding and acceptance of client individuality, needs and context, with affective and cognitive interventions perceived as especially helpful, and decisions based on client choice" (p. 279).

Korhonen reported that she had been aware of the pragmatic and adaptive nature of traditional Inuit life having worked with the Inuit Taspiriit (a self-government institution); however, the stress that both Elders and younger Inuit placed on the empirical assessment of reality and truth and the priority of reason were new findings. She also did not expect the strong emphasis the Inuit placed on individual context, action, and choice because she had been influenced by the notion that reason, future orientation, and individualism are features of modern Euro-American civilization. With respect to the traditional collectivist nature of Inuit culture, Korhonen reported that all group members were expected to follow the rules that affected group survival, but in decisions about other life matters, individuality was stressed. Non-interference in individual and family matters was a general norm. Three dominant themes about humanity emerged from the data: that human beings are essentially similar; that each person is nevertheless unique; and that humans are thinking beings whose ability to reason is their most important tool for a long life.

Although it is reasonable to suggest that there will be differences in values and emphasis between cultures, Korhonen reminds us that there are also fundamental similarities. In a study of culture-specific counselling at a university setting (Robertson, et al., 2015), it was observed that aboriginal clients often prefer to be seen outside of an office setting, feel uncomfortable reporting to a receptionist, feel constrained by a "fifty-minute" hour, and sometimes like to get to know the counsellor before committing to therapy. These can be considered cultural differences to be accommodated but are not the fundamental core counselling values of which Korhonen writes. Both aboriginal and non-aboriginal clients appreciate client centredness, confidentiality, and a holistic view of their situation. Common core values such as respecting the uniqueness of the individual and the need for the individual to find meaningful answers from within suggest selves that have concomitant similarities across the cultures. Thus, we can infer that the traditional self of the Inuit shares certain commonalities with the European self. Supporting the view that certain fundamental aspects of counselling are cross-cultural, Oulanova and Moodley (2010) studied counsellors and therapists who integrate modern and traditional practices in Canadian aboriginal settings. If modern psychotherapeutic and traditional aboriginal counselling practice were based on opposing paradigms, then such integration of service delivery would not be possible.

The self was examined from six different perspectives in chapter 2 with research cited in support of each. The self may be perceived as stable, and the experience of counsellors suggests this self-stability may be problematic in therapy. Emotion or feeling is attached to cognitions that make up selfhood. We may be thought of as constructing our selves, and paradoxically, that our selves are constructed by culture. Social constructionists would have it both ways by suggesting we both create and are created by culture. While there are elements of the self that may be known and understood through evidence, there are also elements of the self as knower or observer that are harder to quantify. A comprehensive view of self should be able to unite these often antagonistic perspectives.

This chapter began with an examination of gender construction differences between Amerindian and European languages as an exemplar of how cultural differences could be expected to translate into differences in self-construction. This assumes that people aboriginal to the Americas had selves, but there has been a body of thought in European philosophy that has suggested that the self is a modern European invention. This led us to examine the Buddhist concept of "no-self" with the discovery that Buddhism found and made accommodations with the self in each culture it visited. A comparison of Western and Inuit counselling methods suggested core similarities of self between the two.

Those who view the self to be a recent European invention do a disservice to non-Europeans by denying their capacity for individual volition. They also do a disservice to the richness of European thought on the subject by denying the interdependence and social aspects of such cultures. For example, in his review of modern European philosophy, Seigel (2005) found a consensus that the self was a compound of bodily, relational and reflective elements, and none regarded the self as independent of social relations. If the most individualist of cultures includes recognition of the collectivity, then the dichotomization of culture between individualist and collectivist is too simplistic. While it would be expected that the self in more individualist cultures may be different from the self in collectivist cultures in some ways, acculturation is highly individualized with respect to both direction and degree (Arthur, 2003; Marin & Gamba, 2002; Organista, Organista, & Kurasaki, 2002).

Five decades ago, White (1969/1990) suggested, provocatively, "We must have a new science: a science of culture rather than a science of psychology if we are to understand the determinants of human behaviour" (p. 182). The attempt to unite psychology with cultural studies has made scant progress since. A mechanism is needed whereby cultural determinants of human behaviour may be understood in a way that also accounts for individualization of acculturative effects, the notion of will, and the capacity of the self for both stability and change. Such a mechanism may be developed from elemental units of culture called memes.

Notes

1   In this work, the term "aboriginal" when used as an adjective to identify earliest inhabitants of an area is lower case but when used as a proper noun is capitalized. With this convention the following sentence is understandable: "The Torres Strait Islanders and Aboriginals (coll. Aborigines) are both aboriginal to Australia." This use allows for a more nuanced discussion of gradients of meaning than would be otherwise possible. For example, in chapter 5 two research participants drew on Aboriginal Spirituality in their self-constructions, a proto-religion that includes adherence to the Medicine Wheel, a circular structure with a distinct presentation. Other spiritualties, aboriginal to the Americas, are possible including some that are not religiously held, and other ancient medicine wheels have been found that do not have the four part structure of the Medicine Wheel (Robertson, in press).

2   An exception being the Pacific coast Salishan and Sahaptin speaking peoples whose languages are either genderless or make use of male and female gender.

3   The Wanapum are a tribe of the Yakama nation in eastern Washington State, USA.

4   There is an important caveat to this oft made generalization about Japanese job security. When a major company downsizes and does not have positions for existing staff, it may ask suppliers, distributors, or other secondary companies dependent on the first to find positions for the displaced employee. This may result in surplus employees and these companies may then make the same request to a third layer of companies. Employees at the bottom layer of companies effectively have no job security. Thank you to Dr. Ronald Camp of the University of Regina for pointing this out to me.

5   The term "Elder" when capitalized in this context refers to a person with an identified role with respect to spiritual practice or healing in Aboriginal Spirituality sometimes referenced as "traditional Elder." I learned the difference between an "Elder" and an "elder" while at the Saskatchewan Indian Federated College (now First Nations University) during the early 1980s. Dr. Ahab Spence, a Cree linguist, Anglican priest, and former president of the Manitoba Indian Brotherhood was on staff. I approached Dr. Spence, who was in his seventies at the time, as my elder, but he could not have the title of "Elder" at the college because he did not practice Aboriginal Spirituality. People who indiscriminately capitalize "Elder" when referencing elderly who are aboriginal to the Americas fail to capture this nuance. Further, the practice of identifying all elders of a particular racial or ethnic group with a special designation would be racist.

6   Korhonen (2002) did not capitalize the term "elder," but she did not discuss the distinction between the general and specific use of the term in her study. She could have been adhering to standard English grammatical usage that does not normally capitalize the term. I made the judgement call that since the participants in her study were both traditional and were viewed as healers in their communities, the term should be capitalized. On the other hand, it could be argued that traditional aboriginal spirituality is not a religion with a prescribed worldview, and if the elderly in this sample followed this perspective then the term would not be capitalized when referencing them.

CHAPTER 4

The Potential of the Meme

I needed one more true and false question for the final exam. I decided it would be: "The majority of people who suffer from Acquired Immune Deficiency come from Africa (T/F)." Even though we had not specifically covered this question in class, the answer was found in the textbook and, besides, I was teaching bright Northern (Saskatchewan, Canada) Teacher Education Program (NORTEP) undergrads. Every student circled "F." If they had only flipped a coin half of them would have had it right! Something must have been biasing them to give the wrong answer. (Robertson, 2001)

Chapter 1 introduced the concept of the meme as an elemental unit of culture and the self as an interlocking cluster of such units. If we view the AIDS concept as understood in popular North American culture as composed of memes, then Dawkins' (1976) suggestion that such units of imitative or replicable culture exhibit attractive and repellent forces on other memes could be used to explain the biasing of the students' answers.

Memetic attraction has been offered when explanations based on self-interest or logic fail. In an examination of the witch-hunt that swept Europe from the fifteenth to the seventeenth centuries, Hofhuis and Boudry (2019) demonstrated that explanations focusing on class or gender benefit are inadequate. Increasingly virulent manifestations of the phenomena consumed people from all classes undermining the economic viability of the communities themselves. They concluded, "the apparent 'design' exhibited by concepts of witchcraft resulted from a Darwinian process of evolution, in which cultural variants that accidentally enhanced the reproduction of the witch-hunts were selected and accumulated" (p. 13).

The suggestion is made that people hold on to irrational beliefs because the complexes of memes (memplexi) involved have superior replicative power compared to competing clusters. Individuals cling to negative representations of themselves because those representations exert repellent force against competing memes. Religions thrive because we are driven to proselytize, casting their memes on both fertile and rocky soil. To its detractors, meme "theory" consists of such tautologies; however, if we can demonstrate a plausible way memes can be thought of as exerting differentially attractive force, then we will have demonstrated the means by which discrete complexes of memes may emerge that can so influence behaviour. We can then make the case that the self is one such "memeplex," and that as a cultural construct it is potentially linked to other complexes of memes. First, we will need to differentiate the meme from other cultural units such as "ideas" and "concepts." Then, in exploring the presumed dichotomy between free will and determinism, we shall see how these perspectives may be united and how a memetic understanding can provide an evolutionary explanation of the self. We begin by building on the concept of the meme as a replicable unit of culture.

The Meme "Meme"

There is little agreement on how the mental construct that is the self attaches, or is attached to, the material entity we call the body. Borghi et. al. (2013) conceived of words as quasi-external devices that extend our cognition.The suggestion that the body uses language to construct a self so as to extend its cognitive reach is compatible with a unitary holistic view. Although the body and mind may be indivisibly "us," the portion that is "mind" is made available through the medium of culture, with extended embodiment normally following routes and patterns suggested by grammatical structure and word associations. Donald (2001) explained, "Any given culture is a gigantic cognitive web, defining and constraining the parameters of memory, knowledge and thought in its members"(p. xiv). Culture not only delimits the interpretive possibilities; it creates the interpreter. Our complex relationship with the culture within which we are embedded places limitations on rational ability while extending the mind's reach.

As with the university students described at the beginning of this chapter, our beliefs and perceptions are biased by nonrational forces. In describing units of culture that exhibit nonrational replicative properties, Dawkins (1976) coined the term "meme"—in part as a derivative of the Greek word *mimetismos*: something imitated, and in part, because the word connotes gene-like properties of replication. As we shall see, this latter association was unfortunate; however, it "has gradually replaced such synonyms as 'mnemotype,' 'idene,' 'sociogene,' 'concept,' and 'culturgen' in describing this phenomena" (Wilson, 1999, p. 148). Despite this replicatory success, it is premature to talk about a "meme theory." True, Blackmore (1999) said the self consisted of complexes of these memes, but since the term was not precisely defined, she was merely restating that selves consist of units of culture—hardly a controversial statement—with her deterministic slant replicating the ideas of earlier behaviourists. In any case, if "meme" is merely a term given to elemental units of culture, their existence is hardly in question. In teasing out the properties of these units of culture, we may come to develop theories with respect to natural forces, in this case a theory about the self, but to do so we must explore the qualities of those units of culture that would make up such a self.

Early proponents of the term "meme" were excited by its analogy with the term "gene." Ridley (2003) noted that such units of culture must replicate with sufficient fecundity, fidelity, and longevity to compete with each other for their propagation to be subject to evolutionary laws similar to those guiding genetic evolution. The lack of a cultural "DNA" directing such replication led some (Boyd & Richerson, 2000; Coyne, 1999) to dismiss the concept of the meme out of hand. They noted memes are often systematically transformed during transmission—a process unlike natural selection; however, such dismissals are predicated on the notion that something like DNA is necessary for evolutionary change to occur. Is it possible that a unit of culture small enough to be passed from one mind to another, but more complex than a simple percept, replicates by processes not analogous to the gene metaphor? To answer this question, we must first consider what we mean by "meme."

A plethora of definitions flowed from Dawkins's rather imprecise initial conceptualization. At one extreme, Heath, Bell, and Sternberg(2001) equated memes with urban legends consisting of entire narratives. Such a definition is not particularly useful since the evolution of similarly sized and larger cultural artefacts we are interested in investigating will be informed by examining what within a given narrative changes and under what circumstances. Unless we view urban legends, religions, ideologies, and narratives generally as complexes of meme particulates, then the concept loses that usefulness.

At the other extreme, Logan (2008) said memes were concepts, and since each word is a symbol representing a mental conceptualization, each word is a meme. With this definition we are left wondering why we would need the word "meme" because "concept" or even "word" would do just as well. If particular units of culture can be demonstrated to be different from "concept" or "word," then its use might have utility.

Dawkins (1976) said complexes of memes come to predominate within a "cultural soup," dependent, not on their utility to their human hosts, but on their replicative ability. Mutations could bring unexpected results: "Scholars of the Septuagint started something big when they mistranslated the Hebrew word for 'young woman' into the Greek word for 'virgin,' thereby coming up with a prophecy 'behold a virgin shall conceive and bear a son" (p. 18).

Steven Pinker (1997), using a global definition of the term, chided Dawkins: "A complex meme does not arise from the retention of copying errors. It arises because some person knuckles down, racks his brain, musters his ingenuity, and composes or writes or paints or invents something" (p. 209). Dawkins (1982) anticipated Pinker by suggesting that cultural evolution may be Lamarckian:[1] intentionality, combined with creativity, may lead to a dynamic within cultural evolution that involves the passing on of deliberately acquired characteristics. Stephen Jay Gould (1996) agreed with Dawkins on the efficacy of cultural evolution, and that such evolution is Lamarckian, but he characterized Dawkins as being a "determinist." This is puzzling given Dawkins's statement, "We have the power to defy the selfish genes of our birth and, if necessary, the selfish memes of our indoctrination" (1976, p. 215). It is likely, therefore, that Gould's (1996) concern stems from a misreading of Dawkins, and this misreading actually supports an argument that there exist attractive forces between memes. Dawkins is an evolutionary biologist with a specialty in genetics and a penchant for using terms such as "replication" when talking about cultural units. These memes (evolutionary biology, genetics, and replication) have connotative meanings of "determinism," with accompanying negative emotional valence in the minds of some, regardless of what was actually said on the subject. Thus, this interaction between Dawkins and Gould may be used as an example of the utility of using a memetic perspective in analyzing discourse.

In fairness to Gould, Dawkins was not clear as to the source or nature of the attractive and repellent properties he attributed to memes, yet these properties are crucial to his cultural evolutionary model. Thus, we are left with the possibility that these attractive forces are somehow inherent within the memetic units themselves, with the resultant notion that "free will" is an unnecessary illusion. Our analysis of his exchange with Gould, however, revealed connotative and affective dimensions of memes held within the mind of the individual affect the understanding of that individual irrespective of referent definitions. While two individuals may agree on the conceptual definition of the word "meme," for one the valence is positive while for the other it is negative, making communication between the two problematic.

Defining memes as "the smallest complex ideas capable of replicating themselves with reliability and fecundity," Dennett (1991, p. 201) suggested human consciousness is a huge memeplex. Since our minds have finite capacity, memes within a given culture would be in an evolutionary struggle for "mind space." Dennett (1995) subsequently added that memes, to be successful, need only replicate, and this replication would not be directly tied to our own survival as human beings. A simple melody or advertising jingle that comes, unbidden, into our minds is obviously a good replicator. The phrase "Play it again, Sam" is a better replicator, and is, therefore, commonly "remembered" in place of the actual phrase "Play it Sam, for old time's sake" in the classic movie, *Casablanca*. A suicide cult that results in the death of its members does not result in the death of the associated cult if the murder-suicide has the effect of spreading the memes involved to other minds. Dennett (1996) also made the controversial suggestion that memeplexi are a kind of life form in an ecosystem of human minds called culture, whose replicatory interest exists independently of our individual or collective interest as a species, thriving by convincing us to abandon our sense of reason except for mundane purposes. This life form exists in a nonmaterial world of our collective mental operations and is enhanced and extended by our libraries, computers, media, and related technology.

Memes are made of words that in themselves are devices of communication and that communication, paradoxically, requires some purposive direction. The use of words to communicate abstractions and conceptualizations and their linkages enhances our cognitive functioning. As we have seen from the exchange between Dawkins and Gould, connotative and emotive factors may drive behaviours that contribute to (or inhibit) memetic propagation. Thus, we can conclude that not all words are memes, and there is a place for the term in our vocabulary, representing a level of complexity that includes connotative association, affect, and behavioural injunctions in addition to a referent describing a simple percept or concept. Thus, for most of us, the adjective in the phrase "the red apple" is not a meme but the term "red" as applied to a political movement might be.

After reviewing 120 million retweets with respect to a Japanese earthquake (2011), a Republican political campaign in the United States (2012), and the "Arab Spring" in Egypt and Syria (2011 and 2012) on the microblogging platform Twitter, and comparing the propagation of those memes with a computer simulation postulating an unlimited number of memes in competition for a large but limited number of minds, Weng, Flammini, Vespignani, and Menczer (2012) concluded that the dynamics of information diffusion meant that a few memes would naturally go viral while most would not, irrespective of their intrinsic values. They noted that the results do not constitute a proof that exogenous features play no role in determining popularity, but that such features are not necessary to explain the observed global dynamics. A random meme, such as the notion that the Arab Spring was connected to democratization, may gain popularity and thereby influence public policy without being grounded in fact. The authors concluded, "While the intrinsic features of viruses and their adaptation to hosts are extremely relevant in determining the winning strains, in the information world the limited time and attention of human behaviour are sufficient to generate a complex information landscape" (p. 6).

Weng and his colleagues actually measured meme dissemination, not meme propagation. Propagation requires both dissemination and internalization. Had, for example, Western populations been predisposed to the notion that those rebelling were terrorists, then the propagation of the notion that the Arab Spring was about democracy would likely not have occurred no matter how widely the meme was disseminated. The meme would not have resonated with the worldview of those encountering it.

Returning to my college of education students referenced at the beginning of this chapter, as a society, we spent considerable resources emphasizing that AIDS in North America is a "pandemic." Attention was given to the concept of "safe sex," which was then modified to "safer sex." Everyone is considered "at risk," except for those who choose total sexual abstinence, with the effect of stalling the 1960s sexual revolution. Further, the notion of identifying black people with negative outcomes has a politically incorrect connotation. Over the preceding decades an anti-AIDS memeplex consisting of such considerations developed in North America that has the effect of repelling the idea that the majority of AIDS cases are in Africa. At the level of affect, the right answer to my exam question did not feel right. The implications of this go beyond university education.

Atran (2002) discussed communication involving religious beliefs as a case in point. In one set of experiments, he asked Christians to write the meanings of the biblical Ten Commandments. Despite the subjects' own expectations, interpretations of the commandments showed wide ranges of variation, with little evidence of consensus. In another experiment, normal subjects and autistics interpreted ideological and religious sayings such as "Let a thousand flowers bloom" and "To everything there is a season." Autistic subjects showed a significant tendency to closely paraphrase and repeat content from the original statement (for example: "Don't cut flowers before they bloom"). The non-autistic controls tended to infer a wider range of cultural meanings with little replicated content (for example, "Go with the flow" or "Everyone should have equal opportunity"). Only the autistic subjects—who lack the degree of inferential capacity normally associated with theory of mind—came close to functioning as Blackmore's (1999) replicating "meme machines."

Defining the Meme Using Selected Studies

Memes have been invoked to explain the size of the human brain (Blackmore, 1999), the prevalence of research into peoples' deficits as opposed to strengths (Fincham & Beach, 2010), the continued use of ineffective therapies in speech pathology (Kamhi, 2008), cults and addictions (Henson, 2002), and the prevalence of religion (Brodie, 1996). This section explores how the meme has been used in research to explore urban legends, environmental activism, and contagion in suicidal behaviour.

Replicatory power in urban legends

Equating memes with urban legends, Heath, Bell, and Sternberg (2001) studied the effect of emotional valence on meme propagation. In an initial experiment, sixty-three university undergraduates rated 17 urban legends, drawn from a database of 112, for emotion-inducing content on a seven-point Likert scale that covered eight emotions. Subjects were also asked whether they would pass each story on to others. The stories that evoked reactions of interest, disgust, and surprise were more likely to be passed on.

In a second experiment, the researchers manipulated the capacity of stories to evoke disgust by varying the content. For example, in one story a man opens a beverage and: 1) notices a dead mouse at the bottom; 2) drinks some beverage before noticing a dead mouse at the bottom; or 3) ingests part of the mouse before noticing it. Forty-two undergrads were asked to read twelve such stories and rate them as low-, medium-, and high-level disgusting. Participants reported that they were more willing to pass along stories rated highly disgusting irrespective of whether the story was thought to be true, plausible, or likely to change behaviour.

In a third variation of this study, three researchers independently rated seventy-six stories for the following seven disgust motifs (coefficient alphas are given in brackets): unusual sexual activity such as bestiality (.96), contact with bodily substances such as feces or urine (.88), violations of hygiene (.76), ingestion of inappropriate food such as rats or bodily substances (.96), violations of the body (.84), contact with proscribed animals (.93). These motifs were then applied to the results of experiment 1. Those stories that had more disgust motifs were more likely to be shared.

This study lends support to the argument that memetic propagation is aided by associated emotions such as disgust. By understanding each legend as a complex of memes, we can allow for a number of different emotions to be associated with each. For example, one additional emotion, mentioned by the authors, might be thankfulness that the related incidents had not happened to the hearer. Another emotion might be a feeling of superiority to those involved. A confounding variable might involve the motives of those passing stories along. For example, it may be that fundamentalist Christians who believe that Halloween is an evil holiday would be more likely to believe, and pass on, stories about contaminated Halloween candy.

The meme in participatory environmental research

Using the definition of "meme" as a unit of cultural transmission containing a specific substantive message, and following consultations with villagers bordering a protected rainforest in central Mexico, Robles-Diaz-de-Leon (2003) created "environmental memes" such as the following:

> "Limpio" (Clean)
> Would you like to have a clean town?
> Everything is better if we make an effort.
> Pick up the garbage off the streets.
> You know the truth about the environment.
> Talk to others about it. (p. 31)

The "Limpio" meme is smaller than an urban legend, but larger than a word or simple concept. As can be seen, it contains a number of concepts linked by connotative, emotive, and behavioural factors. Through the use of questionnaires, people in four separate villages identified separate environmental concerns for each village: 1) garbage in the streets, 2) grey water, 3) burning plastics, and 4) the lack of recreational usage. A fifth village was used as a control, with no environmental issue identified. The researcher initially measured the amount of garbage in the streets, grey water, burnt plastics, and recreational use in each of the five villages. She then selected a different intervention in each village to deal with its environmental issue. In village A, she organized a public meeting where the "Limpio" meme was co-constructed. In village B, she developed a similar meme, without a public meeting, promoting recreational use, and this meme was advertised on posters placed in public locations. In village C, she organized a participatory meeting to discuss the issue of grey water without the specific development of a relevant meme. In village D, the issue of burning plastics was raised in poster form without a public meeting and without meme construction.

Researchers recounted the amount of garbage, recreational use, grey water and burning plastics after a three-month interval and compared the change in each with that of the control village using a measure of covariance. For example, the amount of garbage in the control village increased from 5.46 units per street to 7 units during the course of the study. In only two villages did the amount of garbage decline: the one which involved the participatory (Limpio) meme construction and the village where the issue of burning plastics was raised.

Village B initially had the lowest rate of recreational usage, but after the distribution of memetically based posters, had the highest. No other village recorded a significant variation in recreational usage from the control. None of the towns associated with the remaining two issues (grey water and burning plastics) differed from the control at the post-test.

Robles-Diaz-de-Leon (2003) concluded that the most successful method of aiding people to change their behaviours involved the use of memes, with no difference in effectiveness recorded between the effectiveness of the meme developed through participatory co-construction and the one developed by the researcher alone. The village targeted for the issue of burning plastics produced a significant difference with respect to garbage in the streets. This suggests that there were other confounding variables, such as the actions of informal leaders, for which the study had no control.

Memetic priming for suicide

Marsden (2001) tested the suicide contagion hypothesis that exposure to a suicide meme will increase suicide risk. Since ethical considerations precluded direct experimentation, he exposed the concept of suicide to an experimental group of 67 adult internet users by telling them the study was about "young people and suicide." Both the experimental and control group (who were not told what the study was about) read a text about a hypothetical distressed student and each participant was then asked to estimate the likelihood that the distressed student would commit suicide on a five-point Likert scale. The experimental group rated the likelihood of suicide higher than the control group. This experiment was actually about the effects of priming on the interpretations of an experimental group with no known history of suicide ideation. While priming and contagion may be related, it is a leap to suggest this constitutes evidence of a suicide contagion meme.

Defining the meme

These three studies demonstrate that a definition of meme as a small replicating unit of culture is insufficient. Without a description of the source of an attractive force incorporated into its definition, the meme "meme" remains a tautology. The studies on urban legends and environmental activism suggest connotation and affect as the source of such attraction, which, added to Dawkins's (1976) originating concept, results in the following definition: A meme is the smallest unit of culture having referent, connotative, affective, and behavioural components that may be transmitted from one person to another. Such a meme would rarely, if ever, be copied in its entirety from one mind to another. Atran (2001) concluded that memetic evolution is not possible as it lacks the requisite fidelity for a competition for survival. This is, however, generalizing from a sample of one and there should be no assumption that cultural evolution follows the same rules as those in the physical world.

An Evolutionary Account of the Self as a Complex of Memes

For Blackmore (1999), the self is an interlocking complex of memes, with those including the illusion of free will more successful at replication. If I think that I have freely chosen a religion or ideology, then I will be more invested in membership. If an additional meme to proselytize is added to the complex, then I will become active in spreading it to others. As we have seen, Dawkins (1976) left room for free will, but he failed to delineate a process whereby we could rise above the dictates of our genes and memes. The tension between the view that successful memes or constellations of memes convince us to abandon reason and the view that we have free will reminds us of the social constructionist position of recognizing the power and influence of culture while simultaneously insisting on the individual's power to self-construct. Before constructing a plausible theory of the evolution of the self that would give us the capacity to see through the illusion, we need to examine this paradox.

Dennett's (1991, 1996) idea that we carry within our minds "multiple drafts of reality" in any given moment has application here. We would need to consciously and rationally choose one draft over others to exercise free will. Failure to consider other drafts of reality would indicate genetic or environmental shaping. A being capable of some modicum of free will would necessarily place their self at the centre of each draft of reality, with volitional planning resulting from consideration of probabilities. The hypothesis that a being incapable of volitional planning might nonetheless be programmed to think it has free will necessitates a more complicated process involving malevolent clusters of memes invading and misleading bodies with suggestions of free will. It is unclear in such a dynamic whether "we" are our bodies or the invaders. While it is possible that neither the body nor the hypothesized invading memeplex has free will, the explanation appears inelegant.

Consideration of affect and connotation associated with particular memes helps resolve the issue of incipient dualism. If such affect and connotation varies between individuals, then, at one level of abstraction, it is the embodied individual that is binding particular memeplexi together through individualized emotive valence, but since the process is done within the framework of our cultural experience it is encumbered by such forces. The question we need to consider is whether cultural evolution could have led to individuals capable of conscious volition.

Following an evolutionary model, the characteristics that constitute the modern self would have been only partially present in earlier versions. We can visualize an elemental proto-self co-evolving with an equally elemental culture based on mimetic replication. Once we have a fully functioning self along with a culture capable of reproducing and maintaining such selves with fidelity, providing such a self has some degree of independent will, it is possible to visualize that self engaging in deliberative behaviours that change or "create" the surrounding culture.

We are taught to have selves. Caregivers assume infants have selves with motivations, desires, and unique personalities, and they reinforce this understanding in taught language. As a result, most of us develop a theory of who we are through the interpretation of early life experiences. If our caregivers act in a loving way toward us, we learn we are loveable. The interpretation we bring to our early life experiences serves as a core worldview from which future experiences are referenced and understood. The self becomes the protagonist in an understanding of how the world works. As we saw with the example in chapter 1, practically any self feels better than no self at all. With a self we can relate to others and anticipate their reactions to our behaviours. We can situate ourselves both temporally and contextually. We view adults who have difficulty with these social tasks, such as those with Alzheimer's or autism, as disabled. But in a culture where infants are not taught to have selves and where the language lacks the words to ask "Who am I?" relatively selfless people would be the norm. Such populations must once have existed.

Blackmore (1999, 2000) noted that human brain size far exceeds that which would be required for selective advantage over our nearest rivals, thereby eliminating species competition as the driving evolutionary force behind its development. She suggested a sexual alternative: humans able to display more memes were preferred mates. The resultant evolutionary spiral led to oversized brains for much the same reason the male peacock developed extensive plumage.

Coyne (1999) replied that the human brain reached its present volume approximately five hundred thousand years ago while the proliferation of language-based memes would have begun only thirty to fifty thousand years ago. While this makes the meme hypothesis an unlikely candidate as a driver in the evolution of brain size, it allows for the possibility that memes had a role in the colonization of left hemispheric processes in the development of language. Such a suggestion produces a temporal lens from which we can view memetic evolution; however, the beginnings of the self occurred earlier.

Damasio (1999) said the process of the body monitoring its internal states, necessary for homeostasis, creates a feeling of "me," giving us the ability to react to external stimuli. It may be anthropomorphic to suggest that an organism reacting to a stimulus has a "feeling of me," however, some internal unified response system is evident, and that system would be a necessary but insufficient condition for the creation of selfhood. At some point, perhaps a million years ago, our ancestors developed the capacity to recognize their reflection—a capacity we currently share with chimpanzees and bonobos. Increased mimetic or imitative behaviour would have followed this capacity for self-recognition, but if we define the self as a cognitive self-referencing structure, then these ancestors did not have it. Blind, deaf, and dumb in her formative years, Helen Keller (1905) reported she lacked self-definition and was not fully conscious until she had acquired a language.

Humans appear to be the only species with true language. We take phonemes, which by themselves are meaningless, and combine them to form a virtual limitless supply of words with each word symbolically representing something. Our languages build categorizations and associations. Dogs are canines which, in turn, are mammals. We link words in sentences and stories leading to associations and conceptualizations impossible in a non-languaged culture. Language is like a computer program that extends our mental capacities without the necessity of larger brains. The replacement of "one-sound, one-meaning" signals with a sequential system of phonemes was a foundational evolutionary development. It has been elegantly proposed that two pre-existent systems, an expressive system such as is found in bird-song and a lexical system such as is found in non-human primate calls and honeybee waggle dances, combined to give us human language syntax (Miyagawa, Berwick, & Okanoya, 2013). Thus, early hominids communicated simple memes through mime and one-sound, one-meaning signals with increasing complexity driving brain evolution. That evolution plateaued about five hundred thousand years ago when practical anatomical limits to increasing brain size were reached: larger headed babies would kill the mother and babies born even more prematurely (all human infants are born prematurely compared to other primates) would be in danger of the same fate. Evolution waited for some anatomical change, but instead we got language.

With this vastly improved software, we were able to develop ourselves as "selved" beings—not immediately, of course; the software was running but there was no one to direct the programming. Under this paradigm, our ancestors were true "meme machines," replicating increasingly sophisticated memes and implementing memetic algorithms when triggered by appropriate behavioural stimuli. At some point, a combination of memes answered the question "Who am I?" without the question ever being asked.

An evolutionary perspective allows us to avoid the assumption that the self emerged suddenly. For example, the widespread replication of the Paleolithic Achaean hand axe (D. M. Johnson, 2003; Lycett, 2008) suggests that makers were able to hold the conceptual design of the axe in mind. Similarly, the common Paleolithic practice of burying useful or valuable objects along with the deceased (Duarte, et al., 1999; Riel-Salvatore, et al., 2001) suggests a projected identity that would need such objects. Referencing Paleolithic data, Montemayor and Haladjian (2017) argued that increasingly complex cognitive systems evolved with a capacity for guiding attention while more primal independent perceptual systems continued to operate. The self would be one such evolving cognitive system.

The general acceptance of the notion our ancestors developed selves during the neo-Paleolithic era (Blackmore, 1999; Leary, 2004) is grounded in the period's record of developed art and conceptualized tool making. For example, our earliest toolmaking varied according to the resources available; a suitable rock would be used to hammer or scrape without thought of giving it a specific shape for that purpose. With the Achaean axe, local materials were shaped to fit a particular and effective conceptualization and this design meme was imitated in various locations across the globe. Surely people capable of constructing from an abstract conceptualization had selves! Possibly, but not necessarily the type of selves we experience today.

Following his hermeneutic analysis of early Greek literature, Jaynes (1976) suggested pre-Homeric Greeks were not conscious of a self and were, therefore, unable to exercise self-agency. His most controversial suggestion was when events happened for which their culture had not developed a preprogrammed response, increasing levels of impotent distress led to right hemispheric brain activity. Resultant visions were interpreted as messages from the gods, leading to new random behaviours. If the new behaviours successfully met the triggering conditions that caused distress, they were then added to the culture in storied form, and those stories then encoded into the culture as a new learned response pattern. With a different interpretation of similar data that added an examination of early Egyptian culture, and using a definition of mind to mean a cognitive structure that allows for the notions of objectivity and reason, David Martel Johnson (2003) said the early Greeks and Egyptians did not have minds. Once the mind so defined evolved in a particular population, its adaptive efficacy led to its replication in other populations. Jaynes's (1976) "self" is situated within the cognitive structure Johnson (2003) calls "mind," which in turn are culturally evolved entities. Following an examination of a series of neuro-imaging studies on hallucinatory patients, Rowe (2012) observed, "The change from bicamerality to consciousness does not require genetic modification. The acquisition of a narrative self with an analog 'I' and a metaphor 'me' can be accomplished by culture and learning" (p. 503). As Harre (1984) commented:

> Even if Jaynes' claim … to have identified the moment at which mankind invented self-consciousness as the experiential aspect of novel practices of self-ascription of responsibility for and sources of intentions to perform actions as sometime between the composition of the *Illiad* and the *Odyssey* is fantasy, the fact that his claim is clearly intelligible (and might conceivably be defensible) demolishes the necessary universality aspect of Kant's claim. To put it crudely, we learn to be conscious. … (p. 145)

The development of most of the major world religions occurred during the epoch following the period described by Johnson and Jaynes.

We have seen how the core themes of justice, humanity, temperance, wisdom, and transcendence developed in the philosophical and religious traditions of China, South Asia, and the West (Dahlsgaard, et al., 2005). Earlier, Jaspers (1951) noted that the basis of these traditions flowed from the thoughts of Confucius, Lao Tzu, Buddha, Zarathustra, Moses, Homer, and Plato, all of whom lived during the same period of time (800 to 200 BCE). He named this epoch "the Axial Age," surmising, "This was when the man with whom we live today came into being" (p. 135). Mahoney (1991) called this epoch "a time of turnings ... of unprecedented reflective and spiritual activity ... when humans first 'formally' discovered the universe within themselves and the powers of faith and reason" (pp. 29–30).

Much of the philosophical and religious thought flowing from the Axial Age dealt with concepts such as justice, humanity, and temperance, reflecting the role of the individual in society. It is argued here that the emergence of individuals with a capacity for objective, volitional, and internally consistent thought would have necessitated such a redefinition of roles, and this was a factor in the philosophical outpouring marking this period. As discussed in the previous chapter, the Buddhist doctrine of no-self appears to be a reaction to a volitional self already present ("Buddha", 1980; Nishida, 1921/1990; Sogyal-Rinpoche, 1993), and early Confucian thought dealt with the moral development of the self in relation to the collectivity (Wu, 2017). While the presence of people whose selves were programmed for individual volition might be potentially destabilizing to host collectivist societies, such individuals allow an increased range of responses to problems or opportunities and for time-delineated planning. Thus, societies that incorporated the services of such persons as leaders, sages, or oracles would have had a competitive advantage over their neighbours, but their influence, if uncontrolled could be destabilizing. Religion protected the collectivity by constraining the behaviours of these volitional individuals.

Now we return to the question of how a complex of memes interacting on the body's hardware could result in consciousness. Who is this knower behind what is known, the self-changer behind the self that is changed? The answer might be found in mathematics. With reference to Gödel's theorem, a self-referencing formula that is simultaneously both true but unprovable (mathematically false), Hofstadter (2007) suggested any sufficiently powerful self-referencing feedback loop will create pressure to shift from "the goalless level of mechanics … to the goal-orientated level of cybernetics" (p. 160). He hypothesized the self is such a "strange loop" and that qualities of individuality and volition automatically flow from having one.

The strange loop of the self is at once an illusion and the source of that unique human characteristic that allows us to dispel illusions: our ability to reason. The feedback loop allows us to observe ourselves and simultaneously become aware of our own subjectivity. This immediately presents us with the notion that there is an objective reality, although some of us may retreat into the rationalization that no one can be completely objective—comforting because such a rationalization allows us to keep alive idiosyncratic illusions that could otherwise be challenged. But even the most postmodernist among us define their objective selves in terms of what may be "proved" or "disproved." I put the terms in quotation marks because, of course, what counts as proof will vary, and if we take the logic to its conclusion then nothing (including this statement) can be proved absolutely.

The notion of our own subjectivity leads us to fear the possibility of self-serving illusions. It was the fear of fooling herself that led the suicidal youth described in chapter 1 to cling to negative self-descriptors—she wanted to believe positive things about herself, but she was afraid the positive would not be true and this concern was reinforced emotionally. Having a self can indeed be a curse—we become aware of our mortality, our possible failings, and our terrible responsibility for making our own choices. We are cast out of the innocence referenced in the Garden of Eden myth, and we become aware of our capacity for self-deception.

In ordinary discourse what is accepted as true is negotiated with those around us. I might like to think I am the world's greatest dancer, but I need confirmation of the fact. A Cuban once told me, "You dance like a Canadian," but if I associate with Canadians who happen to support my dancing illusion, then perhaps this particular aspect of myself-definition can be preserved. I may develop conspiracy theories to explain my inability to win dancing competitions. I may rationalize that I am above competition, but the point is, I need some means to convince myself that I am not engaged in mere self-deception or the game is up. While self-enhancing illusions may be a factor in mental health (S. E. Taylor, 1989), we are continually referencing what passes for an objective or evidence-based reality.

The ability to observe one's objective self with a sense of continuity and distinctness was necessary to gain a sense of agency. Using the "strange loop" model of Hofstadter (2007), once self-referencing memes contributing to the notions of continuity and uniqueness are present, then agency will arise. Thus, the notion of William James (1892/1999), that the objective and subjective selves cannot be separated, is confirmed, and the difficulty of Damon and Hart (1988) in finding defining questions for the subjective self that did not lead back to the objective self is explained: The two aspects of self co-evolved and are tightly dependent on each other. This cultural adaptation was so successful in improving problem solving and goal-oriented planning that the self was quickly replicated in all cultures with different manifestations. Thus, while in Japanese culture the self outside of the group is considered incomplete, there is still a self whose relationship to the collectivity is defined.

I have proposed a mechanism by which mind could be said to have evolved out of the brain (Robertson, 2007, 2017). A hominid evolved with the capacity to retain cultural memes learned through imitation. The patterns of such learned behaviour to triggering stimuli became increasingly complex, all the more so with the invention of language. An individual might have a collection of memeplexi leading to different phenotypic behaviour triggered by particular stimuli, and these behaviours were likely, but not necessarily, related to whether or not they increased the individual's probability of survival. Eventually a memeplex evolved representing the self and this allowed individuals to objectify themselves within a larger context. Sensory inputs placed on culturally learned frames of understanding were now related to the individual as conscious thinking. Such individuals learned to see themselves both as objects within a larger context and as activators and animators. This, in turn, allowed for an even more complex cognitive structure: mind. If Jaynes (1976) and Johnson (2003) are right, this latest advance in cultural evolution occurred relatively recently in human history.

As we have seen, Blackmore (1999, 2000) aligned her understanding with behavioural determinism. In such an understanding, the illusion of the self evolved as the clever creation of clusters of memes to enhance their replicatory power. If we think we have a self and our responses are freely determined decisions of that self, then we become emotionally committed to the memeplexi behind those responses, even to the point of subsuming those imagined selves to the will of religious or ideological collectivities. Dawkins was mistaken: we cannot override our selfish genes and our equally selfish memes; we can only be buffeted about by competition between competing memeplexi and the dictates of our genes. There is, however, an alternate memetic view available that situates the self in mind and supports the notion of free will.

Both camps within memetics, determinist and nondeterminist, agree that once our ancestors developed a capacity for imitation, memetic transference became possible. Increasingly complex clusters of memes governed behaviour, but these memeplexi evolved algorithmically in Darwinian fashion—there was no self to guide the process. Eventually, however, individuals acquired self-referencing memes that became preserved in cultures by patterns of social discourse, including grammatical changes to language such as the use of indexical pronouns. With this development children are taught to have selves as part of the process of language acquisition. Further refinements or mutations included notions of volition, individuality, and constancy normative in self-construction.

The concept of individual volition entails a being that is in some sense unique from others. If deliberating involves a future event, then the notion of volition requires a feeling of constancy that the individual may be present in the planned for future. The act of planning requires making choices from possible behaviours while predicting results. What constitutes evidence useful in making predictions may be idiosyncratic; however, once the concept of individual volition is operative, failure invites retrospective analysis. While a range of explanations for failure is generally possible, if a postulated need for increased objectivity leads to greater success in predicting results, then that behaviour is reinforced. Free will is to be found in setting aside habitual behaviours in consideration of new possibilities. While the individual is never truly autonomous with respect to biological and cultural influences, and those "determinants" would create a statistical probability favouring certain behavioural responses, the consideration of alternatives in selecting those that best satisfy personal needs, coupled with the ability to act on those choices, would constitute acts of free will. As Racine (2017) explained, "Free will originates from the first person experience of the world and one's self-constructed understanding of his or her agency in the course of action. Clearly, this understanding is socially constructed, shaped in interaction with others and influenced by cultural backgrounds that nourish interpretations of the phenomenon of agency" (p. 7).

Free will occurs with the capacity to understand our subjectivity by objectifying ourselves to our selves. Once we understand our subjectivities, we can contemplate other perspectives. Once we objectify ourselves, we can imagine ourselves in other contexts exhibiting new behaviours. We can revise what counts as evidence. We can even study genetic and cultural forces. With this information, we have the potential to make choices at variance with both genetic and memetic pressure. While no will can be totally unencumbered, we can direct the change of our personal cultural evolution.

Lamarckian evolution is not dependent upon random mutation but on purposive change. In the metaphor of Johnson-Laird (1988/1990), the self is a software package that allows the organism to stand outside of itself, bracketing presumptions in Husserlian fashion. While all aspects of an individual's horizon of understanding may not be so accessible, some are. It is the resultant approximation to an objective reality that allows the individual to make choices at variance with his genetic and memetic dictates.

Seeking an accommodation between classical behaviourism and free will, Vygotsky (1939, 1986; 2004) suggested that the emergence of higher cognitive processes were brought about by the mastery of the means of cultural behaviour and thinking. Briefly, conditioning processes lead to a "natural memory," which we share with other animals. The historical development of humans, however, "went beyond the limits of psychological functions given to them by nature and proceeded to a new culturally elaborated organization of their behaviour" (Wertsch, 1988, p. 25). These "higher mental functions," including consciousness, have social origins and are governed by a different set of rules than the more primal functions. Elementary functions continue to follow behaviourist principles, thus providing evidence of determinism. But a second possibility exists whereby stimulation may be self-generated internally, leading to new or alternate behaviours. It is in this second level of organization that will may be found.

Vygotsky's (2004) suggestion—"Every product of the imagination, stemming from reality, attempts to complete a full circle and to be embodied in reality" (p. 41)—has a memetic flavour. Our creative and imaginative processes are based in experiential reality interpreted through culture with units of that culture grouped and extended in novel ways, and these interpretive creations then cause the creator to experience "agony" when those creations are not then embodied in reality. Put memetically, complexes of memes assembled in the mind of the individual drive the individual to replication. We may create these narratives based on our motivations, needs, interests, and history, but the suggestion that these narratives then produce emotional responses directing specific behaviours has implications for free will.

To what degree can we say we construct the original narrative? Csikszentmihalyi (1993) defined "flow" as a process of losing your self in an activity, that is, not being self-aware but relying on intuitive responses. If one's self is not present in the construction of a narrative, who or what is controlling the process? If memes exert a differentially attractive force on other memes, the presence of one such unit of culture may attract related pieces of culture without conscious effort on the part of the narrator, thus explaining the concept of "flow." As Nietzsche observed, "A thought comes when it wishes, not when 'I' wish"(quoted in Seigel, 2005, p. 550). According to Price (1999), memetic flow may be compared to natural phenomena:

> A meme in fact, is like the single raindrop. It falls with others upon a pre-formed perceptual landscape. Isolated thoughts gather together in a string—a pattern of co-existing memes— which we might compare to a few drops congregating together in a splash of water. With sufficient mass the splash of water starts to flow into streams and rivers which are, if we like, the connectors between the raindrops and the pools and lakes, if not the oceans, of our thoughts. (p. 78)

Passively accepting flow may allow for the unexamined creation of antisocial, alcoholic, sexist, racist, or terrorist narratives, each demanding a Vygostskian embodiment in reality. Recognizing this dark possibility, Csikszentmihalyi (1993) recommended mental parameters: "If you achieve control over your mind, your desires, and your actions, you are likely to increase order around you. If you let them be controlled by genes and memes, you are missing the opportunity to be yourself" (p. 290).

The mind reels. On the one hand, we are the creation of our genes and memes, and on the other, we are advised to not let them control us. From where does this "true self" that is capable of critically evaluating and directing memetic flow come? Memes or memetic combinations can trigger emotions, including a "feeling of me." At any particular time, perhaps due to familiarity, perhaps due to some objective criteria, a particular narrative is recognized as the captain of the organism.

After a successful psychic mutiny, the new captain declares himself to be the true captain capable of banishing malevolent commands from competing genes and memes that had confounded the old captain.

It is difficult to visualize how such a self-narrative could be capable of establishing objective primacy over other narratives. If we view the self not as a narrative, but as an evolved cultural structure that replicated within populations because of its efficacy at reducing subjective perceptions, then it may be just the vehicle to hold in check both imaginative and relativistic excess. On the other hand, if the self were a cultural structure, it would be affected, if not determined, by cultural grand narratives. Such grand narratives would define "truth" and the self capable of holding such truths. We are left with polar opposites that are both simultaneously true: The self is determined; the self determines.

In summation, the self began as a unified system of responses identified with an organism that evolved through a series of incremental steps leading to self-referencing and a capacity for objective thought. This "evolved self" contains assumptions of personal volition, continuity, and reason, which became benchmarks of what it means to be human. While the capacity to visualize free will allows for its application in some instances, we continue to function primarily as the primordial being of our origins. Nonetheless, the ability to conceive of our individual existence in an objective manner allows us to develop new understandings and new volitional behaviours. As Sagan (1996) observed, "every time we exercise self-criticism, every time we test our idea against the outside world, we are doing science" (p. 27).

Self-definition may be viewed as a kind of hypothesis which we continually test against what we come to hold as evidence. That self-definition can only consist of the materials available at the time, that is, units of culture. The next section explores early attempts to map that self and concludes with the method used to inform this research.

The Implicit Self Made Explicit

For the most part, we live by an unconsciously assumed definition of ourselves that we partially retrieve in specific contexts. For example, if someone were to ask us to do something illegal or immoral and we reply, "I am not that kind of person," then we have retrieved into consciousness that aspect of our selves for the purpose of dealing with that particular situation. If we are faced with the demands of a different situation, we draw on a different part of our self-definition, but this does not mean we are a different person. It means that we are a complex (and evolving) person with values, strengths, and predispositions of which we may only be partially aware. The challenge of this project is to devise a method of cataloguing and mapping the self that allows a holistic view. Finally, the method used to generate the qualitative maps described in the next chapter will allow other clinicians and researchers to generate their own maps. First, I review earlier attempts to map this self and measure their success against what we have learned about the self thus far.

Five overlapping perspectives by which the self may be understood were reviewed in chapter 2: stable, neurological, constructed, socially constructed, and behavioural. The perspective of William James was also reviewed, but he failed to show how cultural and genetic factors interacted to produce the agency, individuality, and continuity in his "subjective self." Since research was found in support of each perspective, a comprehensive representational system would need to be compatible with each. Commenting on the problem of system complexity, Hartman (1995) explained that information overload leads us to "particularize," reduce, and simplify with resultant "damage to the complexity inherent in reality" (p. 112). Such simplifications arrange reality in linear chains of cause and effect, displaying limitations inherent in language more than the nature of the real world. From this understanding, the various schools of psychology necessarily focus on a limited horizon, with each perspective sufficient to the understanding of their respective therapeutic methodologies. The complexity of the self in its totality is not normally broached. While this project is to understand that complexity and thus be compatible with the major themes described in chapters 2 and 3, it should be remembered that a map is never the actual terrain.

Miles and Huberman (1994) suggested that conceptual frameworks in qualitative research be displayed graphically, allowing the researcher to work with all the information at once. Applying this method to the self should allow for the holistic perspective we seek; however, previous attempts to map the self have met with limited success. A review of those attempts will serve to illustrate the advantages of a memetic perspective.

Using weighted vectors of environmental and psychological indicators obtained from the observation of play, emotion, speech, and expression, Lewin (1931) attempted to predict behaviours in children. His conclusion that the accumulation of relevant factors sufficiently known and mapped as part of a dynamic process would allow for the accurate prediction of behaviour, placed him in the determinist camp. He later (1933) modified this stance to suggest the purpose of creating these "psycho-biological fields of force" was to derive all of the possibilities of actual behaviour. Speculation on unconscious drives or forces that may determine psychological makeup was not needed as vectors to illustrate the interplay between observed psychological factors and the surrounding environment was considered sufficient for predictive purposes. Lewin (1943) subsequently declared his "field theory" was not properly a theory at all because it was not falsifiable. He explained, "Field theory is probably best characterized as a method: namely, a method of analyzing causal relations and of building scientific constructs" (p. 294). Maps illustrating the contribution of multiple psychological and environmental factors as "fields of force" were further complicated by consideration of the psychological past, present, and anticipated future of the individual. Since the complexity envisioned resulted in more dimensions than could be represented diagrammatically, Lewin resorted to multidimensional mathematical formulae. While he experienced success in predicting future behaviour, the increasing complexity made replication difficult. Simplified caricatures of his method with limited utility may be found on the internet.

Lewin's predictive successes support a deterministic view of behaviour. One experiment (Lewin & Lippitt, 1938) demonstrated how the manipulation of environmental forces could be used to implant a predetermined result in a so-called democratic workplace setting. Kariel (1956) noted that the leadership qualities required to produce consensus and maximize production in this setting served to undermine labour unions and government regulatory bodies charged with protecting workers.

Lewin's project was not to understand or enhance the self of the individual but to understand those forces that shape behaviour. Ultimately, the project was overwhelmed by variables added in an attempt to accurately predict behaviour without accounting for feelings of individuality, continuity, or volition. A model of self must account for such feelings even if, in the end, such feelings prove to be illusory.

In contrast to the complexity of Lewin's "force field analysis," the "eco-maps" of social work and "mind-maps" in education are exceedingly simple. Eco-maps were originally graphic representations of the systems at play in a client's life, although Vodde and Giddings (2000) adapted it for use with social work practicum students. In commending the use of these maps, Hartman (1995) said attempts to understand the person in his totality involve an overwhelming amount of data which may be mapped so as "to see the client not as an isolated entity, but as a part of a complex ecological system" (p. 113).

The construction of these maps begins with the nuclear family system or household drawn in a circle at the map's centre. Gender is assumed to be a significant variable. Connections are shown to such relevant interacting systems as extended family, friends, organizations, and government agencies with symbols indicating strength of relationship, stress and direction of influence. A genogram outlining an individual's family tree is frequently added on the assumption that it informs current functioning. There is no attempt to predict behaviour based on the mapped environmental or cultural forces. The self is presumed to exist with agentive qualities, but no attempt is made to map this self.

Educational "mind-maps" are not as structurally defined as eco-maps, but generally begin with an undefined "me" in the centre, surrounded by roles, significant others, beliefs, abilities, and other environmental or personal attributes significant to the individual (Budd, 2004; Weeks, 2002). The self-as-knower is placed in a central position and linked to what is known, often including self-characteristics. Mind-mapping has also been used in cognitive behavioural therapy to provide a flexible case summary that helps to prevent important parts of the case from being overlooked (Williams, Williams, & Appleton, 1997). Similar maps have been used in career counselling (Cahill & Martland, 1996) with the objective of developing a richer and more complete aspirational self-story. The self at the core of these narratives remained largely (though not totally) undefined while accounting for cultural, environmental, and situational factors.

Shepard and Marshall (1999) used the idea of mapping to illustrate possible future selves in a group of forty-two adolescents aged eleven to thirteen. Future selves were defined as cognitive manifestations of goals, aspirations, values, and fears. All participants used their "imaginative capacity and self-reflection ... to create a set of hoped-for, and feared future selves" (p. 38). Responses to a set of open-ended questions were placed on flash cards, and maps of these possible future "selves" were then co-constructed.

In these examples of eco- and mind-maps, some aspect of the self is given centrality but is largely undefined. The self-as-knower is assumed. This core self is then pictured as separate from that which is loved, cherished, valued, or to which it is otherwise connected. That which is closest to the person's being is pictured as objects to be acquired, manipulated, or owned. An effective method of self-mapping should replace this assumed duality with a unity that can explain, for instance, the feeling of being attacked when that which is loved, cherished, or valued is attacked, or, likewise, the experience of grief when those who have become central to one's self are no more. Any consideration of the self must acknowledge a unity between elements in self-definition, including interpretive understandings of heritable and cultural factors. Figure 4.1 illustrates my conceptual framework of the self as a body-based autobiographical representation, taking into account genetic, cultural, and interpretive underpinnings, resulting in an implicit representation of the self in cultural units.

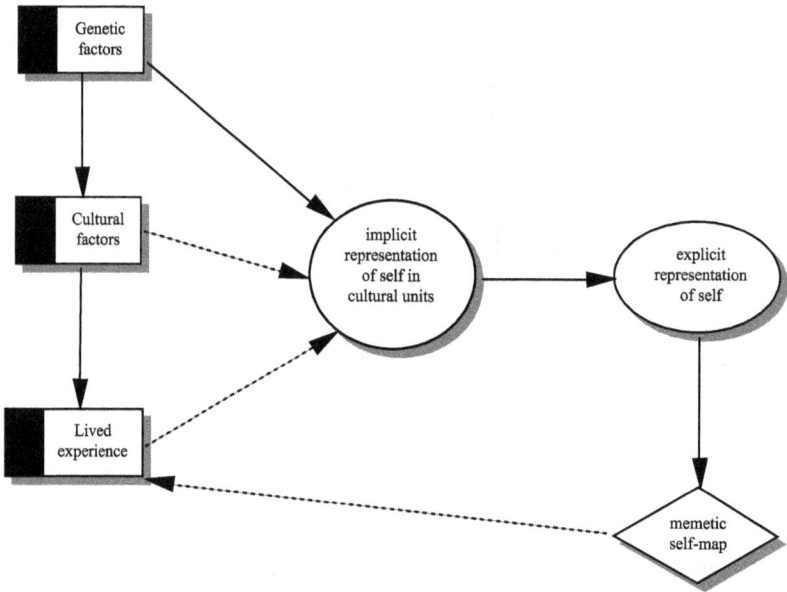

FIGURE 4.1. *A graphic representation of the conceptual framework informing this study showing the process of making the implicit self explicit, mapping that self, and relating the map back to the co-researcher's lived experience.*

Harre (1989) extended the idea that the self is a cognitive structure by describing each self as a personal theory "in terms of which a being orders, partitions, and reflects on its own experience and becomes capable of self-intervention and control" (p. 404). Such a self would exhibit stability while allowing for change on the accumulation of new evidence. Concepts such as "theory" and "evidence" are based on a reality existing independent of one's interpretations. What constitutes evidence may be individualized; but if we stray too far from reality as enforced by physical limitations or cultural pressure, then we must either rein in our "interpretive excess" or face social isolation, perhaps wearing the label "insane." The notion that there exists an external reality to which our self-definition must refer is consistent with the understanding that the creation of the self that allowed for self-objectification also allowed for objective inquiry.

The theory of self on which this research is based begins with the notion that most people have of an implicit self that is consciously defined only when circumstances turn their attention inward. Resultant context specific narratives give the appearance of a self that changes with circumstance. While self-change is possible, we must also consider the possibility that the flashlight of awareness may focus on relevant aspects of a much larger structure, giving the illusion of a person adopting different selves according to context. To understand the self in its fullness we must broaden the focus of our inquiry. A self of which we are not conscious but nonetheless influences our behaviour is beyond self-intervention and control. But while the self is broader than a purely cognitive structure, we may consistently act as though we have certain qualities without necessarily having consciously defined ourselves in such terms. We can combine such psychological forces with the cultural forces of eco-mapping. The self so conceptualized has the potential to define the "me" found at the centre of mind maps while not separating it, homunculus fashion, from those environmental and cultural factors acting upon it. Such a self may have imprecise or diffuse boundaries but would be constructed of cultural units that could be graphically displayed. The method of mapping the self will necessarily include cultural memes comprising a conscious self-definition and a method of displaying relationships between such memes, but it will also require a method of displaying psychological and inferred characteristics.

In chapter 1, the self of a suicidal youth was mapped in units of culture using four prioritized lists of self-descriptors, including perceived roles, affirmations, negations, and values. Self-descriptors that were prioritized as more important (or harder to give up) were deemed to be more central to this client's psyche. Links were drawn between these items based on affective, connotative, or behavioural associations. I have since augmented this method of self-map construction with consideration of personality, pathology, and environmental determinants with successful application to psychotherapy (Robertson, 2016); however, such a prescriptive method of making explicit the self directs the focus of awareness, potentially leaving some areas of the self hidden. Less directive methods were used for the purpose of this research, using open-ended questions like "Who are you?" Units of culture were then distilled from the narratives so obtained by segmenting and coding units or phrases and setting such units against each other according to commonalities and associations. More specifically, transcripts of recorded narratives obtained in interviews were segmented into units of thought with each unit given a descriptive label. Using a qualitative method Miles and Huberman (1994) called "transcendental realism," I placed all units with the same descriptive label together into a "bin." To exist as a meaningful entity distinguished from concepts, percepts, and ideas, memes must exhibit a particular architecture. I declared those bins whose contents exhibited referent, connotative, emotive, and behavioural characteristics to have the necessary architecture. Since memes may share connotative or emotional valence, or since behavioural injunctions may invoke other memes, the structure so described carries a mechanism whereby memes may be said to attract each other. For the purposes of mapping,

I place each code word or phrase identifying a self-describing meme in an oval. Those memes sharing affective, connotative, behavioural, or referent qualities were linked by a line as in the following example:

The biological fact of motherhood is not a meme; in fact, the referent "mother" may not refer to the procreation of children at all, as is the case in some religious orders. The meme "mother" consists of a widely shared referent of that name plus individualized connotative, affective, and behavioural dimensions. For example, one connotation might be that mothers are caring. If the individual whose self is to be mapped shares that connotation and if the same individual develops a separate self-descriptor as a "caring individual," satisfying the definition of meme, then we could say the two memes are linked in a way that mimics attractive force.

The self is not only defined by what it is but by what it is not. Normally, memes that are discordant with memes already constituting the self are repelled. We can imagine, however, contradictory memes coexisting within the same self despite resultant instability or

rigid ⟵——————————————⟶ flexible

tension. For the purposes of generating visual representations of the self, I represented such memes in tension with a double-arrowed line as in the following example:

While it would be difficult to be simultaneously rigid and flexible, it is possible to invoke such divergent self-descriptive memes in disparate contexts. We can also envision maintaining such memes in tension until such time it feels as though one or the other no longer represents who we are. The practice of "sloughing off" such memes would be an important factor in self-evolution.

A second limitation of the method of mapping used in understanding the suicidal youth in chapter 1 was that it left no room for inferred or thematic characteristics. Such characteristics may be inferred by observing behaviours and emotions or by noticing commonalities among diverse memes. The themes so identified were placed in boxes with arrows emanating from them directed toward the collections of memes referenced thematically. Following is an example of how such a theme may be drawn in my system of

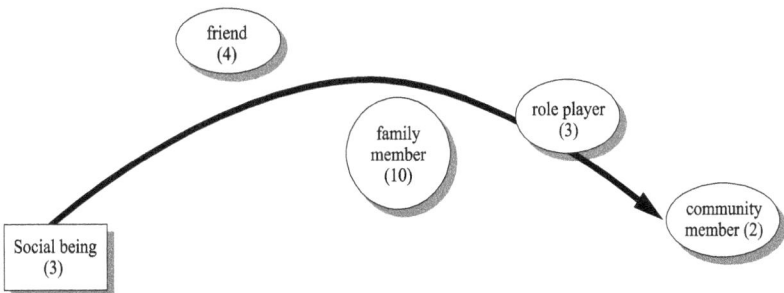

friend
(4)

role player
(3)

family
member
(10)

community
member (2)

Social being
(3)

mapping. The numbers in the ovals reflect the number of times that particular meme was referenced during an initial interview. There is no number associated with the theme "social being" as it was inferred.

The qualitative method I used allowed me to begin with a theory, in this case a theory as to the structure of the self based on previously published philosophical and psychological works. The objective was to confirm, extend, and correct aspects of that theory as new data emerged. In the tradition of Miles and Huberman (1994) this involved amending the method of visual representation to more accurately reflect that data. For example, it became apparent that a self-defining meme could also be a theme. In the following example, the hypothetical individual developed a meme for "Social Being" with connotative, affective, and behavioural elements, but that meme also acted as a theme for a cluster of associated memes. I represented such thematic memes with a diamond shape:

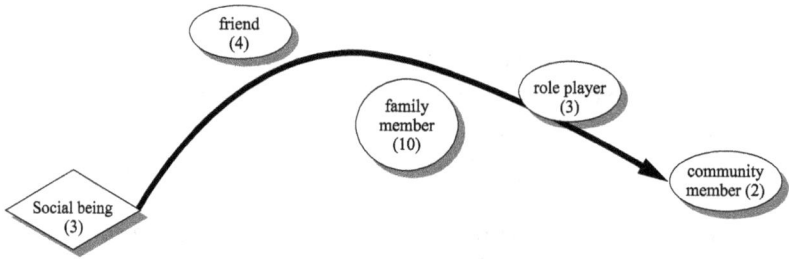

A second modification of the data involved the assertion of participants that emotional centres, separate from any self-defining meme, were essential to their self-existence. Such emotional centres were not considered part of their cognitively defined self, but could nonetheless trigger a focus on specific aspects of their selves with associated behaviours. Such emotional centres, and other psychological characteristics and dispositions not part of the self constructed by the individual, were represented by a box with flags on either side as in the following example:

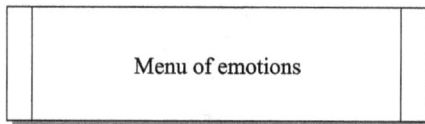

Menu of emotions

Given the literature, particularly from the narrative school, it was not unexpected that participants would present with context-specific "mini-selves." It became apparent during the study that the naming of these mini-selves would aid in the discussion and resonance of the mapping exercise. Such mini-selves were named with those names placed within a cloud, as in this example:

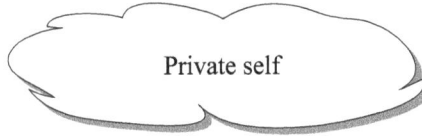

It was anticipated that by using the concept of the meme with its attractive and repellent properties, the self could be mapped in a way that represents both its stability over time and its capacity for change. Once I isolated memes from the stories people used to define themselves, I needed to connect those memes in ways that were meaningful to the persons so mapped. The use of themes and emotional valence assisted in providing this holistic view. The contents of the individual self-maps were not preconceived. Each participant presented their individual and unique theory of themselves, perhaps making their implicit theory of self explicit for the first time.

To enhance the credibility and authenticity of the results, a balance was sought for gender, ethnicity, and socioeconomic status in participant recruitment. Similarly, some balance was sought between urban and rural populations and for education level. It was also considered beneficial to have participants from both traditionally collectivist and modern individualist cultures. The eleven participants in this study ranged in age from 24 to 59, with an average age of 37.3. Eight of the participants in the sample were resident in a metropolitan centre and three were resident in a small community in northern Canada. Four participants were university students, six were employed away from the university, and one was unemployed. The sample was equally divided by gender: five females, five males, and one transsexual. With respect to nationality, eight were Canadian, one was Chinese, one was Russian, and one had joint Canadian–US American citizenship. The racial composition included seven Caucasians, two people of aboriginal North American ancestry, one Chinese and one person whose mother was of a group recognized as aboriginal in Canada (Métis) and whose father was Caucasian but who self-identified as neither of those categories but as "Canadian."

Three cycles of data collection were conducted over a seven-month period. All interviews were audio taped, and initial interviews were transcribed and analyzed with the aid of a qualitative software package. During an initial interview, participants were asked to talk about their selves with prompt questions available for use if needed to generate full and rich self-descriptions. The open-ended conversational style allowed for a full exploration of themes. The initial interviews lasted one to two hours and produced from thirteen to twenty-five pages of transcribed text. The transcripts were then divided into segments, and those segments were coded for the main ideas in those units. These descriptive codes were then examined for the set of properties used to define memes. Codes that did not fulfill our definition of a meme were either discarded or included as properties of existent memes. Separate memes appearing in the same segment were considered connected unless the participant was contrasting those memes. Memes that referred to other memes explicitly or implicitly in their referent, connotative, affective, or behavioural dimensions were also considered connected. The combination of having a finite number of categories (memes) that were connected to some, but not all, other such categories allowed for a mapping of those categories. Such maps were prepared by the researcher and returned to the participants in a second interview.

During the second interview participants were invited to discuss ways that their initial maps could be strengthened, and to share any thoughts that came to mind. They were also invited to reflect on events in their past that helped make their present selves. They were asked if there had been any changes that had occurred since the first interview and whether looking at their map led them to think of changes that they would want to make to their selves.

Participants were given a subsequent third interview and were invited to comment on their revised self-map. They were asked for any new insights they may have had with respect to themselves, and whether any changes occurred to who they were since their previous interview. They were also asked to elaborate, clarify, or explain ideas previously expressed that were not adequately understood by the researcher. They were asked about their feelings of empowerment and whether those feelings had stayed the same, increased, or decreased as a result of their participation in this research, and they were invited to share any other impacts this research may have had on them.

Qualitative research allows for participant voice, referencing the social constructionist notion of the self as a narrative. The first question to be answered by this research was whether the self-narratives were represented in a way that reflected who participants were holistically. The final two chapters examine the data for implications on self-structure and for psychotherapy. I shared my good fortune on having such a diverse and insightful group of subjects with my then teenaged daughter. She replied, "Dad, everyone has a fascinating story if you listen so that they can get it out." As you read the stories in the next chapter, you may reflect on your own self and understand the beauty and the complexity within.

Notes

1 During the nineteenth century, Jean-Baptiste Lamarck proposed a theory of evolutionary change, in opposition to Charles Darwin's "natural selection," in which acquired physical characteristics were thought to be inherited by offspring. This theory as applied to physical evolution was discredited with Mendel's discovery of the gene; however, an argument has been made that it could be applied to epigenetics. (see: Jablonka & Lamb, 2014).

CHAPTER 5

Mapping the Self from Personal Narratives

Maps of the selves of eleven individuals were prepared by applying the method developed in chapter 4. Only the final self-map for each participant is reproduced here, except for two examples, illustrating developmental change that occurred during the course of the study. The edited narratives of each participant have been reproduced to give a sense of the person behind the maps.

This chapter is organized into four groupings: Finding One's Self through Sports, The Aboriginal Self, The Humanist Self, and Two Selves from outside North America. These groupings emerged from the data and may be used to gain further insight on the spectrum of self-creation within North America. It cannot be inferred that the two selves from outside North America are necessarily representative of selves in Russia or China but they do provide an interesting counterpoint, to the North American sample.

Finding One's Self through Sports

The three research participants featured in this section were North American Caucasians whose successful participation in sports preceded positive psychological transitions. While the extent to which their membership in an "individualist" culture impacted on their willingness to undertake developmental transitions cannot be known from this study, it is significant that each required an outside objective measure (excellence in sports) to change their self identities.

As we saw in chapter 1, the person we believe ourselves into being may have un-endearing characteristics. In each of these three vignettes, positive change to a negative self-definition was framed by the individual as a discovered "true self." Thus, "Chantelle" no longer defined herself as a criminal, "Magdelynn" refused to define herself as disabled, and "Brent" stopped defining himself as lacking in intelligence because each had always had, within, the attributes to succeed in socially useful, empowered, and self-actualizing ways. While it would certainly be difficult to argue that they had lacked the potential to succeed, potential is not the same as identity. Nonetheless, their old selves now felt to be "false" and to always have been so.

From Criminal to Counsellor

"Chantelle" said she had been "a rotten little child." As a youth, she became involved in violent crime, often drug-related, and she spent a number of years in youth correctional facilities. She was not successful in parlaying her training in this "breeding ground for better criminals," and her dual Canadian–US American citizenship, into profitable criminal activity, and she landed in adult prison.

Our initial interview resulted in thirty-two codes that satisfied our definition of a meme. Almost a quarter (eleven) of the forty-six segments of text comprising the interview were coded for the memes "student" and "athlete." Chantelle said she loves most sports, but her failure to take advantage of a four-year baseball scholarship to Colorado State University out of high school suggests that sports had not resulted in a pro-social self-definition during her teenage years. As an adult she became a boxer as an outlet for her anger and frustration, and she turned professional following eight successful years at the amateur level. Becoming an athlete gave her the confidence to become a student. At the time of this study, she was pursuing a master's degree in counselling psychology. Her thesis research was on the role of hope in women's prisons. She reported that the inmates in her counselling practicum related well to sports analogies: "It's one thing to watch it on TV, but it's another thing to actually to be in the ring, take the pain, and deliver and stay focused, and ahh, if you kind of put that in terms of life, a lot of these people have been through some painful past and you know, they're able to take that but also to have some positive energy about and move forward. ... "

Figure 5.1 represents Chantelle's self-map completed after her second interview. Both "athlete" and "student" are united by "proud"

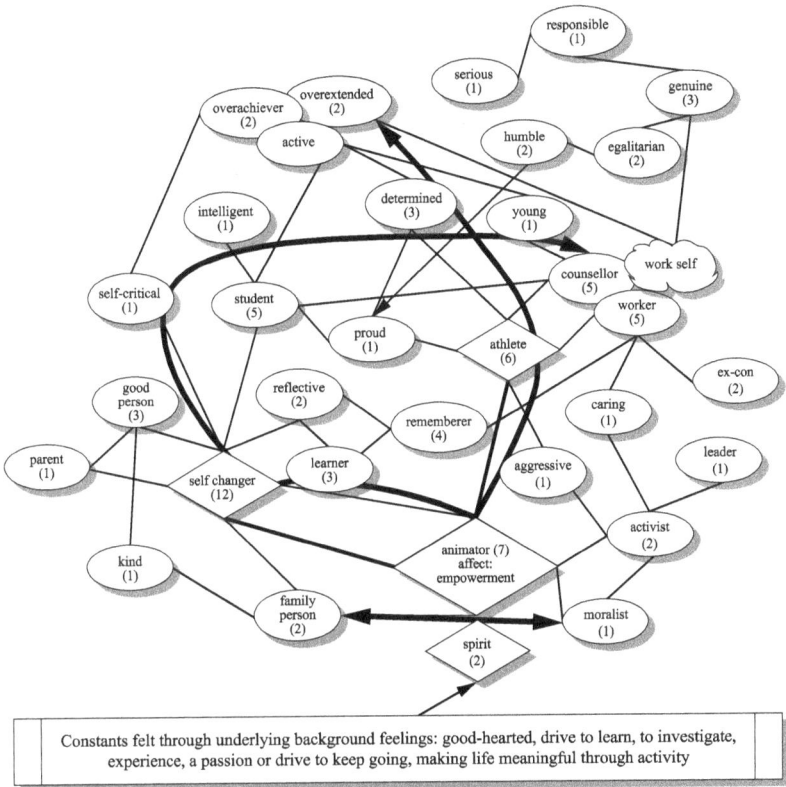

FIGURE 5.1. *Revised memetic self-map of Chantelle with amendments flowing from her second interview (with no further changes resulting from the third interview).*

as these represent roles in which she exhibited pride. "Athlete" is illustrated with links to "determined," "counsellor," "worker," "animator" and "aggressive," and it is shown in a diamond-shaped box, illustrating it as both a theme and a meme. "Animator" is also represented as both a meme and a theme. Chantelle's narrative provided examples of empowered animation within moralist, activist, athletic, learner, family, and self-changer contexts. Her drive to accomplish, she said, came from her spirit, which in turn was a function of emotion-related constants such as being good-hearted, being driven to learn, and having a passion or drive to "keep going" despite obstacles. These constants are represented by a bar at the base of her self-map with directional arrows illustrating their importance in animating her being. "Self-changer" is pictured as flowing from empowered animation grounded in spirit, but it was not always present in her self. While she credited sports with giving her the self-assurance she needed to attend university, she credited her pregnancy with her decision to stop criminal activity: "I think the biggest thing in my life was my son and he is seven now, and I would say that he was kind of like my saviour that when I found out I was pregnant it was. ... Suddenly I wasn't just being reckless and just living for myself and I actually, I needed to start caring about something, and he provided that for me, so, like, when he was a baby I wanted to do everything I could to be a good person. ... "

Although her son was taken into foster care, Chantelle continued with her life-building changes. Her "Work Self" persona was a planned, developmental change involving the belief that she could succeed by pursuing socially acceptable goals. Memory provided a feeling of constancy in a life marked by change. She reported that her memories give her the feeling that one person is having all of these varied experiences.

During our second interview, four-and-a-half months after the first, Chantelle said that her pride had previously involved being arrogant, overconfident, and rude. She subsequently discovered that she could be proud without "throwing it in others' faces." While noting that being proud in a nonaggressive way was necessary to her self, she said she would move the "proud" meme to the outside of the map and move "humble" toward the middle to illustrate the importance she placed on that attribute. The attempt to do so failed in a way that showed that self-map construction is not simply subject to arbitrary thinking. "Proud" was connected to her roles as athlete and student, which were central to her being at the time of this mapping. Since a self-map is a representation of lived experience, moving "proud" to the outside of her self would necessitate that she devalue her accomplishments as a student and as an athlete. Instead, we shifted "humble" to a more central position than had originally been represented, with a unidirectional arrow connecting it with "proud" to represent how the latter meme is moderated by the former.

During our second interview, Chantelle reported that one of her brothers had recently died, and she felt torn between guilt for not connecting with her family and her desire to distance herself from the family's drug culture. She concluded that she could not risk becoming co-dependent. A new meme, "moralist," was added to her map to include the idea that she avoids actions supportive of the bad behaviour of others with tension between it and "family person."

Chantelle was asked what drives her to take on more than she can reasonably expect to handle (represented by the meme "overextended"), and to excel. She replied she has a lot of energy, and that if she happens to "take a night off" she finds herself "sitting at home" wondering what to do with herself. Her mission is to make her life count. She explained that work and recreational activities with friends "count" while passive activities like watching TV do not count. Her self-map was elaborated by adding "making life meaningful through activity" to the bar representing "underlying constants." In addition, the meme "activity" was added to a cluster that includes "overextended" and "overachiever."

When asked what future changes she would make to her self-map, Chantelle replied, "I kind of like my map; it fits in with who I am. I like the bottom part, the constants, the passion to keep going." She said she would like to reduce athletics in importance, especially as it is related aggressiveness and competitiveness while maintaining an active but less intense athletic life.

Chantelle reviewed her revised memetic self-map again five weeks after her second interview, commenting, "It's how I would describe myself, it's perfect." When asked if she had any new insights about who she was, Chantelle said her spiritual aspect is strong, and she has had time to reflect on this. She reported having explained to her surviving brothers that she needed to keep her distance from the drug culture they represent. She had not talked to her parents, insisting that she would not be talking to them, ever.

"Empowerment" was noted as a theme on Chantelle's self-map. She said she had not felt empowered as a child, and she had been a "shy foster kid." Then she stopped going to school and became involved in criminal activity. She said the process of "getting clean," going to jail, having her son, and then starting university contributed to her self-empowerment. She said this research led her to reflect on her values and how they connect with her life.

Athlete via Wheelchair

"Magdelynn" initially described herself as "all these fractured pieces," living a "Forrest Gump life … floating along wherever the breeze takes me." She used to be different:

> Before I crashed my motorbike and ended up in my [wheel]chair,
> I was very goal orientated, like I had this to do and that to do,

and right before my crash, I just kind of completed all these things from my five-year plan, got my education degree, and, like, was teaching and was like, 'Okay, I've finished the end of this, now what?' so I was in the process of trying to think what I was going to do for the next five-year plan, and then I crashed my bike …

The segment about having a "Forrest Gump life" was coded as "environmentally driven" and "flexible." She explained that while family has always been important to her, she realized after the accident it is not something for which you develop in a "five-year plan," but it is something that you live; "it happens." More segments (seventeen out of ninety-three) were coded for "athlete" than any of the other forty codes applied to those segments, yet this too was a product of her "Forrest Gump life." She had not previously defined herself as an athlete. She had played hockey, but she did not see herself as being skilled. After the accident, on the suggestion of a friend, she found wheelchair basketball:

I'm not a quad, but I am not really paraplegic either, because I do have these two limbs, but I don't have any balance, so I can use my limbs if I'm not falling over and smashing my head on a table or whatever is in line for me to hit. So anyway, haphazardly, I just kind of found wheelchair basketball, and it was like, "This is the greatest" because you could strap yourself in your chair, and the chair is made so it doesn't flip over very easily so I was, ahh, I could play this …

After playing the sport for a year and a half, she made the Canadian women's national basketball team. That is when she began defining herself as an athlete who was both "environmentally driven" and "flexible" (figure 5.2). "Environmentally driven," "context dependent," and "role player" form a thematic "Relativistic" core that allows flexibility in taking advantage of her "Forest Gump" opportunities. A thick link between "gimp" and "athlete" illustrates a strong relationship (associations in more than two segments) between the two.

The second-largest number of interview segments (twelve) from Magdelynn's initial transcript were coded for the meme "gimp." She explained that she preferred calling herself a "gimp" to disabled "because, in my mind, when you think of disabled, disabled alarms

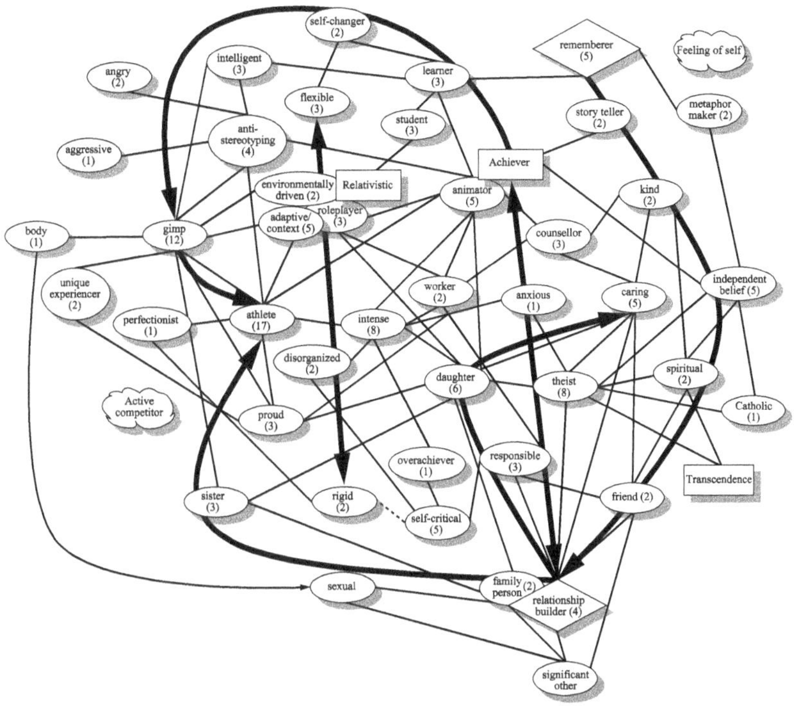

FIGURE 5.2. *Revised memetic self-map of Magdelynn with amendments flowing from her second and third interviews.*

can't do anything; like, it doesn't function. So I don't see myself as disabled 'cause I can do a whole lot of things that able-bodied people can't do." Magdelynn wore this "gimp" label as a badge reinforcing her self-identification as a "unique experiencer." She believed no one is quite like her, and no one would experience events in quite the same way.

The meme with the third-largest number of segmental codings (eight) is "intense." While this quality is necessary for success as an athlete, Magdalynn applied this quality to life generally, and she became an "overachiever" as an athlete, daughter, and worker. In her drive to succeed, she attempted to do many things simultaneously with the result that she did not get everything accomplished. This created anxiety and a new self-descriptor: "disorganized." Her inability to master all her lofty goals led to her initial description of her self as "fractured."

Magdelynn was raised Roman Catholic—baptized as an infant, confirmed as a youth, and a regular churchgoer with family. She was sent to an all-girls Catholic school in Saskatchewan, Canada, which she described as, "like, way out in the middle of nowhere." After her accident, pastoral care people come to see her on a regular basis, but she reported their prayers were unhelpful. She would humour them because she was "too tired and weak to fight anybody." She continued, however, to have a belief by faith that there is a supreme being:

> I always believed that there is something out there, I don't know if it's, like, the Catholic god 'cause I could not understand why, like, the Catholic Church wasn't tolerant of, say people with a different sexual orientation. That bugged me and I was like, "You say you're all fine and good and you're, like, shunning all these different people. Why is this?" so I was like, "it doesn't make any sense because something is supposed to be all loving, why are people getting discouraged and getting pushed away, and then when you have Catholic priests who are, like, traumatizing little kids. What is that?" Like, I could not wrap my head around that, so I thought, "I am out of here. I quit this." So, I only go to church with my mom and dad to kind of appease them.

Magdelynn sometimes expressed her theistic belief ambivalently: "I have a hope that there is, like, a higher power that is all-loving and there is an absolute acceptance of people." Her spirituality, expressed by being good to others, was connected to this theistic belief or hope, and was represented visually by connecting "caring" to "theist," "daughter," and "counsellor" in her self-map.

Subsequent interviews revealed changes that were already accommodated in the initial self-map. She had stopped playing for the national basketball team, but she still defined herself as an athlete. She had felt "fractured" during the first interview because her emphasis on sports at the national level left her family and boyfriend neglected. She decided her priority was to develop these relationships to feel "whole." Magdelynn's animator meme, central to her sense of achievement, was shown as connected to family and learning as well as to sports. Her meme "self-changer" connected to flexibility, which, in turn, connected to "adaptive/context" within a "Relativistic" cluster. Thus, a mind mechanism is represented whereby she was able to make changes outlined between the first and second interviews without making substantive changes to her self.

During our second interview, Magdelynn reported more confidence in allowing others to know who she was with the result that she became less of a role player. As a result, a link between "athlete" and "rigid" was deleted. A link between "rigid" and "perfectionist," an association suggested by her wanting things "just so," was added. Magdelynn also said she would add "sexual" to her meme-map, and she viewed her sexuality as connected to being attractive, life-giving, and complete.

Magdelynn explained her belief in a higher power allows her to be confident in the future despite her realization that she cannot "do everything under the sun." She expressed faith that "everything will work out; or if not, it is all part of some master plan that explains why, somehow, it is not supposed to work out." She wanted to feel nurtured by a higher power, and she wanted the children with whom she was working to have that feeling as well. The connection between supernatural belief and doing good for other people was anticipated in Magdelynn's initial self-map, but I sensed that in her internalized theistic and spiritual belief she was attempting an understanding that transcended both her physical limitations and the limitations of a materialist interpretation of nature. This led to a new interpretive or thematic code labelled "Transcendence," pictured in figure 5.2 as feeding both her theistic and spiritual selves.

At the end of the second interview, Magdelynn suggested adding another meme to her self-map: "significant other," reflecting her role as a partner to her boyfriend. She said he provides a calming and supportive influence that allows her to be how she feels inside. She reported reciprocal dreams of having a family. The new meme, "significant other," was added, connecting to "sexual," "Family Person," "Relationship Builder," and "Friend."

During our third interview Magdelynn said that the new "Transcendence" thematic code "hit the nail on the head," and that she wants to leave a positive legacy based on that theme. She said she now sees herself more as a mobile than a "fractured pie" with different pieces that move and rotate as a unit. She felt more in balance with her real values being more consistently applied across contexts as compared to when she began her participation in this research. Thus, when she was in Toronto playing basketball, she was comfortable refusing to play a role that involved drinking and partying. She explained she wants to be the same person "no matter what." This feeling of being uncomfortable with context dependency implies a need for a unitary self.

Environmentalism and Competence

"Brent" described himself as a "packrat." He kept so much memorabilia that he did not have space in his house for usual furniture such as sofas and chairs. He feared that if he lost the memorabilia, he would lose the memories. A "rememberer" meme is pictured as a diamond in figure 5.3 to signify its importance as a theme. Links connect it with "reflective," "animator," "student," "storyteller," and "self-changer," but a thematic line was also drawn to other aspects of himself such as "self-aware," "friend," "caring," "family member" and, of course, "packrat."

Another theme recurrent within Brent's narrative was represented as "Takes self lightly." This theme was closely associated with "humorous," which he used in his roles as a student, teacher, friend, leader, and broadcaster. He explained it helps keeps his thoughts "in balance," and helps him to preserve relationships and reduce stress. He credited his reflectivity with developing a "long view" of the world, especially with respect to environmental issues.

Being an environmentalist gave purpose to Brent's life and was associated with a drive to understand the world around him. This theme is represented in figure 5.3 as "attempts to understand," and is associated with "empathetic," "flexible," and "positive spirit." As an example, Brent recounted his attempt to understand a former girlfriend who had ended their relationship after she saw his house. He recognized her values as different from his, and he resolved to deal with some aspects of his "packrat" behaviours. The meme "flexible" was a relatively recent addition to his self: "I am much happier than I was then. I think by letting that rigidity go I'm able to be flexible with myself, be patient with myself, be understanding, allow myself to fail, allow myself to move on and particularly with other people. ... I thought we had to be one way. I was a little more rigid in my thinking when I was younger."

The theme "Attempts to understand" is associated with empathy and flexibility and is drawn to connect disparate elements of his self, including "environmentalist," "teacher," and "animator." Brent honed a sense of himself as an empowered "doer." Being an athlete is important to him, but he was also an elected leader in his cycling association, taught classes in swimming, and was an activist in promoting environmentally sustainable lifestyles.

Brent said he was not close to his family. As a youth, his parents did not understand him and were not proud of him. He had adopted

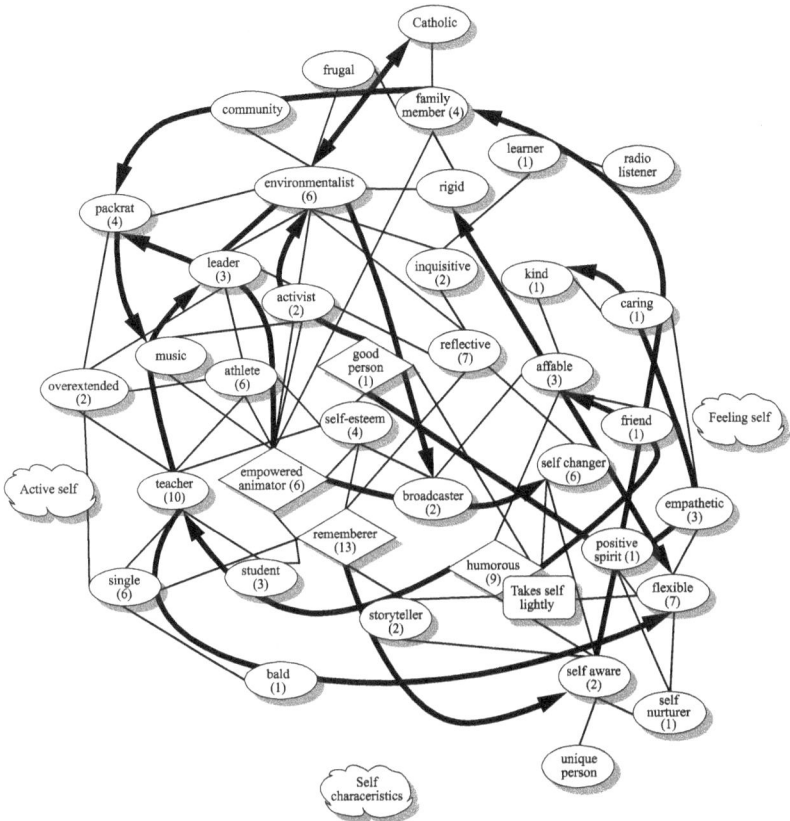

FIGURE 5.3. *Final self-map of Brent showing the number (in brackets) of segments in which memes occurred during the first interview and revisions following subsequent interviews.*

a "punk rocker" lifestyle and became "heavily into environmentalism." He did not use Styrofoam or plastic cutlery and rarely ate beef because of the high energy demands and wastefulness of these products. He did not establish a career until he was in his thirties and lived a frugal existence. He had not sent his family Christmas or birthday cards, but he recently began talking to his parents "almost weekly." He eschewed flowers because they die. "Family member" is represented as having a link to "animator" because he has controlled the amount and nature of the contact with his family; but it is his memories that give "family member" a continued place in his self.

Brent shared that he would like to have a child of his own someday if he could find a suitable partner. He worried, "I have never had a [serious] relationship, and that starts to surprise me as I come into my late thirties." He explained that at first, he had not been ready for a relationship, and when he was ready, he did not know how to meet eligible women. Then he met someone on the internet:

> I was on Lava Life, and you have to buy credits in order to, in order to communicate with the other person anymore than simply sending them a smile, as it were, and I thought about it for awhile because you can exchange a smile for free and I thought I am a bit ... I question these things. I thought I preferred to meet someone the old-fashioned way, but this woman was fairly good-looking, and I liked her profile. ... I actually bought some credits. We met. I thought she was quite attractive. I thought we were on the same wavelength, and we started dating, and that was quite shocking to me actually because I had never been on a second date.

Brent said he believed that his "packrat" tendencies and being overextended in his roles as a broadcaster, athlete and teacher contributed to her decision that they were not compatible. This led him to re-examine some aspects of his self. "Self-esteem" was used as a label for a meme developed within Brent's self, representing the quality of thinking positively about his existence and his ability to affect himself and the world around him. He reported that he had not developed the level of self-esteem he needed to pursue a career as a teacher until he was well into adulthood:

> I was in a swim class at the university and I was simply taking courses because I wanted to stay active. And a teacher that I had, the swim instructor, who is a prof, said to me at the time ..., "Have you ever swam [sic] masters?" and I had, and I said, "Yeah, I did at my old school." And she said, "You ought to consider teaching swimming," and I thought, "Wow, she thinks I am good enough to teach," and then bugles started blowing, then I started to think ..., "Wow, I can do that."

Subsequent to successful experiences as a certified swimming and, later, cycling coach, Brent enrolled in a college of education. Although he had only taught full-time for one year prior to his participation in this research, he identified himself as a teacher in ten segments, the second most common reference to himself in the initial interview. He said he brings two distinctive qualities to his students: his sense of humour and his drive to understand others. Brent's self-map includes three "mini-selves": a feeling self that includes such memes as "caring," "empathetic," and "positive spirit"; an active self that is centred on the meme "empowered animator"; and "self-characteristics" such as "bald" and "single."

Brent's initial comment, on reviewing the first draft of his self-map four-and-a-half months after his first interview, was that it represented him well, but he would connect "positive spirit" and "good person" more tightly, and he would also connect "good person" with "environment." He said "good person" represents a theme that runs through a number of memes in his self-map. It was, therefore, defined as a thematic centre in his revised self-map. The interpretive theme "Attempts to understand" was incorporated into Brent's definitions of "good person" and "empathetic." Put simply, this revision recognized that Brent's empathetic self flowed from his attempts to be a good person rather than the reverse.

Brent explained that to teach in the publicly funded separate (Catholic) school system you have to get a priest's letter documenting your faith. This was a problem for him because he had not been living the Catholic faith nor had he been attending church. His old high school motto was "goodness, discipline, and knowledge," and it so happened that the school to which he applied had the same motto. He suggested this motto represented his personal connectedness to the divine, yet he had the feeling that the interviewing vice-principal probably realized his faith was not strong.

Brent explained he does not accept much Catholic dogma, but he believed one could be Catholic and hold views different from official church doctrine. He said the church should be more progressive on environmental issues: "If we are not environmental, how can we care for the sick because the environment is making them sick." A good person, he explained, reflects on what he does and considers other peoples' feelings with respect to outcomes. Brent said many Catholics are good people and you can trust them, but many miss the broader picture: the connection between being stewards of the planet and environmentalism.

Although Brent would not describe himself as a devout Catholic, since he still defined himself as such with the term, it was added to his revised self-map connected to "family person." A tension line was drawn between "Catholic" and "environmentalist" illustrating conflict between the two. A meme for "community" was added, connected to "environmentalist" in recognition of his participation in that community. The meme "good person" was amended to include the idea of reflecting on one's own actions in consideration and respect of others.

Brent also said he would add "radio listener" to his self-map connected to "learner." He explained that he listens to the Canadian Broadcasting System (CBC) regularly for both news and music. He would also add another meme, "music," to his self-map. Music represents, for him, activism, empowerment, storytelling and at times, humour. Memes for "radio listener" and "music" were added. The meme for "music" was linked to "activism" and "empowerment" and was placed along a thematic line emanating from "humour."

Brent noted the inconsistency of a fellow teacher who recycles newspapers, but garbages paper from his classroom without recycling. To Brent, this suggested someone not totally committed to the environment. The fact that Brent would take note of this discrepancy and interpret it in a way suggests rigidity connected to environmental issues. A meme for "rigid" was added to his self-map and connected to "environmentalist." This meme may be understood as being in conflict with another aspect of his self, "flexible"; therefore, a tension line was drawn between the two.

Brent explained that the woman he met on the internet forced him to look at himself. She had felt uncomfortable in his house because it was cold and without furniture. He began dating another woman who owned a dog. He bought the woman a dog brush to deal with its shedding. He also insisted that she should stop smoking. She accepted the mess at his house, but he attempted to make his home more welcoming. His memorabilia that helped him retain associated memories included old newspapers, drafts, books, notes, tapes, and even dated clippings from his hair after haircuts. He discovered that by taking digital pictures of such items he was able to throw them away while retaining the associated memories, and doing so gave his apartment space in which to put furniture.

Brent traced his difficulties in making relationship commitments to his childhood. He described his birth family as very oppressive and identified this as a source of his own rigidity. By re-establishing a relationship with his parents, he felt he was working on this rigidity. They subsequently established a joint account with him so that he could purchase a townhouse but, "Even now I wasn't able to tell them I bought a new car. I was afraid my parents would not approve because I lost money on the trade-in."

Brent said a fellow cyclist had been murdered immediately prior to this research. He had begun sensing the deceased person's presence, awaking during the night prior to our second interview afraid that he would see a ghost. He felt guilty when another cyclist said the deceased "could be an asshole sometimes," because he found himself agreeing. He began thinking about what people might come to understand of him if he died. He noted that while the deceased believed in cherishing each day, he was also filled with a deep-seated anger.

Brent explained during our third interview that his sense of community came from people who were activists on environmental issues. He was involved with a student newspaper and part of a cycling community, and he organized races as part of that community. His radio show promotes activism. He said that he is also part of a teaching community. As a result of this information, his participation in his cycling and teaching communities were added to the behavioural aspect of his "community" meme.

Brent said that for seven ears he did not have a television, and he felt good about this decision, but the internet had now begun to unprofitably occupy his time. He described the internet as "a strange addiction," and he suggested he is more productive without a computer. Signs of Brent's frugality had been interpreted as a function of his environmental concern for the planet in the preparation of the first and second versions of his self-map, but this new information suggested that his frugality with respect to the purchase of possessions and the expenditure of his time constituted an ethic related to his upbringing. Although compatible with environmental activism, such frugality could exist independently. Thus, a meme for "frugal" was added to a third version of Brent's self-map linked to both "family" and "environmentalism."

Brent said the quality of taking himself lightly had its roots in elementary school. He enjoyed making people laugh, and he saw this as an effort to make people like him. He was shy when he went to high school, but he discovered that almost everyone else was also shy. This knowledge gave him the courage to take risks and be humorous. While attending university, he noted that the people he respected took themselves lightly. He also learned to appreciate there are multiple perspectives, and he tried to replace a tendency toward rigidity with the understanding that people are merely doing the best they can with the knowledge they have.

Brent credited his mother for instilling in him the idea of self-empowerment by insisting that he take responsibility for his actions. He said his sense of empowerment increased during university: "When I said I would do something they expected you to do it." He became interested in the power of positive thinking and discovered he could empower himself in sports by reaching inside and finding an inner strength. This same inner strength was now helping him in his quest to remake himself into someone who is less rigid, more tolerant of opposing viewpoints, and less demanding on himself.

The Aboriginal Self

An indigenous Mapuche from Chile told me that to be considered as an Aboriginal in his country one has to live a traditional lifestyle. A person with Mapuche ancestry who, like himself, wears suits and works in a bank in Santiago had chosen to be non-aboriginal. This definition assumes a static or essentialist culture: aboriginality is based on active membership in an aboriginal community practicing a defined aboriginal lifestyle.

Situated at the opposite end of the American continents, Canada's definition of aboriginality was once similarly cultural. In its *Indian Act* of 1876, an Indian was defined as a male of "Indian blood" who is a member of an Indian band, the wife of such a person or their children. One could "cease to be Indian" by becoming enfranchised into full Canadian citizenship. Those who obtained a university degree or women who married non-Indian men would automatically cease to be Indian by virtue of a presumption that they had ceased to live a non-aboriginal way of life. Amerindian people in Canada have successfully argued that such provisions are discriminatory, and that they should be able to keep the advantages of Indian status such as on-reserve tax-free status, hunting and fishing rights, and various income subsidies while having the full rights of Canadian citizenship. With this development, the definition of Indian has necessarily changed from culturally based to racially based. People of mixed ancestry who were raised in Indian bands and trace their ancestry to those aboriginal people who signed treaties with Canada or were otherwise recognized as Indians by 1985 are considered "full-blood" for the purpose of considering "blood quantum."

The Métis, a people of mixed ancestry who identified with neither Amerindian nor European cultures, were recognized as an aboriginal people in the Canadian constitution of 1982. Their definition was primarily cultural: Métis self-identify and are accepted by a Métis community, but the allocation of benefits not available to non-aboriginal Canadians has introduced pressure to restrict the number of people who are permitted to identify as "Métis." If the self is a cultural construct, then issues of blood quantum do not decide issues of self-definition. One of the participants in this study, "Judy," is not included in this section because she did not identify as being Aboriginal despite her mother's ancestry as part of a community that is recognized as Métis. She was like the banker in Santiago, culturally European, but unlike many with her genetic background, she refused to claim Métis status.

Is there such a thing as a self that may be identified with the aboriginal inhabitants of the American continents? "Trevor" thought so and began a quest to find his "true self" by calling on the traditions of his ancestors. He sought guidance from Cree Elders, went on a vision quest, became a traditional drummer and singer, and participated in rituals such as sweat lodge ceremonies, traditional feasts, pipe ceremonies and sun dances. Here we have a return to the notion of an essentialist traditional culture to which one must return to maintain one's aboriginality.

Religiously held belief may maintain a culture's distinctiveness while under threat of being overwhelmed by another. An argument may be made that at least some traditional aboriginal spirituality was nonreligious in nature (Robertson, 2014b), but a codified set of beliefs and practices sanctified by a supernatural power marks religious thinking. Such a sanctified set of beliefs known as Native or Aboriginal Spirituality has been commended as an alternative to Christianity (Robertson, 2011a, 2011b). What if a non-aboriginal person converted to this faith-based codified belief system and how might this affect their self construction? If there is such a thing as a distinctive aboriginal self, can a non-aboriginal person have one? "JohnB" never claimed to be an Aboriginal, but his example is useful in examining this possibility.

Finally, "Tina" grew up in an aboriginal community in northern Saskatchewan and although she accepted herself as a Métis person, nothing in her self-map would strike one as being overtly aboriginal. Her concerns were practical and centred on family. Perhaps the original Métis were not concerned with identifying with a culture but were simply building communities to survive in their environment. With this view, culture is not static but evolving with no true proto- typical self. We can only seek to build an optimal self for our times.

"Against the Wind"

Trevor was a single Amerindian Cree male in his twenties. His self- narratives were delivered in the storytelling traditions of his people. Thirty-eight memes were identified from 110 segments and are pro- duced with connecting associations in figure 5.4. There is no obvious starting point pictured. Someone with a strong sense of chronological order might start with the gender roles he learned in childhood tak- ing care of two younger siblings while his parents drank heavily. An essentialist might start with the core of who he is, an empowered per- son whose sense of self-worth is tied to action. A psychologist might be tempted to start with "self-esteem," coded for more segments than any other meme (ten). I started with the interpretive or thematic code "Rememberer" because his recounted memories seemed to provide meaning and direction. Trevor talked about how memories become "learnings" and contribute to a sense of constancy:

> Interviewer: What is in you that stays the same?
> Trevor: I had a discussion about this with one of my friends; she
> was actually an ex-street worker, and she has changed her life
> around; it was the experiences, the experiences stay the same.
> Interviewer: So, you know it's you because your memories
> remain?
> Trevor: Not only that, it's there, but also what you learnt, the
> learnings.
> Interviewer: The learnings?
> Trevor: Ya. You know, it's like a little kid learning to walk ... just
> because he can walk doesn't mean he's not him. He can
> expand on it, and add things on to it, maybe he will run,
> jump, maybe he'll skip, swim, or bike. It all adds on to it, but
> it's still the same.

"Against the Wind" was identified by Trevor as his Indian name. He recalled that it was both symbolic and an example of family humour: "I got that name when I was young, and what that meant was I was always going against some beliefs; I would be strong enough to stand up for what I believe, basically. ... But the whole reason why I got that name was because my uncle, who is not a traditional native guy, observed me when I was kid, and I would always piss against the wind. And that's pretty much who I am, ya know, more stand-up."

Much of Trevor's learning was informal and introspective, captured by the statement "I learned about myself from myself." The idea that everyone is unique in the way they experience and interpret events is incorporated into his meme "unique experiencer." His self-definition was grounded on his interpretations of old experiences. Memories of being the child of alcoholic parents led him to define himself as a potential alcoholic. He described his career as an addictions worker as "me trying make sense of myself and my childhood."

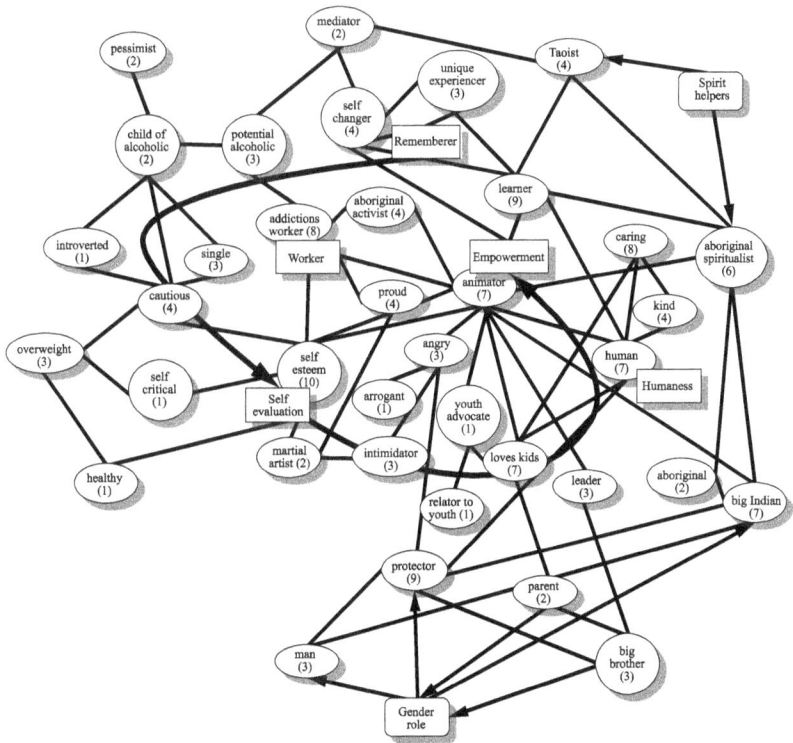

FIGURE 5.4. *Memetic self-map of Trevor resulting from the segmentation and coding of his initial interview, showing the number segments coded for each meme (in brackets).*

Trevor's "cautious" meme included a tendency to discount other peoples' compliments, a trait associated with low self-esteem. He associated caution with both introverted and single. While "self-esteem" might not ordinarily be thought of as a meme, in this case it represents the quality of feeling positive about oneself, and it is something that Trevor has worked on frequently by drawing on his Indian name, using positive affirmations, and by challenging himself to attempt new behaviours. He made "self-esteem" into part of who he is to diminish the effects of those parts of his self that are self-critical.

A "Self-evaluation" theme was added to Trevor's self-map that represents a reflective tendency touching on "self-esteem," "cautious," "arrogant," "self-critical," "loves kids," and "human" memes. For example, he recognized an "intimidator" component to his anger. One time he chased a "john," a customer of one of his friends, with a baseball bat. On another occasion, he threatened a father who had hit his child in a shopping mall. In his evaluation, this method of curbing the behaviour of wrongdoers was ineffective and potentially self-defeating. During the course of our study, he transformed his need to redress wrongdoing into political action.

Trevor traced his anger with people who abuse children and women to his childhood experience of protecting his younger siblings. He learned that to be a man was to be "judge, jury and executioner." He surmised:

> I am a big Indian, and no one is really going to mess with a big Indian. ...
>
> So then I thought, 'What's it mean to be Indian?' and I thought, 'warrior,' so I did some research, and I realized back in the old days we used to go on vision quests, so I went on a vision quest.

With the guidance of Elders[1], Trevor became a drum keeper and a powwow singer, but he embraced the Taoism of his martial arts instructor along with Aboriginal Spirituality.[2] He said both traditions guide his behaviours and relationships with a premium placed on the ability to feel. A woman he dated was prescribed medication for a mood disorder, but while those pills stabilized her mood, "She stopped taking the pills because she wanted to feel something; she wanted to feel human." As an experiment, he visited a doctor with ambiguous complaints and was prescribed antidepressant medication. His interpretation was that doctors overprescribe to treaty Indians because their medication is paid for by the federal government.

Trevor befriended prostitutes to help them "be able to feel again, being able to think about things other than their addiction." He saw even their lies as signs of progress toward humanness "because one has to feel something such as fear in order to prompt the lie." Eventually, he decided it was not his job to help female alcoholics and prostitutes find their humanity, but the theme remained: Being human has to do with acknowledging and acting on one's inner feelings. He also concluded that being human includes a capacity to engage in social relationships. Trevor felt incomplete when single.

During our second interview, Trevor described his initial memetic self-map as "an awesome picture." He said the inclusion of the meme "aboriginal activist" in his initial self-map was "almost prophetic" because, although he would have not given himself that label two-and-a-half months previously, he would now. The meme had been apparent in earlier segments dealing with his responses to prescription drugs, prostitution, child abuse, and addictions; however, now he was focused on lobbying elected governments, explaining, "It was like igniting a fire that keeps me focused on something bigger than myself."

His activism had inspired him to write poetry and songs critical of society and greed. It seemed that "Rememberer," "activist," "empowerment/animator," and "caring" had converged to create a new meme, "artist," within Trevor's self. Directional arrows from those initiating centres were added to his revised self-map (figure 5.5) showing this relationship. He intentionally replaced the overweight meme with the less pejorative "big." The meme "single" was changed to "dating" with the understanding that he was not sure about the future of his new dating relationship. A directional connection between "dating" and "self-esteem" was used to indicate he relied on dating for positive affect.

Trevor said sex trade workers also need relationships to validate their humanity, but they cannot allow themselves to feel or trust. By denying or repressing their human emotions, they become less human. People who are prescribed mood-modifying drugs are inhibited chemically in their capacity to feel and are also made less human. Male gender roles and addictions were similarly restrictive. "Humanness," as a theme that focuses consciousness on a range of memes in his self-constellation, was added to figure 5.5 with a thick directional arrow highlighting the associations triggered by that theme.

Trevor's animating impulse led him to attempt to redress perceived wrongs with such aggression that he described himself as "capable of being an asshole." Recognizing that using his size, martial training, and arrogance to intimidate others was a denial of their

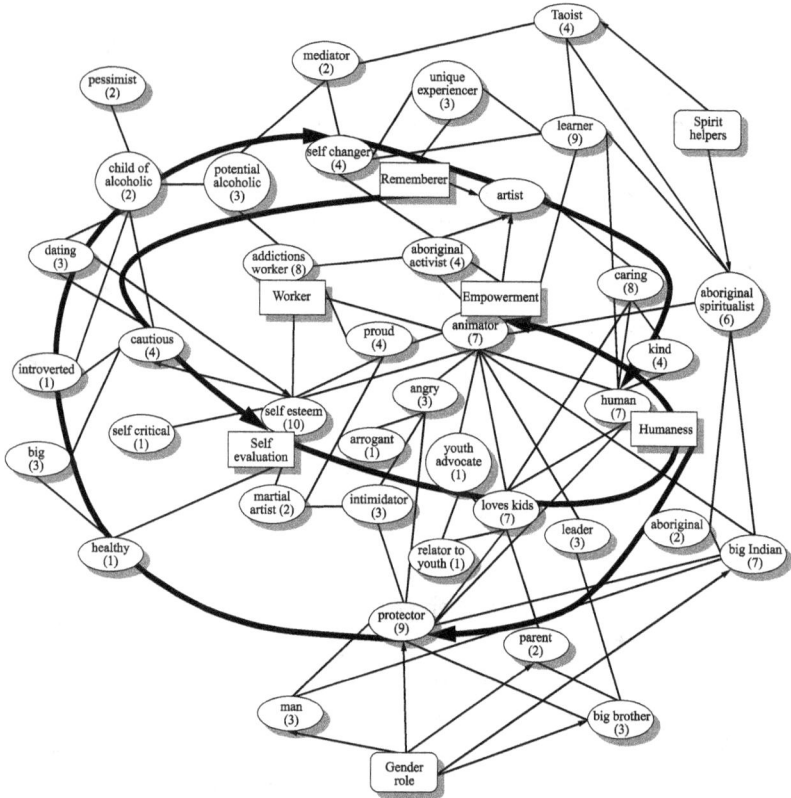

FIGURE 5.5. *Revised memetic self-map of Trevor resulting from his second interview (with no further changes resulting from the third interview).*

humanity and his own, he decided to modify this behaviour. This could be taken as an example of his "self-changer" and "learner" memes overruling initial intimidator tendencies. He accomplished this, in part, by sublimating his aggressiveness into political activism, which became more central to his self-definition.

During the three-month period between the second and third interviews, Trevor's uncle stabbed his father, inflicting serious wounds. While his father was in hospital unconscious, Trevor told him that he forgave him for being "a lousy father" and that he loved him. He thought his father heard this because he experienced father-son bonding once consciousness returned. He said he had been very angry with his uncle but then thought, "If a tiger attacked a deer would you blame the tiger?" He explained his analogy by observing that his uncle was an alcoholic and an illicit drug user, and his father had been trying to get him to "sober up." His uncle's reaction was the reaction of an alcoholic and a drug user, not a fully human person.

Trevor was in an auto accident during this period, and the woman he had been dating asked him for money while he was hospitalized. He decided that she had been using him as an enabler in her alcohol and drug abuse and ended the relationship. He concluded that he was too "needy" with respect to being in a relationship, that alcoholic women had "come on" to him "like a bee to honey," and that he had been attempting "to use honey to attract butterflies." Trevor said participating in this research had helped him visualize possible changes to his self. He explained, "I think the map is in my head."

White Renegade

During colonization, people of European ancestry who joined Amerindians in their way of life were often referred to as "white renegades." Laws were passed by colonial administrations with imprisonment, torture and even death meted out to Europeans who "went native." Although the traditional aboriginal economy has vanished, there are still non-aboriginal people who prefer indigenous beliefs and practices to those of the majority culture. This is the self-story of one such individual.

JohnB was a Caucasian male in his fifties in a common-law marriage to an aboriginal woman. He began his interview by talking about racism. He said young children are open to playing with anyone, but they may learn racist stereotyping from their families and schools, and that this had happened to him growing up in a "typical German-Catholic community in Saskatchewan." This was JohnB's only reference to his German heritage, but eight out of a total of seventy-nine interview segments were coded "Catholic." His first experience knowing a non-white, non-Catholic person led him to question the church's teachings. He had been taught only Catholics could go to heaven, but he decided she was as good, and as entitled to heaven, as anyone.

Challenging the church's authority over spiritual matters led to a more general life theme, "Challenger of authority" which was seen in the memes "cynical," "inquisitive," and "independent thinker." This progression from German-Catholic to "Challenger of authority" is pictured in figure 5.6.

"Independent thinking" was a focus of as many segments (eight) as "Catholic." JohnB recalled that when he was in the first grade, his mother, who was a caretaker at the school, would periodically break

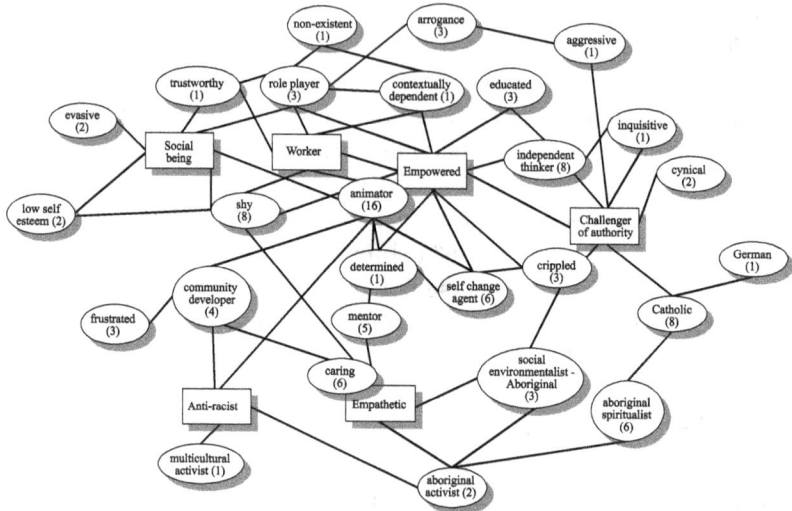

FIGURE 5.6. *Memetic self-map of JohnB resulting from the segmentation and coding of his initial interview, showing the number segments coded for each meme (in brackets).*

into the school records to see how he was achieving in relation to the other students. If he wasn't at the top of the class, he would be given extra lessons at home. He told his mother, "That's wrong and you're telling me not to lie, and not to break into things and not to steal but you are doing it."

JohnB was born with a club foot. Despite accepting the label "cripple," he drove himself to overcome his physical limitations in sports, thus displaying a competitive spirit associated with an initial sense of empowerment. Sixteen segments of the transcribed interview were coded for "animator." Although initially this animator meme was associated with challenging church and parental authority and with becoming a competitor in sports, later it also became associated with social activism and self-change. In the course of self-reflection, JohnB found that he played different roles in different situations. Although this may be thought of as empowering, it also gave him the sense that who he is, is contextually dependent. Since he appeared to be different in different contexts, he worried there was no real person behind his animator self, that in some sense he did not exist.

As a work supervisor, JohnB was required to direct, educate, and evaluate with competence. Conversely, he described himself as "a social idiot," and he avoided being with people when not at work. Low social self-esteem is pictured in figure 5.6 as connected to evasiveness and being shy. This shyness was countered, in part, by a drive for social justice understood as being part of the meme "aboriginal activist." He introduced non-native friends to aboriginal people to overcome negative racial stereotyping. He engaged in educational and community development activities in his adopted community. JohnB's activism on aboriginal issues suggested an impulse toward compassion and caring. Six segments were coded for caring, and the meme was presented next to a more general theme labelled "Empathetic," linking his roles as a mentor and as a person concerned with the social environment.

JohnB connected his belief in Aboriginal Spirituality to his Catholic upbringing. In his understanding the aboriginal "Creator" is the same god as is worshipped by Christians. He suggested that Christianity represents a corrupted form of Aboriginal Spirituality: "I think where Christianity has gone astray is … going way back hundreds of years, when Christianity went across Europe basically raping, plundering, pillaging, they say Christianity was basically a land grab, but Christians, even from the beginning of time, have been very powerful, have ruled with money, with power over people."

JohnB practised his spirituality by connecting with nature and through mystical experiences in ceremonies such as the sweat lodge: "It seems strange that a little white boy is going to sweats, and jokingly I call them spooks and I'm going, "Oh, they are back in there, the spooks like me," but the spirits seem to come to me always more than even aboriginal people."

JohnB agreed with the historical evolution pictured on his self-map: he became a challenger of authority based on early family and church experiences and this, in turn, influenced the development of his worker and social selves. He offered the insight that this "pushed" the centre (the animator-empowered core) to happen, uniting an otherwise fragmented self. He suggested there is a chronology with three or four context dependent selves evolving at separate times. As a result of this insight, selves 1, 2 and 3 were added to represent the different "persons" JohnB presents in different contexts. He said his German ancestry did not influence his affect or behaviour with the result that "German" was eliminated as a meme.

Given that memetic self-maps represent a changing self at a particular time, and given that JohnB did not believe in much Catholic dogma and did not participate in Catholic ceremonies, it was considered possible that the meme "Catholic" should also not appear on his self-map. He explained he still viewed himself as a kind of general-ized Christian who believes that Aboriginal Spirituality is closer to original Christian teachings, but he had used the term "Catholic" reflexively because that is how he was raised. One interpretation of this conversation is that JohnB made a mistake, and the meme coded "Catholic" should be given a different label. Such an interpretation would flow from an assumption that there are meanings essential to certain terms and that to be a Catholic one must believe in, for exam-ple, the infallibility of the popes. Another interpretation is that the meme which has been labelled "Catholic" in JohnB's self evolved, but that the label remained. He spontaneously thinks of himself as a Catholic with the understanding that early Christianity is compatible with modern Aboriginal Spirituality. Following this interpretation, "Catholic" remained a meme in JohnB's self-map, but its connotative meaning was amended to include the idea of a generalized primal Christianity.

JohnB reported a decrease in shyness as he grew older, but still he feels more comfortable in smaller more intimate groups. To repre-sent this decrease over time, broken lines replaced solid links between "shy" and three memes that no longer evidence shyness to the degree to which it once occurred. He said that "competitiveness" and "sports" were important memes that allowed him to overcome his shyness as well as part of his lifestyle.

JohnB objected to the coding of "frustrated" as a meme. He explained he was not a frustrated person, but he would sometimes become frustrated in certain situations. "Frustration" was not, there-fore, a meme by which he defined himself, but an emotion he sometimes felt in certain contexts, and it was eliminated as a meme in the second version of his self-map (figure 5.7). His notion that frustration is related to personality traits suggested that a menu of emotions was embedded in his personality. A bar representing the emotions that he highlighted was added to the base of his self. Thick directional arrows were then drawn connecting these emotive options to memes that may elicit an emotive response and trigger a context-specific mini-self.

JohnB had not mentioned spirituality until I asked, at the end of our first interview, if he reflexively hid his spirituality from all but his closest friends. He replied, "True," and added, "I need to see closeness to share it. Unless people know me very well, they don't get into my inner bubble." I concluded from this that spirituality appears to be a theme that originates on the Aboriginal Spiritualist/theist/storyteller

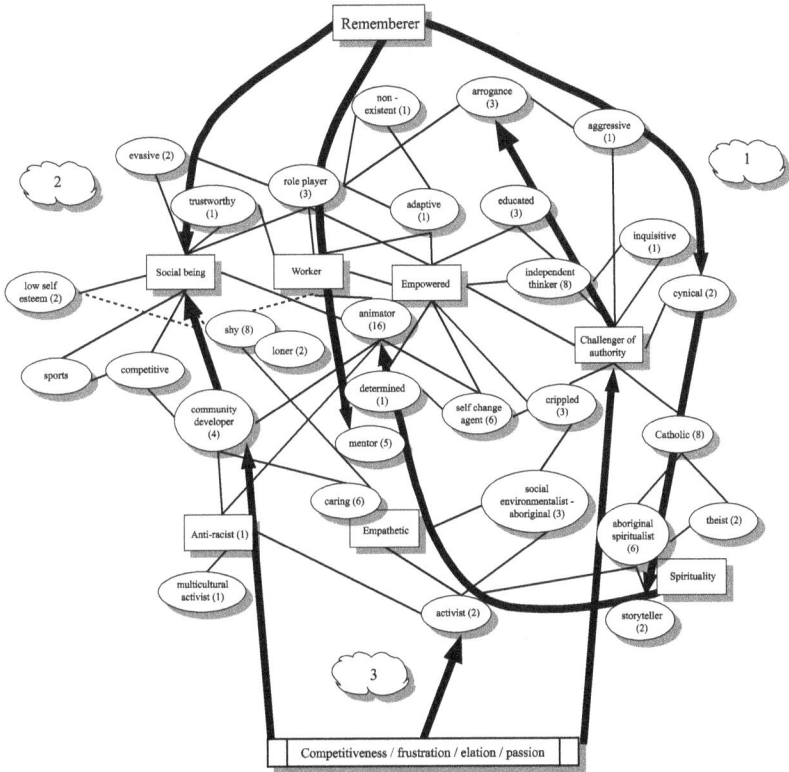

FIGURE 5.7. *Amended memetic self-map of JohnB following his second interview (with no further changes resulting from the third interview).*

side of his mind and directly influences his activism and animator centres without always being apparent to others. A "spirituality" thematic code was added to JohnB's self-map.

JohnB's spirituality contained many references to nature, and he said (in our first interview) he sometimes likes nature more than he likes people. He elaborated that people can get very frustrating "because they have the ability to think and to stand you up." He said violence in nature, as in a storm, can be beautiful, but violence in people is "quite ugly." He added that in nature it is easier to see yourself as part of a bigger process. Identification with something transcendent was incorporated into JohnB's conceptualization of Aboriginal Spirituality.

During our third session, JohnB said that while his revised self-map is complex and difficult to follow, "It captures everything." When asked if he had any new insights as to who he was, he said, "I thought that was your role!" He said he is biased when it comes to who he is, and by asking others one would get a different perspective.

A Métis Mother

When asked to tell me about herself, "Tina" said she was in her twenties, had three children, was married, and that she likes to clean. She said that talking about herself was difficult, but her responses gradually lengthened, producing fifteen pages of transcript. The numbered memes in ovals in figure 5.8 were induced from this initial transcript. Unnumbered memes and the bar at the base were added after the first interview.

Love was an emotion Tina associated with being a mother, daughter, and a sister and was also given to other children not her own. Had she described herself as a "lover," then that might have qualified as a meme in its own right, but she did not. On the other hand, "love" is very much a theme in her life and is represented in her self-map as a box. Other thematic centres represented include "Family Person," "Decent Person," "Empowered," and "Learner."

The meme "mother" was identified in eleven segments in Tina's initial transcript, more than any other. Ensuring her children had many toys constituted part of this meme. She also ascribed to it responsibility for their safety and care. This had led to excessive worry for her children's safety and extensive restrictions on what they were allowed to do. "Mother" is shown as connected to memes labelled "caring," "anxiety," and "paranoid."

The meme "mother" had such force in Tina's self that she credited it with saving her from binge drinking on two occasions. As a teenager she rebelled, left home, dropped out of school, experimented with drugs and drank to excess. She reported, "Getting pregnant made me sober up and smarten up." This child died in infancy, and in her grief she began binge drinking again. "I got into alcohol really, really bad, probably months straight. I was only sober for two days." Then she discovered that she was pregnant again: "The only time that I actually changed was when I found out I was pregnant, and then I couldn't drink. I couldn't go out. I couldn't do all that stuff, so I actually had to sit down and relax."

All four segments in which Tina described herself as paranoid were associated with her children. She would not allow her children to play in the bush behind their home. Her husband slept on a couch

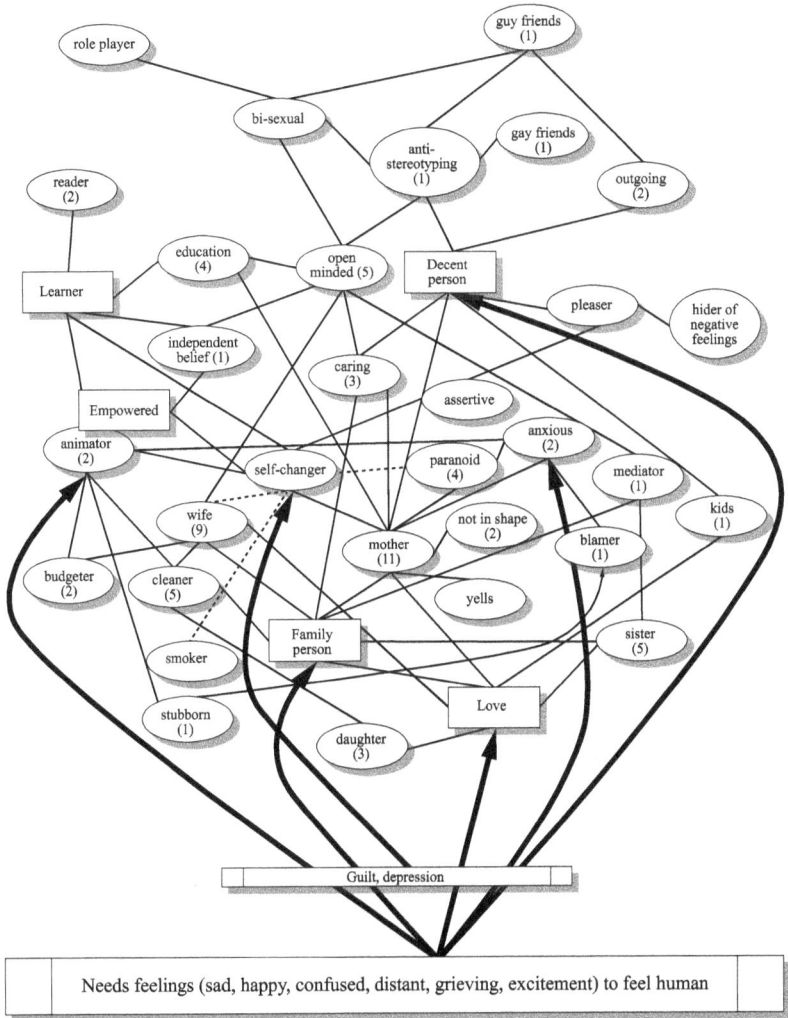

FIGURE 5.8. *Revised memetic self-map of Tina resulting from her second interview (with no further changes resulting from the third interview).*

so that she could be close to their baby at night. She awoke frequently to listen to her baby breathing. She worried when her children were out of sight.

Tina's anxiety was also associated with motherhood. It is possible that the referent words "paranoid" and "anxiety" represented the same meme, but the decision to code the two as separate was subjectively based on the understanding that she had previously been diagnosed as having an Anxiety Disorder, and part of her self-definition was some-one who suffers from this condition. At the time of this study, she was no longer taking medication or attending counselling. When she rec-ognized panic symptoms, she would go into a separate room and talk or will herself out of it, leading to a sense of empowerment. The second most referenced meme in Tina's map is "wife," and connections were formed between it and memes for "budgeter," "cleaner," and "open-minded." She admitted to "spoiling" her husband:

> "My best friend … lives on the farm, she grows her own grain, makes her own butter, makes her own bread, takes care of her man, stuff like that. I like doing that. I just won't let my husband touch my vacuum cleaner; I like cooking for him. I don't think he's ever done laundry. I just enjoy doing that for him. I enjoy cleaning and taking care of my household. My best friend … thinks I spoil [her husband] too much, and I know I do, and she says that makes him lazy, and I know it does, but I don't care."

"Wife" is also connected to the interpretive or thematic codes "Family Person" and "Love." These two themes with their surrounding memes presented as her core self. Tina reported that she experiences considerable stress as a result of the importance she places on her roles as "budgeter," "cleaner," and "mediator."

The "mother" meme is also connected to the interpretive or the-matic code "Decent Person." She recognized that failure in any of her primary roles would threaten her self-identification as a decent per-son but the most closely associated meme with this theme is "open-minded." It was coded for just five segments but had associa-tive connections with seven adjoining memes. For example, Tina has the role of mediator in her family of origin because she can see alter-native points of view, a quality that she defined as part of being a decent person. This quality also leads her to care for and befriend people of minority status and to defend students who have been ste-reotyped negatively by teachers. Similarly, she has defended gays and lesbians in her community. She said being open-minded enhanced her ability to "get along with" her husband, and it contributes to her belief in the importance of education.

Another centre in Tina's self-map was that of being an "anima-tor," defined as someone who gets things done. This meme was only mentioned explicitly in two segments, but it was implied in her self-characterizations as being "stubborn," a "budgeter," and as a self-directed learner. The capacity for self-animation implies the interpretive theme "Empowerment."

While looking at her initial self-map, Tina mentioned that she is a "yeller." Her children listen to her husband when he talks normally, but she has to yell for them to listen. In response to this information, I added a meme "yeller" to her memetic map which was attached to "mother." I considered merely adding this as a descriptor of what it means to be a mother, but I obtained the sense from Tina that this is not how she would define mother.

Tina reported self-change at her second interview held three months after her first. She said she was not as paranoid as she used to be, and that she was no longer trying to please everybody. She said she was giving her husband chores at home, and he was helping out with things like laundry and bottle-feeding their baby. These changes, and her new capacity to say "no," allowed her some time to relax, which she realized she had not done before. She was now working part-time to help out with finances, and this has forced her to get up earlier, resulting in her having breakfast with her eldest son. He told her, "I like it when you have breakfast with me, mom," and this led her to realize she had been sleeping in, partly because she had been "a little depressed." She also said she cried during her recent birthday. She had worked "so hard" to make everyone else's birthday special, but she had to buy her own birthday cake.

As a result of this new information, we added memes for "self-changer" and "assertive" to Tina's self-map. A dotted line between "self-changer" and "assertive" was used to indicate that she still relapses into non-assertive behaviour, as indicated by her response to the failure of her family to adequately remember her birthday. A meme for "pleaser" was included, indicating Tina takes care of others' needs but often neglects her own, and we attached this meme to "Decent Person" as the core of this tendency to please others is the feeling that she is a good person when she engages in this behaviour.

The most striking addition to figure 5.8 was an emotive element beyond that afforded by the memes themselves. Tina had admitted she could not take her children to a mall because of social anxiety, yet she said she does not like the way she feels on medication because she "should be feeling everything." With further questioning she said, "Because that is part of life. To feel is part of life. … That's who I am."

She added that a repertoire of emotions such as "sad, happy, mad, confused, distant," are necessary to feel human.

Tina admitted to bouts of depression and guilt preventing other emotions from surfacing. When these emotions are overpowering, she hides from others and attempts to generate positive thinking. The repertoire of accessible human emotions is represented by a bar at the bottom of Tina's self-map with green arrows flowing to and through various memes that are frequently triggered or, in turn, trigger, these emotions. A second bar is represented above the base bar representing the depression and guilt that block other emotions.

During our second interview, Tina said she was bisexual, and that she thinks more like a guy than like (straight) women, whom she described as judgmental and controlling. Men had always been more accepting of her. She added that lesbians are easier to get along with than straight women because "they know who I am." Her husband has not been jealous of her male friends but has been jealous of a female friend. Tina said her sexuality contributed to her open-mindedness. She added, "When me and [her husband] did our vows we made sure that 'faithful' was not in there because that's not realistic." Her husband has had sex with a female friend with her approval, but she said that if he was to lie and sneak around, that would "break my heart." As a result of this discussion, we added a "bi-sexual" meme to Tina's map with connections to "guy friends," "open-minded," "role-player," and "anti-stereotyping."

Tina was invited to elaborate on her self-description as "stubborn." She replied, "I like my house in a certain way; it's my way or the highway." Tina believes her children are a reflection on her, and they have to be well mannered. She blames people when they do not live up to her expectations. As a result of this elaboration, we moved the meme "stubborn" to a somewhat more central location in her self-map and added a directional arrow from "stubborn" to "blamer" indicating a tendency to blame when she does not get her way.

Tina was invited to elaborate on her experience that having children had profoundly changed her twice. She explained, "Before I had kids it was all about me. I didn't care about anyone else. I learned it wasn't about me—it was about him. If I didn't take care of him, no one else would." When reminded that not all women change their lifestyle when they discover that they are pregnant, Tina said that she did not want her children on welfare and dropping out of school and that her family valued children.

When invited to share new thoughts or feelings, or ways of seeing herself as a result of developing her self-map, Tina replied, "After the first interview my head was so clear. It was relaxing. I was clear-headed for a good two days after that." She went on to say that she realized that different things made her who she was. In answer to the question "Does looking at this map of yourself lead you to think of changes that you would want to make to your self?" Tina replied, "I am going to spend more time on me and not try so hard to make everyone else around me happy." She added that the guilt she feels when she relaxes, and the fact that relaxing reminds her of depression, inhibits these changes.

During our third session, Tina suggested that the revised map summarized who she is, and that she had no new thoughts or feelings associated with the map, which she now described as "pretty cool." Denying change, she said that she is the same person she has "always been." Being pregnant with her fourth child led her husband to take on more chores. She explained with a smile, "When I'm pregnant I get spoiled."

Tina said that the process of participating in this research had neither empowered nor disempowered her; she had always considered herself an empowered person. The process of this research made her think about who she is and how she sees herself. It made her think about things she wanted to change, such as having negative feelings, being a blamer, being paranoid, and being a smoker.

The Humanist Self

A past president of the Humanist Association of Canada said organizing humanists is like trying to herd cats—they all insist on going in their own direction. His comment was directed to a convention of Humanist Canada, whose national membership, at the time, numbered less than one thousand. We might assume that the 22% of the Canadian population who consistently declare themselves to have no religion but have not joined a humanist organization might be even more difficult to herd. Nonetheless, most of these people operate by secular moral and ethical standards (Buckman, 2000; Dawkins, 2006; Howes & Mazurk, 2006).

The three research participants grouped together in this section rejected the notion of the existence of a god-directed ethic, and each asserted a secular morality developed using rational methods. The three could also be said to share a nonreligious spirituality consisting of a belief in a higher purpose as evidenced by service to others, a belief in the unity of all things as evidenced by science, awe and enjoyment at the manifestations of nature, and a valuing of human life. Despite these commonalities, profound differences emerged. "Pangloss," for example, was committed to retributive justice, while "Judy" preferred to focus on understanding and mitigating the effects of social conditions leading to dysfunctional behaviours. While espousing atheism and humanism, "Fredelle" saw the world through the lens of victimization and identified not with an official humanist organization but with the Unitarian Church. Future research may reveal that the aspect of individuality present within the self is accentuated in the humanist self. Such accentuated individuality could lead to nonconformity and a predisposition to not follow leaders or social conventions. On a hunch, I asked one of the participants, Judy, if she has a pet. She does. It's a cat.

Not Métis, Not Humanist

"Judy" defined herself by what she was not. Although her mother was Métis, she was not. Her views were humanistic, but she refused the label. As a youth, she decided, despite her upbringing, that she was not Catholic. Despite a long and successful career in the field, she was not a social worker. Each negation necessitated the construction of alternatives culminating in a sense of uniqueness.

Judy described herself as a responsible, mature, fun, kind, friendly, loyal, smart, pet lover. Each descriptor involved decision-making, which implies a decision maker. I asked if the decision maker changes over time, how would she know it is still her? She replied that her self ultimately rests on a feeling that it is still her, and the decisions she makes "feel right." Thus, a "feeling of me" forms the basis of Judy's self, represented as a bar at the base of figure 5.9. From this flows a sense of empowerment that, in turn, leads to animation.

Five out of sixty-eight segments from Judy's initial interview were coded for the meme "animator," which also appeared as a theme driving such memes as "self-changer," "intelligent," "reflective," and "independent thinker." She placed importance on intelligence, as "it gives me some ability to understand what's going on around me, and I value it." Judy's life was also a product of environmental forces driving her in particular directions. For example, "worker" was mentioned in seven segments, but she felt that early experiences forced her into

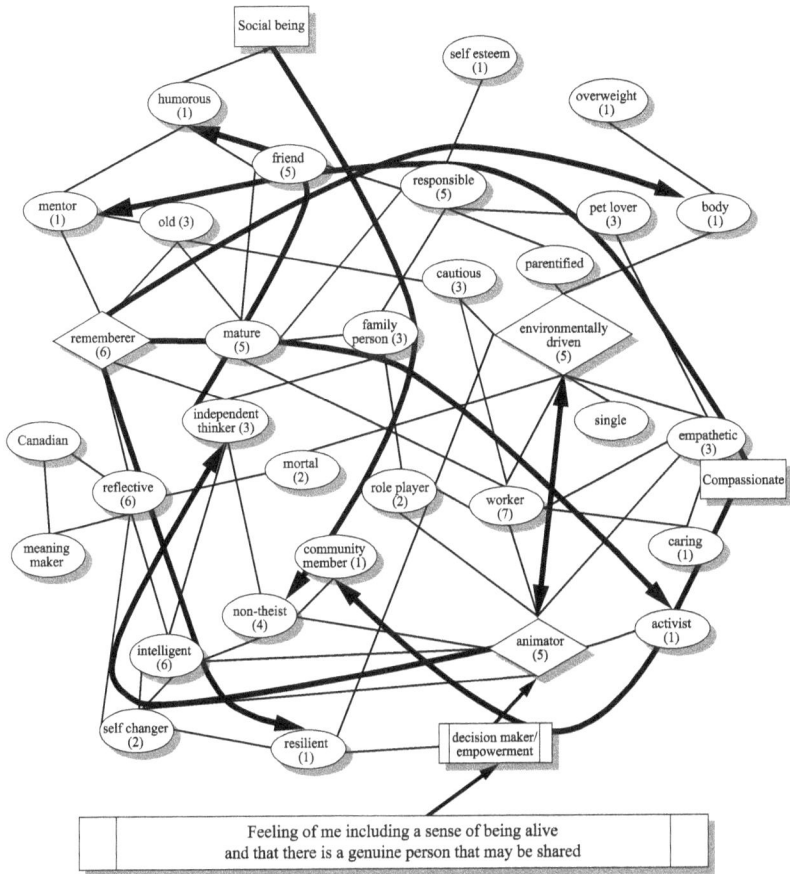

FIGURE 5.9. *Revised memetic self-map of Judy resulting from her second interview (with no further changes resulting from the third interview).*

her career path. Therefore, there is tension illustrated between "animator" and "environmentally driven."

The theme of remembering seemed to permeate Judy's entire self. She said by remembering reflectively we gain an understanding of who we are and why. This helps her to become resilient when facing life's challenges. One becomes more mature as one collects experiences, and this allowed her to become more of a family person. Her memories of interactions with people in poverty led her to become a social activist. Her memories helped her establish lasting friendships. Even the body, she said, develops memory from repeated use, as when neural pathways become entrenched.

Another theme represented in Judy's self-map is "Social being," inferred from her discussion of contexts in which she is humorous, kind, friendly, family-oriented, and a community member. Defining herself as "the family connector," she saw herself as the person who brings her family together. As a role player, she differentially applied skills such as levity, seriousness, and responsibility for the purpose of enhancing the well-being of others.

Judy resisted self-definitions attributed to her by others. For example, she declared that she is not severe and unfriendly despite feedback from her friends to that effect. She admitted to being non-expressive, especially in her younger years. As she grew older, she showed her inward friendliness by becoming animated, making eye contact, smiling, and talking more so people will see "what has been inside all along." But she still has difficulty with small talk: "I hate the trivial. When people are, you know, in social gatherings and they are talking about silly nothing things, I can't do that. You know, if you want talk about something serious, I'm your man. ... I'm not a good social chit-chatterer."

Despite having a successful career, spanning decades, in which she rose to management positions, Judy did not define herself as a social worker, although she acknowledged that she is "quite good at it." She believes the root causes of social ills to be broader than her profession appears willing to acknowledge. She explained it is more difficult to say what you are, as opposed to what you do. She said no one is interested in this deeper question, so engaging in a process of self-mapping is useful in developing self-knowledge. She explained she "fell into" social work as a young, single parent who needed an income, but would have preferred being an artist or a lawyer. This is reflected in the meme "environmental driven."

Judy was also not a "Catholic" despite being raised in the Church and having attended a separate school taught by priests and nuns. She began questioning Roman Catholic teachings in grade 10 when a priest presented, as church law, instructions on how long and in what way couples could kiss. She remembered thinking that if this teaching was wrong, then other church teachings may also be wrong. She decided she was the kind of person who needed evidence for belief, and she decided the very idea of a god was not logical.

Judy did not identify as Métis because she was not raised in that community. While being open about her aboriginal ancestry she did not define herself as Aboriginal because, "Blood does not drive you. For me the Métis part is overwhelmed by a lot of things."[3] She hoped someday it would be possible to simply define oneself as "Canadian." A "Canadian" meme was attached to both "meaning-maker" and "reflective."

Judy also refused to define herself as a humanist. Although she had joined an association of humanists, she found the label to be unhelpful or misleading since some people have a distorted view of what it means. The referent label of the meme was, therefore, changed to "non-theist."

Judy said she did not think she had changed in the five-month interval since our first interview. For her a constant was "genuine," defined as recognizing "the good, bad, and indifferent within self." The idea of genuineness was added to her "Feeling of Me" base. She added that maturity involves knowing and believing in one's self and in making an effort to relate to others in positive ways.

"Kind" had been added as a meme on Judy's initial self-map, but Judy explained it was not a word she uses frequently because it is included in empathy and compassion. A review of her first interview revealed references to compassion in Judy's definitions of pet lover, friend, empathetic, caring, and activist. "Compassion" was added to Judy's revised self-map as a theme uniting different aspects of her self and incorporating the idea of kindness.

Judy had mentioned being "parentified" several times during our initial interview in reference to her having taken care of younger siblings. During this session, she added that she tends to become protective toward people to whom she is not related. As a result of this conversation a new meme, "parentified," was placed in her self-map, connected to "responsible" and "environmentally driven." The meme "single" was added and attached to "environmentally driven" after Judy explained that she preferred that term to "widowed."

While discussing her own mortality, Judy explained basic necessities, such as having a home, are important, but accumulated possessions would give her no pleasure at all. In answer to the question "What is important?" she answered: "Awareness that you are alive, that everything that happens is meaningful and that you have the opportunity to experience it. Fun is important but possessions are not." As a result of this interaction, "meaning maker" was added to her self-map and attached to "reflective." The sense of being alive was added to the baseline "Feeling of Me" upon which her self is built.

Judy said the quality of self-empowerment was always present in her, even though as a child she was encouraged to listen and do as she was told. She said the process of participating in this study reminded her that she is stronger than what she might sometimes think. She believed she has the resources to do what she wants to do, and her change from Catholic to non-theist reflected this. Her action in taking her grandchildren to a church to appreciate the music demonstrated, "I don't have to throw out everything. That which is beautiful I can appreciate." She said her self-map represents somebody she wants to be.

Judge, Jury, and Executioner

Pangloss, the central character in Voltaire's eighteenth-century book *Candide*, explained all developments with the phrase "all is for the best in the best of all possible worlds." As increasing misfortunes befell the protagonists, this philosophy of optimism became untenable, even laughable. "Pangloss," the participant in this research, did not exhibit unbridled optimism. According to this Pangloss, we are both determined and limited by our memories. Memories of his adolescence in British Columbia, Canada, defined him:

> My parents were both drinkers. I knew that I wouldn't finish high school if I stayed at their houses. They were split up ... hostile to education. ... So, I moved out and had this East Indian landlord. This Sikh fellow had a bunch of conditions. ... I had to attend every day of school unless I was sick, and if sick I had to stay in the house, and my grades had to either stay the same or get better, and if they got worse, I had to move back in with one of my parents ...

"Rememberer" was a theme that permeated his self-definition, and this theme included "metaphor maker," "story teller," "self-critical," "learner," and "moralist," as presented in figure 5.10. He remembered acting on his moral outrage as a young man:

> I saw my sister and there was blood coming out of her ear. I come from a violent family, and I knew what that meant immediately ... it was my drunk brother-in-law that I never really liked. I dragged [him] downstairs by the shirt. I weighed 220 and ... I had big legs. He was a radio reporter; he didn't have much of a chance. My father had just seen my sister; no words have been said. ... It's

eerily quiet, and I brought him into the middle of the living room downstairs and there's a deer hunting rifle up on the wall. I grabbed the rifle; I went to my dad's bedroom, and I got the bullets … my dad held him and I spoke for the first time. Now my dad never let me take the lead, he was the cop; he was in charge, and I told [the brother-in-law] if he wanted to live he would turn around right now and walk out the front door, and not look back, and that the gun would be trained on him until he was out of sight.

Pangloss said he would have killed his brother-in-law without remorse had the man not followed his exact instructions. His role as protector and intimidator were activated even though he was not particularly close to his sister.

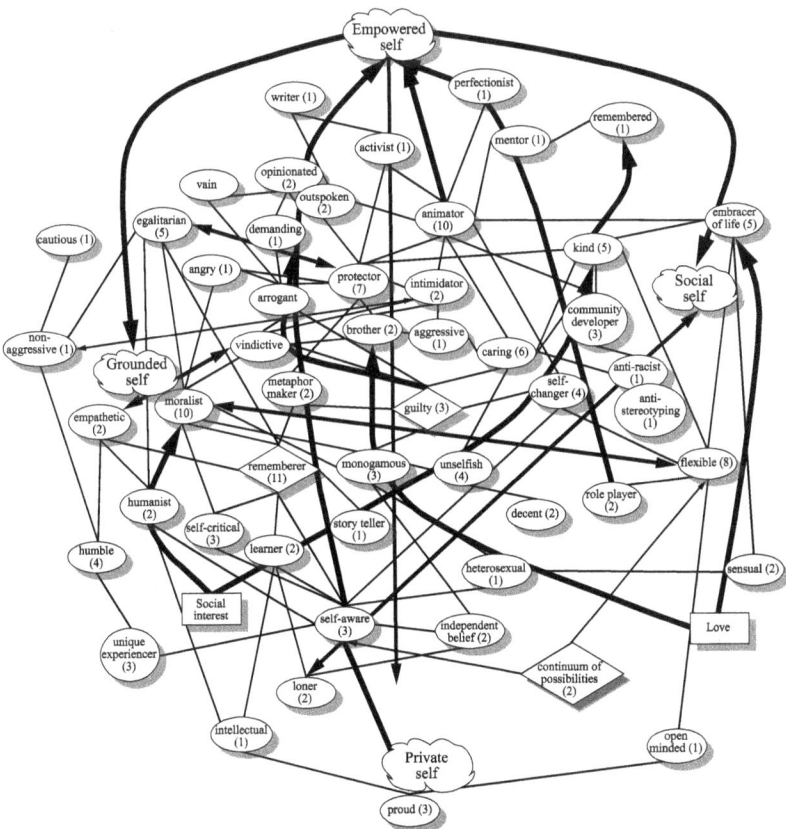

FIGURE 5.10. *Revised memetic self-map of Pangloss with amendments flowing from his second interview (with no further changes resulting from the third interview).*

Pangloss would continue a quest to vanquish evil people later in life. The meme "community developer" points to social interest but also contains an element of reciprocal altruism. He is happier when focused on making his neighbourhood and his world better, reporting, "Every day I am ready, willing, and able to make a positive difference in somebody's life."

In contrast with seemingly rigid moral ideals, Pangloss also advocated the idea of flexibility to the point of accepting chaos. He said if you hold onto your goals in the face of changing circumstances, "not only will you be thwarted, but you'll piss everybody off around you ... as the field changes, change your target." Thus, flexibility enhances empowerment along with enjoyment in life. This flexibility leads to what he called "some weird kind of continuum." He said he is mostly not hateful, selfish, or racist, but that he can be all of these things. An implication of this "continuum of possibilities" is that in certain contexts he could be substantially a different person. "This moment, right now, oh yeah, it's me looking at you. Tomorrow, I'm going to have a memory of looking at you." He pondered, "What is this thing that is experiencing stuff?" He concluded that he is only partially self-aware, but that his awareness includes being self-critical, a learner, a humanist, heterosexual, sensual, having independent beliefs and having unique experiences. Although no one trait or characteristic is uniquely his, the combination makes him unique:

> You wanna know what makes me unique, it depends on who you compare me too. Compare me to a whole bunch of people who were raised Anglican and taught Sunday school, and were kicked out of the church, and got a philosophy degree and became stagehands after a TV career, we would all be the same. You know it depends ... what makes me unique? Throw me into Niger and I'll tell you that it's my big belly, my height, and my white skin. Throw me in women's studies at SFU and I'll say it's the testes. Throw me on stage and I'll say it's that I read books without pictures, [laughs] sorry that's a bad thing to say, there is a high level of illiteracy in stagecraft.

This self-awareness gave Pangloss a sense of having a "private self," such that he could become a "community of one," living the rest of his life with books and having his groceries delivered. He reported he is, with his failings, proud of who he is. In particular, he is proud of his curiosity and willingness to change his mind in the face of contrary evidence. His "Empowered Self" theme is presented as permeating his entire being, but it is grounded in the values he applies, and it activates and animates his social self. A number of memes are in conflict. For example, Pangloss's "egalitarian" meme may be in conflict with his "protector" meme with the latter requiring him to place himself in a superior role over others. Similarly, his "intimidator" meme is in conflict with "non-aggressive," and "moralist" is in conflict with "flexible."

Pangloss said he was nervous and excited about his second interview: "I woke up with tense stomach muscles … how would he assess me?" He refused to accept the idea that this research was not about individual assessment. The question in his mind was whether the assessment would be ingratiating or whether I would say things he did not like. He concluded after a review of his initial memetic map that this "assessment" was ingratiating. He reported surprise that he did not see "vindictive," "arrogant," "vain" or "self-centred" in his self-map and said he did not think he hid these things from the researcher.

When asked to give an example of his vindictiveness, Pangloss talked about urinating on the grave of an aunt after her funeral and telling her he would do so when she was still alive. He said this gave him the feeling of having punched a bad person in the nose. He was angry with her, not because of the way she treated him, but for how she treated other relatives. He also mentioned destroying the tax records of an employer, and then calling Revenue Canada to accuse the employer of tax evasion. The employer had docked two other employees' wages when they pulled people out of a burning car and had to be themselves hospitalized. "Vindictive," in his mind, equated the kind of rough justice he gave his brother-in-law.

Arrogance is conjoined with vindictiveness because the latter involves acting as "judge, jury, and executioner." Pangloss said he does not consult with the people being wronged; he just acts. In answer to a question about who made him the protector of wronged people, Pangloss replied that he tends to be more skeptical and introspective than people around him. Thus, he has a "leg up" on most, and while his superior knowledge or ability may be fact, knowing that fact is arrogance. Still, he "cannot stand people who are arrogant."

The memes "moralist," "protector," "intimidator," and "aggressive" seemed to flow from the incident Pangloss had described in our first interview involving his assault on his sister's ex-partner. The second interview revealed that these memes were not sufficiently negative to represent him the way that he represented himself at the time. Memes for "vindictive," "arrogant," and "vain" were connected to "moralist," "intimidator," and "aggressive." Pangloss's insistence that he be seen negatively in some ways suggested a thematic quality to his meme "guilty" and a thematic line was created binding the above-mentioned memes to each other. The new meme "vindictive" is in tension with the meme "empathetic," so a tension line was drawn between the two.

Pangloss was unable to voice any changes to his self that had occurred in the five months since our first interview. He said that he is still "unreasonably happy and surrounded by love." A "Love" theme connecting "sensual," "embracer of life," "heterosexual," "monogamous," and "brother" was added. He was impressed by SunTzu's first dictum: "No battle plan ever survived first contact with the enemy," but Taoism is too naturalistic for him. He suggested that he is more comfortable with existentialism because it emphasizes personal choice and is "out of fashion." The idea of being contrarian was added to his "animator" meme.

Pangloss said he applies a "yardstick" to everyone he comes into contact with, and he expects them to live up to their capabilities. He recognizes perception can be wrong, but he demands that people "be human" in their dealings with others. He admitted this is being "judge and jury," but insisted, "As grown-ups we are supposed to make moral evaluations."

I noted an inconsistency in Pangloss showing understanding for some people who made poor decisions as a result of life circumstances, such as his parents who were said to have done the best they could, while being demanding of others. He explained that the sins of his deceased aunt occurred over decades when she was surrounded by love, yet she remained devoid of gratitude. He wondered if a twelve-year-old boy could see she was wrong, why could she not see it?

Pangloss explained that a humanist viewpoint is centred on a non-supernatural world with special emphasis placed on reason and dialogue, which evokes a secular ethic of maximizing happiness. He said reason and dialogue can solve most human problems, and we can learn to live together. "The Western spiritual ethic," he suggested, "is too heavily dependent on punishment in another realm, but a humanist ethic involves being good simply because one wants to be good." Pangloss suggested if he were not a humanist, he would have a narrower worldview. As a result of this information, the ideas of opposing supernaturalism, but supporting reason, dialogue, ethics and goodness were incorporated into his "humanist" meme.

Pangloss said being heterosexual "narrows my sexual behaviour but not my ability to love." He loves both men and women and finds there is a strong correlation between liking someone and finding them attractive. As a result, "Love" was added as a theme that permeates various aspects of his self.

After reviewing his amended self-map, Pangloss said, during our third interview, "What struck me was how indelibly uninterested I was in finding out from someone else what I am." Pangloss said he pays attention to himself only to the extent of its utility and is not studying himself as a subject. He said, referring to his second interview, "I was determined to convince you that there were negatives in my personality, so I presented an inaccurate picture." He was invited to make the picture more accurate.

Pangloss expressed the concern that if meme-making depends on qualities that are extrinsic, then it cannot represent those intrinsic elements of self of which he is not aware. He shared he can exaggerate things to the point of dishonesty, using examples that reinforce whatever image he wishes. "All is marketing," he said. He said he was looking for some kind of independent "assessment" that would serve to cut through the "marketing." During this interview, he agreed it was logically possible to describe a self without assessing it, but he added, "This flies in the face of a million years of human evolution." He asserted that we evolved to make judgments, often in crisis situations with minimal information. He did not have a concern about my judgment of him at the beginning of this research, but now he decided he liked me, and my opinion of him matters; therefore, he wanted to present himself in a positive light. On the other hand, he did not want to lie about himself because then what is liked is the lie and not the reality. Positive statements may be seen as a step in negotiating a relationship "like courtship," he said, and there exists a fine line between the reality and the lie. When asked how he resolves contradictions in his self he said, "I don't know that I have to resolve conflicts between contradictory parts of my nature. I am utilitarian in my ethics. I want to know the effects of my actions."

Pangloss explained individual members of society sometimes have to step in and exact retribution even though we would like others to take care of it. Some matters, such as cranky neighbours, are not police matters. This view may be in conflict with his egalitarian value, but, he remarked "Being an adult involves holding two contradictory ideas in your head and not needing to resolve them." When asked to recount from where this sense of empowerment came, Pangloss recalled his attempted suicide. A girl, with whom he had made love, had sex with another youth the following night. He swam into the Pacific thinking that if he was too tired to swim back, he would drown, but some friends in a canoe saw him, presumed that he was caught in the tides, and paddled out to save him. He did not remember being pulled into the canoe. While in hospital he thought that the reason he tried to kill himself was he had been living for the approval of others, but he observed that everyone was as wretched as he was. He became more selfish, and this led him to become more generous toward others. He noted that the more he knows himself the easier it is to understand others. Increased empowerment resulted from increased self-awareness, coupled with an awareness that others were like him in some important ways. Nonetheless he concluded, "I have never been a good sage to understand how I make changes in my life. ... I am not my own grand subject. The key to happiness is finding something greater than yourself and dedicating yourself to it."

Born in the Wrong Body

Fredelle was a Caucasian with some Amerindian heritage who, as a male to female transsexual, identified as part of a third gender. She explained that regardless of the extent of her sexual transition, her history precluded knowledge of the genderization of those born and raised as female, and that transgenderality incorporates both female and male personas. Despite this self identification, she expressed a preference for being referenced by female pronouns and this accommodation was made except when referencing that part of her psyche she considered to be male.[4]

Fredelle presented two themes within her self that were pictured as being in opposition to each other: a male side she named "Fred" and a female side she named "Fredelle." These two personas or mini-selves are represented by clouds in figure 5.11 with those memes associated with each lying in the general area of the thematic persona. In all, twenty-seven codes were applied 123 times to one hundred segments of transcribed text. Thirty segments were coded for the meme "feminine," but Fredelle does not look the part. She explained, "There's absolutely nothing female or feminine about my physicality, so the only part of me that is genuinely feminine is the mental and consequently the spiritual, the emotional, the results of my mental activity. That is where my femininity resides; my goal is to be female and feminine, it's not necessary to pass as a female and be feminine."

Fredelle identified the qualities of being loving, sensitive, and caring as feminine. She viewed her sexuality as feminine, and she wanted to relate to her lover in a feminine way as opposed to an aggressive, dominant, and strong masculine way. She admitted her idea of femininity exists in her own mind and may not be universal. Other memes she associated with being feminine include being cooperative, hopeful, nonaggressive, and multicultural. "Multicultural" includes acceptance of diversity and difference. She viewed "male society" as enforcing rigid conformity.

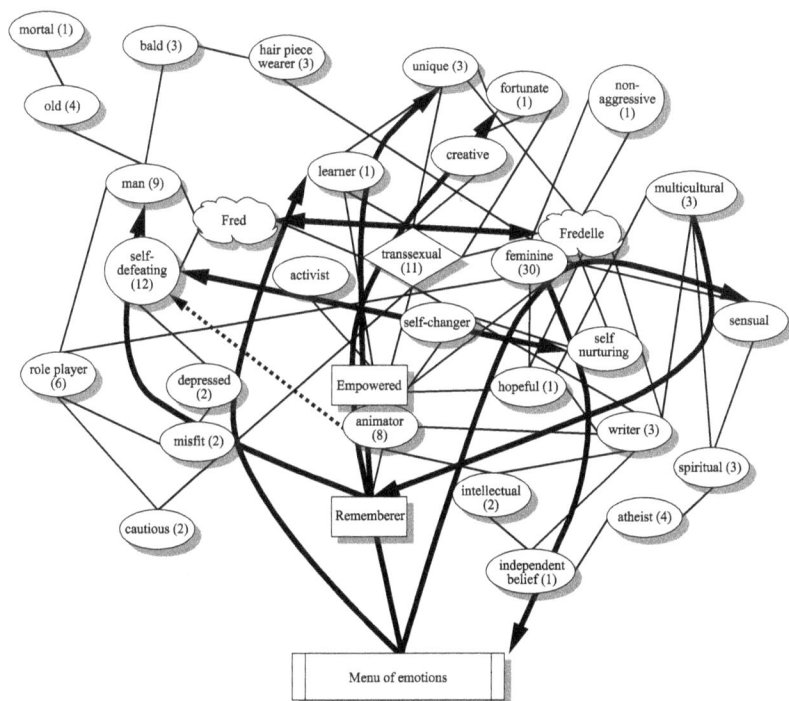

FIGURE 5.11. *Revised memetic self-map of Fredelle with amendments flowing from her second and third interviews.*

Fredelle's initial self-map was as pictured in figure 5.11 without the menu of emotions at its base, the thick directional arrows emanating from it or the theme "rememberer." It was also without the tension lines between Fred and Fredelle and between "self-defeating" and "self-nurturing" which were added subsequent to our second interview. During her second interview, Fredelle argued emotions are not properly part of the self and are to be monitored and controlled by a rational mind. She felt safer following logical cognitive pathways such as those illustrated on her self-map than "jumping around" as may happen when one acts and thinks from emotion.

The male side of her self, represented by "Fred," featured memes that for her had negative connotations such as "depressed," "bald," "old" and "mortal." She viewed the parts of herself that are "unavoidably masculine" as "dead weight," and this understanding led to ritualized self-defeating behaviours: "I don't wanna be a success as a man. I will do whatever it takes to not succeed as a man, and I know that is a conscious decision on my part, but it might be an unconscious decision in that I've never allowed myself to succeed openly in social or business or even romantic things. I've always wanted to sabotage Fred. ..."

"Transsexual" is presented as the core meme uniting the "Fred" and "Fredelle" personas in one self. She includes in her sexuality a form of "transgenderality," having fantasized being passive and feminine with both male and female partners. She tried unsuccessfully to be "gay" because, from her perspective, homosexual people are more accepted in society. She concluded, however, that transsexuality is core to her being—the source of her uniqueness, creativity, and learning. She decided to work for societal change, so transsexuals may gain the rights that homosexuals have attained.

Social activism implies a sense of empowerment, and eight segments were coded for an "animator" meme from the initial interview. This sense of empowerment was related to Fredelle's "coming out" by presenting her transsexuality to her church. Having gained acceptance in a Unitarian congregation, she began organizing a transsexual presence in other forums, such as annual "gay pride" parades. Although this event represented a positive transition, the act of undermining herself to deny success under her "Fred" persona also represented a kind of empowerment. The connotation of "role player," however, was disempowering as she had felt compelled to play a male role due to her physical man-form while working in the oil industry.

Self-defining memes that imply empowerment included "intellectual," "community member," and "leader." In defining herself as an intellectual, Fredelle stated she prefers the world of ideas to manual labour. Her transsexuality contributed toward independent thinking that, in turn, led her toward atheism. She felt a need to be part of a community, and that need was served by her membership in the Unitarian Church, a community that accepts the notion of atheistic spirituality. Fredelle's spirituality involved a belief in the interconnectedness of nature, which she viewed as a universal force without awareness, and community. She began building a transsexual community and speaking out for transsexual rights—activities that suggested the incorporation of a "leader" meme into her self.

Fredelle said her initial self-map accurately depicted the disproportionate imbalance between her two centres: Fred and Fredelle. She noted that Fredelle contains "all the good things about me," and she concluded that she would be a better person to have lost Fred. She said Fred is connected with being depressed and a misfit and added, "Nature is not necessarily just. Nature cares only about reproduction of species; it cares nothing for quality of life. Nature screwed me up with this Fred stuff."

Fredelle had an orchidectomy during the five-month interval between our first and second interviews, and she reported "tears of joy" with the removal of the first testicle. She considered her testicles to have been an insult to her, and with their removal she felt more like taking care of her body. Her impulse to engage in self-defeating behaviours was reduced because "No testicles will benefit from my efforts to help myself." She noted there had been nothing her self-map about health maintenance or self-care, but with the surgery came self-nurturing. She explained, "Nature wants you to reproduce. I am getting back at nature because I am now non-reproducible. I wanted to force nature to say 'I screwed up when I put Fredelle into a male body."

As a result of this information, the meme "self-changer" was added to Fredelle's self-map, situated between "animator" and "transsexual." The solid line connecting "animator" with "self-defeating" was changed to a dotted line reflecting the change that she is no longer attempting to sabotage "Fred" by neglecting his/her health. Further, a meme for self-nurturing was added.

Although Fredelle planned to eventually travel to Montréal to have gender reassignment surgery, she said she could be happy with a penis as she does not find the penis to be as offensive as testicles. After an operation to remove her penis she will be physically a female with an artificial vagina, but she said she will still be a transsexual because of her history and memories. This was her first indication that memories are essential to her self, and the theme "Rememberer" was added to her self-map.

Fredelle said it is not possible to resolve the dichotomy of Fred and Fredelle and become both simultaneously. Fred was understood as the enemy within that cannot be combined with Fredelle. The 'I' William James identified with the animating principle is on the Fredelle side of the ledger. There can be no real battle between the two because Fred has no animating 'I." He is simply a repository for unwanted characteristics. Despite this consideration, Fredelle admitted, "The real me was both the Fred and the Fredelle. They formed a committee that could not get along. A hidden controller was a result of that conflict. I may still have some conflicts in the future, but the conflicts will have shifted from being internal to external. Fredelle can now take on anything. She is no longer being undermined by Fred."

Fredelle reviewed her revised self-map approximately five weeks after her second interview. Despite her earlier claim that emotions were not properly part of the self, she experienced happiness that her father's germ line dies with her because "He was a vicious man." Consequent to her orchidectomy, Fredelle reported feeling free of her past with a concomitant openness to emotion. She reported "tears of happiness" when observing a young boy at a mall. She now associated her former less emotional self with maleness, and she described her new emotional functioning as a "wonderful time of change." The bar representing a menu of emotions was added to her self-map.

Fredelle said what empowers her is knowledge, confidence, courage, and vision and this resulted in a new-found optimism. Following quadruple bypass surgery, she decided, "life is too short to allow the corporation to dictate who I was." She began telling more people about her transsexuality and enjoying her body more. She explained that to feel the feminine aspects of her body, such as her long hair, are a wonderful experience. She said the army shaves the heads of soldiers to remove their individuality, but she, with her hair, has reclaimed hers. She described short-haired people as "mean and vicious."

Fredelle said spirituality equates with connectedness and all of the items on her feminine side can be used in building this spirituality. She discovered she can now look at a woman and admire her without physical sexual consequences. Previously she would become aroused and would masturbate, which she viewed as a physical price for attraction, adding, "To me it was hell to be sexual."

Fredelle said that the experience of participating in this research empowered her to be physically free. The night before our final interview, while installing a bathroom cabinet, the lyrics to a Phil Oakes song came to her, "I want to give all that I have to give; cross my heart and hope to live." She noted that she hadn't been putting the effort into life, but now, "I see myself as a woman at the beginning of her second life."

Two Selves from Outside North America

Although this research precludes making any general knowledge statements about the specific cultures (Russian and Chinese) from which these exemplars are drawn, it is not insignificant that it was possible to map a self from each, and those selves shared certain characteristics with North American selves. While it is tempting to look for difference, it is also instructive to note similarities between American and Asiatic selves. The Siberian Russian "Nick" accentuated qualities of individualism and competitiveness not equalled in the selves of the North American sample. It is reasonable to speculate that European Russian culture was influenced by western European thought beginning with the reign of Peter the Great and accompanying ideas of individualism gradually permeated the Russian Empire. The collapse of the Soviet Union, which occurred during Nick's early childhood, would have given additional impetus to notions of competitiveness within a capitalistic paradigm, but these understandings would have necessarily been idealized versions of the Western experience. Such speculations constitute a narrative that requires further corroborative research.

Although elements of self-change and volition formed part of her self-map, "Maomao" placed greater value on a core self emphasizing deference. The method used in this research encouraged self-reflection, and by our third interview Maomao had developed a rationale explaining why she preferred to have others make decisions for her. This could be the signature of a collectivist culture, but that would raise additional questions as to why none of the participants from North American aboriginal cultures exhibited this trait.

My own linguistic limitations affected the results in this section. The interviews were conducted in English, a language in which these two participants were still attaining fluency, limiting the number of concepts they were able to communicate. While every self-map should be considered to be a simplified version of the actual territory, these maps were further simplified due to language constraints.

A Competitive Spirit

Nick was an ethnic Russian in his twenties, born in Kazakhstan but mostly raised in Siberia. He was attending a Canadian university at the time of this study. Ten of the segments from Nick's initial interview (out of forty-one) were coded "animator." He lauded individuality in self-definition, noting that during Lenin's time, 20% of the Russians were revolutionary while 20% were conservative. Lenin was said to have described the 60% who were neither as "muddy water." Nick said he respected conservatives more than those without opinions, and that you define yourself through your actions: "You have a choice to behave like an ordinary man or behave like a little bit different from ordinary man, ... [if] you have chosen how to behave yourself; it's more interesting."

Nick linked his animator self with a competitive spirit: "Everybody wants to be best. Sometimes you can find a man that is better than you. Ok, you should develop your skills more to be competitive, to be such a man." Six segments were coded "competitive" while an equal number were coded "self-changer": "If I see I'm not right in some situation, it's ok, I know the quality which I should develop." The memes "animator," "competitive," and "self-changer" are shown as linked in figure 5.12, forming the core of Nick's self.

In figure 5.12, the thematic code "Empowerment' is linked to "competitive," "self-changer," "adaptive," and "spirit" selves. Nick uses his intelligence to adapt to new situations, and he defined his spirit as an underlying positive confidence in his abilities and future. He carries his competitiveness into his social self. A "Social Self" was inferred from his "learner," "worker," "student," "husband," and "friend" memes. He uses humour and acts according to context. Playing different roles can change how he defines himself, thus "role player" was linked to "self-changer."

A counterpoint to Nick's empowerment is his sense of being "environmentally driven." He reported adapting to Canada's "slower-paced, relaxed" culture with some difficulty. "Environmentally driven" is linked to "reflective" because through reflectivity he comes to understand the nature of his environmentally driven self, and thus comes to have some sense of control over the process. Nick reflected, "Who can tell you what me is me? For example, my interior voice of

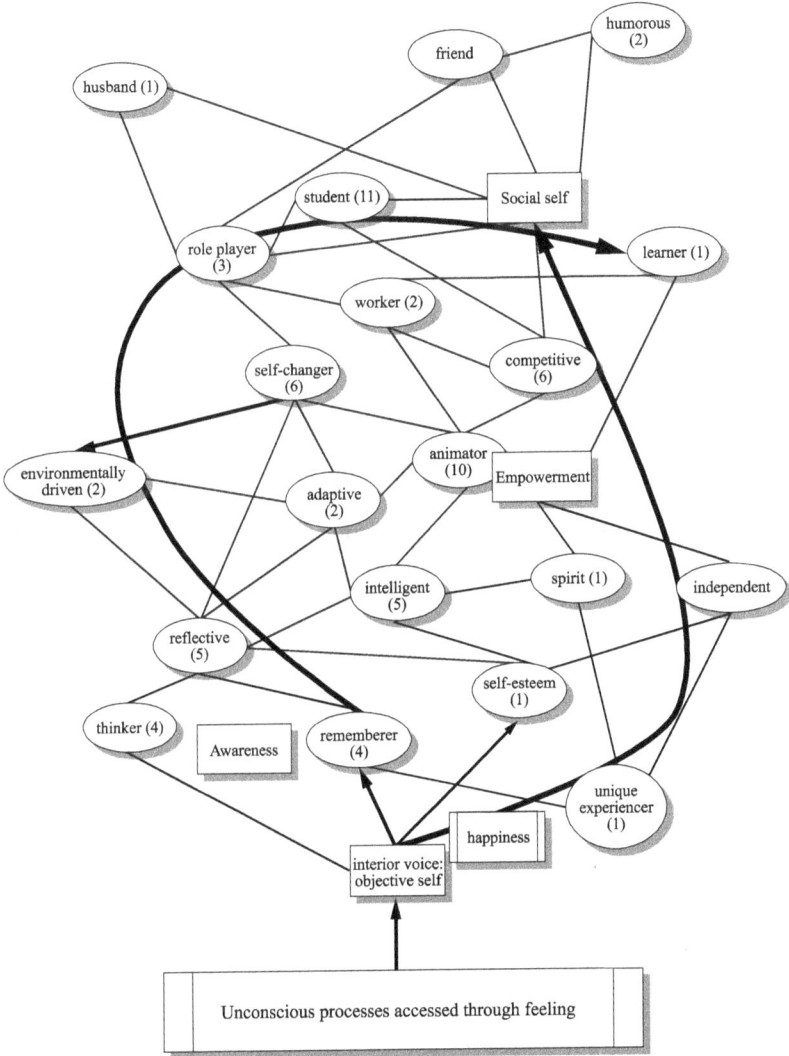

FIGURE 5.12. *Revised memetic self-map of Nick with amendments flowing from his second and third interviews.*

course it's me. … for example, who can prove what you is you? You're asking yourself, 'Is it true what who is me is who I can remember when I was three years old, is it me again?' and you know because your interior voice is what tells you."

Nick revealed that this interior voice flows from an unconscious process accessed through feeling, which forms the base of his self-map. The interior voice, connected to unconscious processes, lets him know he is the same person while exercising different aspects of his self across temporal and situational contexts. It was Nick's view that this inner voice, reflecting internal feeling states, tells him what memories to access. "Rememberer" is also represented as a theme that connects to "reflective," "environmentally driven," "role player," "student," and "learner."

Nick's first comment, on reviewing his self-map created from the initial interview, was that the pieces may be thought of as fitting together like parts to a narrative or story. Describing himself as a "social guy with many friends," he said his social self should be given more centrality. He also suggested that his spirit included a drive to try new experiences. As a result of this new information, a new meme, "friend," was added, connecting to "role player," "humorous," and "Social Self."

Nick said that he was calmer than at the time of our first interview. He had been in cultural shock and frequently angry at delays that were not of his doing. Canadian bureaucracies did not appear willing to resolve mistakes and are inflexible. Nick complained they are too slow, and the people in them do not want to work and do not want to understand. In Russia you can give bribes and complain to get people moving but not in Canada. He attempted to explain his needs and deadlines to Canadians, but they still did not speed up. Irrespective of these difficulties and his reaction to them, he did not define himself as an angry person, and he reported experiencing less anger by accommodating his expectations to this different reality.

The frustration Nick felt with the Canadian pace is related to his sense of empowered animation. He believed this came from his child-hood when he had pneumonia, but he refused to restrict his physical activity. When sent to Siberia from Kazakhstan, he became involved in cross-country skiing and running and learned, "If you are good, you could do many things." As a student in Russia, he thought that it would be good to see the world, and his academic chair suggested that he go to the United States. Although many people had difficulty obtaining visas after the terrorist attack in the United States known as "9/11," he was successful. He interpreted this to mean that if he "antic-ipates something, it will happen." He suggested this sense of empowerment came from inside himself.

Nick reported a feeling of constancy through temporal and con-textual change and asked, rhetorically, whether it was possible for him to know if his self was different than it had been. He replied that he could not be cognizant of such difference. Although he may feel differently at times, since he is owning the feeling, that which does the owning gives a feeling of constancy, and he would be unaware if that which does the owning changed. He said no one part constituted himself, and he speaks of "my arms," "my body," and "my mind." He noted the implication that he, the owner, exists independently of his possessions, including his body parts. He concluded he was "a closed system that is indivisible," and that which observes and is capable of objectifying parts of his self is associated with his "interior voice," which gives him a feeling of constancy.

Nick described happiness as "a background goal" needed to obtain other goals. For example, if one wants to be a leader, that goal cannot be achieved without happiness with oneself. In reply to a supplemental question asking whether the happiness of others is a goal for him, Nick said if people in his environment are not happy, he cannot be so; therefore, his attempts to cheer others is for his own benefit. He described happiness as a process goal but not an ultimate goal. He said you cannot have but one goal in life because once it is reached there is nothing left, and this results in a loss of well-being.

To Nick the central question for everyone is, "Okay, what can I do with my life?" To Nick, this translated as, "What do I need to do … to be happy?" Finding meaning and purpose are two ways of becoming happy. He knows when his accomplishments are sufficient because he feels it, and that feeling is translated by his inner voice. "Happiness" was not represented in figure 5.12 as a meme that describes who he is but is drawn as a goal to which he aspires, and it was drawn as overlapping with "interior voice" to represent an aspect of himself that carries on a dialogue, letting him know how proximate this goal is and its relationship to primary goals.

Nick had said he could be rigid, tough, and good during the first interview, and he was asked to give examples. He said he is sometimes rigid when he and his wife have different views. He is tough when sometimes she fears a new experience, and he pushes her into that experience. Sometimes, when he tries to be attentive to her feelings and says, "don't worry," she thinks he is still pushing her. This behavioural description was added to Nick's "husband" meme.

Nick said he feels it is too calm in Canada, and he would like more stimulation in the form of gathering new experiences. He added he needs positive feedback with regard to his social self, yet he would not like to be defined by the feedback—he wants internal knowledge defining himself positively. This would involve becoming less environmentally dependent and being, essentially, the same person regardless of context.

Nick said he had gained self-insight from his participation in this research. In an exercise as part of a university course between the second and third interviews, he discovered that he is humorous, intellectual and open-minded—qualities already represented on his self-map. He said it is interesting to get feedback from others but added it would be good to not have to depend on others for one's opinions, and this quality should be added to his map. He described the experience of participating in this research as novel and unique, giving him increased ability to talk about and explain himself.

I Am Robot

Maomao was from a city in the interior of China. She was in her twenties, unmarried, and without children. At the beginning of this study, she was a student at a Canadian university, but by our second interview she was employed as a bank systems analyst.

Maomao responded to the invitation to tell the researcher about herself by talking about the city in which she was born and raised. She described it as the middle city of the middle province of China and said it had been that country's ancient capital on thirteen separate occasions. She described several local historic and cultural attractions in detail, and she suggested the interviewer visit her city if he ever travels to China. She then talked about her parents and her extended family in the city, listing each of their occupations. She described her elementary, middle years, and university education in China, and then detailed her university dissertation thesis in Canada concerning an application of computer graphics to Chinese calligraphy. This led to a detailed description of her grandfather, who is a famous Chinese calligrapher. She mentioned some of his teachings before reverting to a discussion of the difficulties in replicating two-layered calligraphic brush strokes using an algorithmic computer program. She discussed the difficulties of defending such a thesis and how she hoped her parents would be able to come from China to attend her convocation. She then permitted the interviewer to ask a second question.

Maomao's initial monologue is summarized in some detail because it presents a core of what she felt a person, not of her culture, should know to better understand who she is. She felt it was important for the interviewer to know something about her city of origin. She both identified with and had pride in that city, and this is represented in her initial self-map (figure 5.13) with "territorial" representing, not possessiveness, but identification. "Territorial" was interwoven repeatedly with family. Seventeen out of eighty-two segments were coded for "Family person." Maomao's role as a student was emphasized in her initial statement and the meme "student" was coded for fourteen segments of her total initial interview. It is linked strongly with family as her family directed her student career, including both her areas of study and the location of those studies.

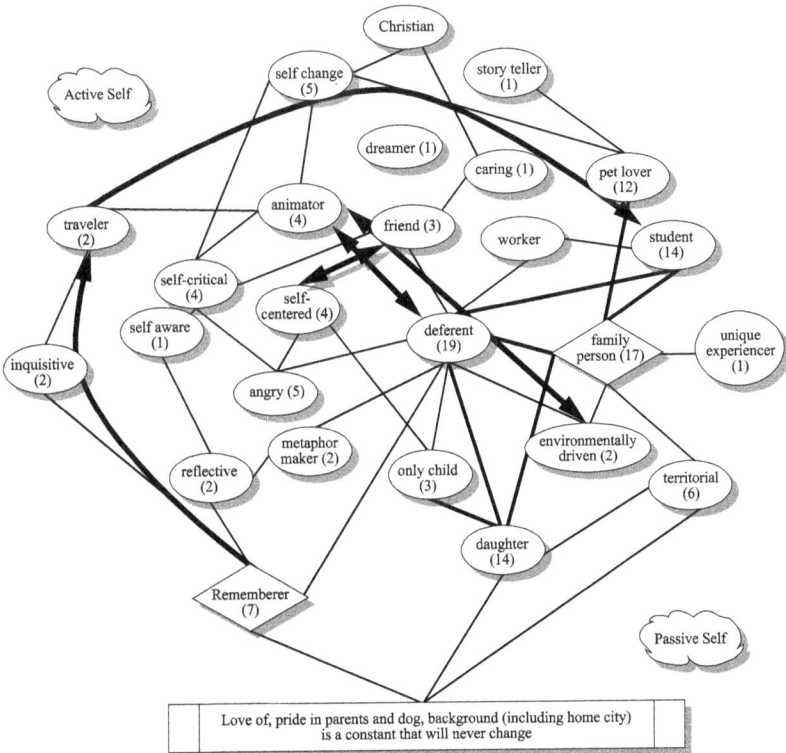

FIGURE 5.13. *Revised memetic self-map for Maomao with amendments flowing from her second interview (with no further changes resulting from the third interview).*

More segments (nineteen) were coded for "deferent" than "family member," although the two are linked. The behavioural dimension of her meme "deferent" is to submit to the decisions of significant others. Maomao said even small decisions, such as what to wear on a daily basis, had been made by her parents prior to her leaving home. Her decision to major in computer science was not hers, and she never liked the subject. Although her interests were in astronomy and medicine, she respected the direction of her elders. Maomao said she panicked during her first two days in Canada because she had no ready access to her parents. With the help of her landlord, she obtained a cell phone and a computer, and parental control was re-established. Even her dissertation topic involved deference—in this case, to her supervisor. She reported, "I still cannot make decision, so found like before, I want to listen to the command." When the decision of a significant other differs from her wishes, she feels sadness, but when peers enforce a decision she does not like, she feels anger. She said being deferent does not bring her happiness: "I found that maybe twenty years of my life, it's just ... I am like a robot. I just listen to the command, but at that time I found it hard to make a decision myself, and I found it so hard, for even just very simple, very easy things."

"Deferent" was associated with her anger when denied what she wants, and it was also linked to "metaphor maker" as a result of her self-description as a robot. She also saw deference as a consequence of being an only child and her parents "caring too much." Every day, on her return from university classes, she had to call her father to assure him she is back home. "If I forgot to call my father, he calls me," she explained. Maomao said her role as a good daughter involves more than deference: "The other thing I want because I hear a lot, friends ask me to go to Ontario, or eastern Canada, like Toronto, or some other places for travel together, but I don't. I didn't go with them because I want to travel with my parents."

The meme "pet lover" was coded for twelve segments. Buying a dog while living in Beijing was the first major decision she recalled making without being deferent to anyone else: "Before I graduate from Lanzhou University, which is my undergraduate study, my dream is, I can have a dog. I dream not (for) a cat or a lot of money, but it's that I can have a dog, and after I graduate I found a job at Beijing, and I have my own small room, and so I buy a dog, and it's a very small one, it's a Peking [Pekingese] dog."

Maomao developed an interdependent relationship with her dog: "It is very cold in Beijing. It's a lot of, it's a very big wind, so where I was thinking my dog is waiting for me and is so hungry and so lonely at my home, I would feel very strong, energetic and do not feel so cold. I just ride my bicycle very fast, and when I go back home my dog is always waiting for me."

Added significance accrued to Maomao's first independent act because her father was not fond of dogs. Nonetheless, she was able to convince her parents to accept the dog when she returned from Beijing, and entrusted its care to them when she left for Canada. The dog died, but Maomao was told her father lost twenty pounds in his grief. He bought her another dog and gave that dog the same name, Maomao. Losing her first dog led her to change the way that she treats other people, "They should be treated good to everyone because one day you will lose them."

Maomao blamed herself for the death of her first dog even though she was not in the country at the time. She derided herself for her difficulty in making decisions, for displaying anger, and for being impatient. "Self-critical" combined with "self-change" to create action. She investigated taking astronomy at university. She devised a plan to go back to her old university in China to visit friends before letting her parents know that she was returning, so they would not have an opportunity to invoke an alternate command. She explained, "The thing is I cannot ask my parents exactly what I want because they would not allow me to do something, and I am old enough, I think."

Her capacity to be self-critical led to self-awareness and reflectivity. She analyzed her memories with an awareness of her history of deference, her difficulties in making decisions and her self-centredness. She remembered her travels and her curiosity in exploring new places, coded in figure 5.13 as "inquisitive." She remembered the things she has changed, and would like to change, about herself, and she remembered her first dog. Thus, her memories helped to unite various aspects of herself, depicted as a thematic line flowing from "Rememberer."

Maomao's account suggested potential conflict between her "animator" and "deferent" memes. Similar tensions are pictured between "friend" and "self-centred," and between "self-change" and "environmentally driven." These lines of tension display a conflict between her passive and active selves. On reviewing the self-map created from her first interview, Maomao agreed with the representation of her passive self as more prominent than her active self. She recalled her mother always helped her prepare for examinations while other students were responsible for their own studies.

In the five-and-a-half months between the first and second interviews, Maomao's parents had arrived from China for her convocation and an extended visit. Maomao said she looked for work when she graduated because her mother "nagged" her about it "every day." Maomao said she now defined herself as a worker and less as a student, and a new meme "worker" was added to her self-map.

Given her level of passivity, Maomao suggested that "environmentally driven" should be represented more centrally in her map, acting to repress her "animator" decision-making capacity. While her negative feelings associated with deference could be understood as a contaminating cross-cultural effect, Maomao said she also had this robot-like feeling at Lanzhou University. She had surreptitiously registered for a class in astronomy and said she would have found a way to pursue this interest had she stayed in China. By our second interview, Maomao was working and had her own apartment. She had complained that the Canadian family with whom she had initially stayed drank too much, but she had made some "church friends" who did not drink. She said she had stayed with the drinking family because she liked the girl who lived in the home, and the mother of the girl was very nice. Maomao said she now considers herself to be a Christian, and "church people" say that you should help other people because it is the good thing to do. She said in China goodness is defined by the law. The "church people" also taught her to pray, and she said she found prayer to be helpful when under stress. As a result of this information, a new meme for "Christian" was added to her map linked to "self-changer" and "caring."

Maomao reviewed her revised memetic self-map approximately two months after her second interview. She once again agreed with the prominence given her passive self. Her parents had returned to China, and she reported more of her time was being spent at home on the internet, watching television, and listening to music. She said although she feels comfortable in a passive role, she can with effort be self-activated and she had begun to decide for herself whether she would return home or stay and study. While she can make decisions on her own, she said she prefers to not do so. Being deferent allows her to do other things because she does not have to take the time to gather all the information she needs to make a good decision.

She said her parents enjoyed their time in Canada, and they planned to return the following summer. They approved of her conversion to Christianity and had attended church services with her.

She reported an understanding of her self as a result of her participation in this research, and she would like to change some "bad habits." She said she was now more aware of her personality.

Notes

1 Traditionally, individuals would seek out an elder person with the knowledge they sought and offer that person tobacco and cloth as a way of commencing their special relationship. Becoming an Elder, then, was a function of the people who recognized them as such from the available pool of elders. More recently some Elders have been appointed to salaried positions by institutions such as the First Nations University of Canada.

2 Aboriginal Spirituality (capitalized) is defined here as a belief system prescribing certain actions based on faith, thus taking on the some of the characteristics of a religion. When not capitalized, it references practices that may have been traditional, but were open to change on the basis of context and evidence. For more discussion on this distinction, see (Robertson, 2014b).

3 In Canada the Métis, a people of mixed genetic heritage who identify as neither Amerindian nor Caucasian were recognized as an aboriginal people by the Constitution Act of 1982.

4 Transsexual people who identify as a "third gender" may now be identified by alternate pronouns. At the time of these interviews non-binary pronouns such as "ze" were not commonly known and their use was not discussed with Fredelle.

CHAPTER 6

Memes, Themes, and Humanness

Everyone in this study, including people from both individualist and collectivist cultures, had a self. While it would be exciting to find a culture of people who did not have selves, this is unlikely. A self is necessary for objective thinking, self-empowerment, understanding the motivations of others, situating oneself in context, and forward planning, and any society without these capacities would be at a competitive disadvantage. Of course, it would not be necessary for all members of a given society to have these attributes; indeed, using the concept of the self developed here, people with Alzheimer's, classical autistics, and young children do not have one. But as inferred from the evolutionary account of self presented in chapter 4, a dichotomy between self and no self is too simplistic—there are many possible selves with the one capable of objective volitional thought being only the most recently evolved manifestation.

The advantages to having a modern, albeit three millennia old, self are bought with significant costs. As we saw, Maomao recoiled from the stress of being responsible for her own decisions. The sense of an individual self also ushers feelings of isolation from other humans with an accompanying need to negotiate and maintain a place within society. Interpretive emotions such as shame, embarrassment, and humiliation are not possible without self-referencing. Not insignificantly, enseleved people also become cognizant of their mortality. At a societal level, a potential danger of selfhood is the placing of individual interests ahead of the interests of the collectivity, thereby potentially destroying the society that nurtures and gives us collective strength.

This chapter begins by with an examination of the selves mapped in chapter 5. While the cognitivist view has a long and useful tradition in psychology, dating from the classical works of James and Mead, the role of emotion in animating aspects of the self needs consideration. The resemblance of the self-maps in chapter 5 to small-world networks is considered. Since the modern self, at least with respect to the cognitive construct that forms an essential part, is interpreted into being, the relationship between the self and the primary purveyors of culture to the individual, the family, and community, is examined. A majority of the participants expressed the belief that some qualities were needed to be fully human, with happiness often linked to a transcendental goal. Notions of happiness and transcendence are discussed with particular reference to the role of religion. Finally, I conclude this examination of the emergent theory of self with a holistic understanding of the evolved mind-body relationship that some readers may find surprising.

The Cognitive View: The Objective and Subjective

The cognitive self is sometimes called "autobiographical" because it is constructed from memories used as evidence to construct a working model or "theory" of self, situating the individual within a worldview: "Autobiographical memories unite cognitions, affect, and goals into a goal-driven construct known as the working self. The working self is able to track goal progress over time through the principle of adaptive correspondence and is simultaneously able to ground current goal pursuit in the context of the person's life through the principle of self-coherence" (Beike & Crone, 2012, p. 318).

In this examination of the remembered narratives from which selves were constructed, recurrent units of meaningful culture were mapped. Properly speaking, a meme must be held in a person's awareness before it can constitute part of his cognitive self. When people tell me who they are, they often begin with their work, their family status, where they live, and sometimes they add psychological attributes such as "intelligent," "friendly," or "inquisitive." These are roles and qualities that may be seen to be true and are objectively verifiable in the feedback we receive from others. As previously discussed, William James divided this "objective self" into four basic components: physical, social, active, and psychological.

In this research, self-maps containing memes referencing some physical attribute were indicative of a physical self, while memes placing the participant in a social community were seen as evidence

of a social self. Memes that included activity as part of their definition, such as "athlete" or "protector," were interpreted as evidence of
an active self. Memes referencing personality, thinking, or feeling
were deemed to be evidence of a psychological self. Using this system
of categorization all participants had active, psychological, and social
selves, although in one case the social element was inferred. Ten of
the eleven participants incorporated social selves into their being.
Fredelle was the exception despite her continuing involvement in the
Unitarian Church and the transsexual community. She recalled a history of painful social experiences which plausibly led her to deny a
conscious social self despite ongoing social activity.

Three participants—Maomao, Nick and Pangloss—did not
include memes representing their physical selves. That we do not
need to include reference to our bodies in our self-definition is consistent with the approach of Charmaz (1990), whose clients dealt with
conditions of severe physical illnesses by not admitting their physical
selves into what she termed their "dialogic selves." Their wasted and
deformed forms were not considered to be representative of who they
truly were. Similarly, those who believe in an afterlife seldom picture
themselves as continuing on into eternity with physical deformities
or mental deficiencies.

James pictured the obverse of the objective self, the subjective,
as having three components: agency, uniqueness, and continuity.
This subjective self cannot be observed directly but may be inferred
from the objective record or from self-reported felt experience. Thus,
if the objective record shows purposive action, self-descriptors that
demonstrate the actor's willingness to undertake interventions with
an expectation of success, we can infer an animating impulse leading
toward goal-directed behaviour. While all selves in this study had an
animating or volitional component, several also evidenced its passive
opposite. Maomao's passive self represented the major part of her
self-definition. Similarly, the selves of Nick, Magdellyn and Judy contained memes labelled "environmentally driven." The fact that the
active self may be modified by passive or "environmentally driven"
memes suggests a psychological mechanism whereby the quality of
agency James attributed to our subjective self may be set aside.

Once we discover that we can accomplish our goals we come to
see ourselves as "doers" or "accomplishers." The label "animator" was
used to represent participant self-identification as someone who
engaged in planned purposive action to achieve goals. JohnB, Trevor,

Pangloss, and Nick ascribed positive affect to such agency, linking it to their self-esteem. "Animator" was referenced by JohnB and Nick more than any other meme. In Pangloss's self-map, "animator" was the core of a large cluster of memes that as a unit were labelled his "Empowered Self." Trevor's animator meme formed the hub of his self, connecting with eleven other memes in spoke-like fashion. "Self-changer" was referenced twelve times during Chantelle's initial interview, compared with seven references to "animator," but both memes imply agency, with "self-changer" representing the animating principle turned inward.

The relative importance of the animating principle varied between individuals. Five participants (Tina, Fredelle, Magdelynn, Brent, and Maomao) identified memes or themes other than "animator" more often, with the suggestion that these other memes were more central to their self-definition. For example, nine segments were coded for "wife" and eleven were coded for "mother" from Tina's initial interview, and together with other memes they formed a cluster with the thematic code "Family Person." Thus, "Family Person" was presented as more central in her self-map. Similarly, Fredelle's self-map was more centred on "feminine" and "transsexual," while Magdelynn emphasized "athlete" and "gimp." To Brent, memes for "rememberer" and "teacher" were more central to his self-definition, although the role of volition, particularly with respect to self-change, was important. This may be contrasted with the experience of Maomao who, like Tina, pictured family as core to her self, but unlike the others in this study, she eschewed volition as a desirable attribute.

No one meme or theme appeared to be central or dominant in Judy's self-map, although "animator" appeared to be in a favoured position, flowing from a "Decision-Maker/Empowerment" theme that in turn flowed from the "Feeling of Me" base of her self-map. On the other hand, Judy moderated or limited her animator self by declaring it was not always operative, and she placed it in opposition to "environmentally driven," which she referenced an equal number of times. Magdelynn, Chantelle, and JohnB modified the effect of their animator memes in similar fashion. Magdelynn found she had a "Relativistic" cluster of memes that included "environmentally driven," "context dependent," and "role player"—all of which served to reduce her sense of empowerment. The relative importance of this cluster declined during the course of this study as she attempted to apply a more consistent self cross-contextually. Chantelle identified an (other) "determined" meme working in opposition to "animator." JohnB also found he could be context dependent, and he worried this could mean he was nonexistent. Although all of the participants incorporated a meme for animator with an accompanying theme of empowerment into their self-maps, most tempered their animator memes in some ways. This served to recognize they may, at times, passively accept environmental or contextual limitations to their empowerment. These individuals recognize their sense of agency has limitations and that they are "other determined" in some ways.

Ten participants asserted their uniqueness by stating that no other person could have the totality of their collection of experiences and qualities. Judy said her combination of experiences and values was situated within a specific extended family, so family identification aided in her sense of uniqueness. Pangloss shared a combination of contradictory characteristics, such as his "outspoken bravado mixed with humility," leading to his sense of uniqueness. Magdelynn described herself as being "the most gimped," having "the most heart," and being "the most tenacious" of anyone she knew. Brent and Maomao first mentioned negative qualities or indicators (for Brent his singleness, for Maomao her anger) and then added a collection of positive attributes, the combination of which made them unique. Trevor volunteered that even if someone else had exactly the same experiences, each would still be unique because their perceptions of those experiences would differ. Only Tina was ambivalent when asked, "Do you see yourself as a unique person?" She replied, "Kinda." Then she added that she was more open-minded than most people. This could reflect a desire to not appear "too different" from others.

The logic of having a self implies that each self will be felt to be individual, unique in some ways. When asked to support this individuation, people seek to contrast themselves with others. There may be a tendency to define our unique selves with adverbs like "most" and "more than," thereby cultivating a sense of self-importance.

All eleven participants in this research admitted to feelings of constancy. Tina said she avoided taking medications for anxiety or depression because those feelings represented who she "really was." With the implication that this constant or genuine self may not be totally understood, both JohnB and Pangloss expected the researcher would find objective truths about their selves of which they had been previously unaware. Judy referred to a genuine self, but qualified it by making it experiential—the constant self is dependent on entrenched neural pathways. "The genuine," she emphasized, includes recognition of the "good, bad and indifferent" within. Brent said he once thought he had to be a different person in different contexts, for example a "strict disciplinarian" within the context of teaching, but he now brings a constant authentic self to different contexts. Chantelle said putting up a front leads one to appear inconstant or context-determined, with the implication that if one exhibits one's "true self" one will be less contextually dependent.

If we each have an authentic self, could we have been different? JohnB said, "I can't even imagine how I would be different. ... Because it wasn't the path I chose. Maybe I would have ended up in Calgary as an oil company executive." He then suggested he may not have been happy in such a scenario. He reported the feeling that, regardless of his earlier choices, he would have eventually settled in some northern community similar to the one in which he actually does reside. Similarly, Fredelle said she would always be a transsexual regardless of the changes she makes to her body because of her memories, and she could not have been other than transsexual unless she had been born into a female body.

Maomao said her true self was passive while admitting that this self was a product of upbringing. Nick said, despite feelings of constancy, it would not be possible for him to know whether the self-as-knower was constant—he could not be cognizant of changes occurring at that level. Despite this qualification, Nick echoed the Jamesian "I" when he said his inner voice told him he was the same person across contexts. Magdelynn did not know what, if anything, was in the middle connecting her "fractured pieces," but she felt less fractured as she participated in more interviews.

A total of nine participants referred to a constant or "true" self or implied the existence of one. Six of these individuals referred to their memories as a source of constancy. Two (JohnB and Tina) implied that there were self-characteristics with which they were born. While admitting to feelings of constancy, the remaining two participants (Nick and Magdelynn) suggested that these feelings could be illusory.

In chapter 2, we came across the notion we have multiple selves that we selectively present in different social contexts. While several participants admitted to being different in some ways according to context, only one (Pangloss) suggested this was a preferred way to be. A majority sought consistency across contexts, and even Pangloss admitted to some core element of self that provided continuity.

In summation, all three components of the Jamesian subjective self and three of the four components of the objective self were confirmed in this study. Constancy and uniqueness appear to be felt experiences with agency more related to the objective record. That objective record is maintained in memory with the sense of agency or empowerment reinforced from memories showing volition. The sense of constancy was also reinforced with a set of memories maintained and considered unique to the individual. Thus, memory is an essential component to selfhood.

While constancy could exist independently of volition, it is difficult to imagine volition without an element of remembered distinctness or individuation, implying that a person, separate from others, is carrying out a particular act. In their developmental study of children and youth, Damon and Hart (1988) found evidence young children attribute both continuity and distinctness to unchanging innate characteristics, and they are nonvolitional. As we have seen, constancy may be confirmed by the identification of characteristics common to past and present selves, or it may involve the preservation of unique remembrances. Distinctness gradually evolves to include reference to unique subjective experience, while agency becomes attached to personal and moral evaluations. In this study, volition or agency was represented by the terms "animation" and "empowerment." Every participant, including those from non-Western cultures, incorporated an animator meme indicative of individual volition, and they stated they felt individually unique in some ways. This study is supportive of the historical scan completed in chapter 3 indicating that far from being a Western invention, the self with volitional properties is common across cultures. While this structure may be cross-cultural, the values placed on aspects of that structure vary.

All of the research participants voiced narratives as to how they overcame adversity in becoming who they were. They also recalled initiating developmental changes to themselves. For example, eight reported changing their religious beliefs, motivated by a desire to become better people in some ways. The remaining three told stories of how they had initiated change to become better parents or spouses. This would seem to support the research purporting to demonstrate self-efficacy (Bandura, 1999; Bandura, et al., 2001; Wiedenfeld, et al., 1990; Witkiewitz & Marlatt, 2004). Maomao's self-depiction as a programmed robot, and her subsequent decision that this was her preferred way to be, may give us pause to question the universal role of self-efficacy in building mental health. Her decision to become a Christian could have flowed from her earlier programming where both goodness and action were other-defined. Without the direct support of her family and community, she was open to finding a substitute family and community to give moral direction within the new (Canadian) context. On the other hand, although she preferred to not make her own decisions, she did not consult with her parents prior to her religious conversion. It is as though her self's maintenance needs initiated an act of volition that would not be countermanded by consultation with the usual authority. Thus, we are presented with the paradox of an other-determined self acting independently to maintain itself as a determined being.

Fredelle's planned developmental change was unique to the study. She had previously unsuccessfully attempted to live as both a heterosexual male and as a homosexual "gay." While sexuality may have a biological connection at the mental level (LeVey & Hamer, 1994; Whitam, Diamond, & Martin, 1993), Fredelle demonstrated an ability to fight her physical biology when she took hormonal treatments to enlarge her breasts and when she engaged in an operation to remove her testicles. One interpretation flowing from this is Fredelle's transsexual self sabotaged prior attempts to integrate into the heterosexual and gay communities. The language used here betrays a false dichotomy. If Fredelle's self is transsexual, then Fredelle is transsexual and there is no other entity within her self to oversee the earlier changes she attempted. "Fred" was simply Fredelle's repository for unwanted characteristics—it had no will of its own outside of male hormonal functions. The core of Fredelle's transsexual self must have felt innate—an unchanging constant. Thus, her developmental change was an act of self-maintenance.

All of the participants were able to recount childhood transitions. This supports the notion that the self develops interpretively and experientially from units of culture associated with those experiences. Thus, the self begins within the embryo of the family and is refined as the individual expands into the community. Evolutionary change happens as memes are modified, new memes compatible with existing self-defining memes are added and old peripheral memes are discarded. However, fundamental change involving the construction of a totally new self would be extremely rare. There would be no one internally to oversee such a construction as the existent self that would occupy this role is itself the object of deconstruction.

All of our participants related stories of childhood and adult transitions that contributed to making them who they were at the time of this study, supporting the proposition that the self is a developmental process evolving from early childhood. Ten of the eleven said their self-maps resonated with them, with the implication the method used here produces self-maps to which they could relate. The same ten reported that they felt empowered to make future changes to their selves with five of these stating they had felt so empowered before the study commenced. If therapy involves self-change, then the method used to create memetic self-maps may be an aid in identifying desired change irrespective of whether the client felt empowered to do so prior to the mapping exercise.

Chantelle provided an example of relatively slow evolutionary change to her self. She started boxing as an outlet for her anger, and she confirmed her ability by defeating opponents. A counsellor assisted in helping her decide that she had the will and ability to develop a socially useful life for herself. She expanded her horizons by deciding to become a better mother and a counsellor within the corrections system, and she began making choices to meet these goals. Each change built on her self that was existent at the time with accumulative effect. The evolutionary change was Lamarckian (accumulated change based on deliberately acquired characteristics) as opposed to Darwinian (accumulated change based on the survival value of random mutations).

Brent gave another example of this gradual evolutionary change. He had defined himself as having low academic ability as a result of early academic failure; however he came to believe he was good at certain sports. A swimming instructor whom he respected suggested he coach swimming. He found he both liked and enjoyed coaching, and this led to him considering a career as a teacher. His subsequent success led to him to reinterpret the cause of his earlier academic failures. After this success, he began re-establishing contact with his parents.

The universality of an animator meme within the participant population is consistent with Jayne's (1976) argument that the self is a culturally evolved structure that proved to be so successful in empowering people that it was replicated in all cultures. Volition allows us to examine and thus improve our selves and is evidenced by memes showing us as animators in action. The physical entity, the body, can act or react without the self, but the existence of a map or theory about who we are allows us to approach life's issues and problems in new ways. In Vygotskian fashion, the dynamics afforded by self-creation result in a different set of rules than those inherent in classical behaviourism. Although every participant's self had a centre of animation and empowerment, none had specific centres that corresponded with constancy or uniqueness. It is possible constancy and uniqueness are felt conditions necessary to animate the entire self-structure while generating resistance to change.

Several participants said they could be context dependent, with some (Chantelle, Magdelynn, Trevor, Judy) seeking to present a consistent self across contexts. Contained within these grand narratives of the self were remembered stories of feeling, constancy, community, volition, and individuation. Within that broad framework was room for variation. The maps of five participants (JohnB, Chantelle, Trevor, Pangloss, and Nick) showed an animator meme with an empowerment theme at the core or most central part of their selves. Their stories showed a predisposition to act deliberatively and forcefully when meeting life's challenges. The maps of Tina, Fredelle, Magdelynn, Brent, and Maomao showed other centres more core to their felt being. Their lives, as interpreted from their stories, reflected these differences. In Maomao's self, the animator meme was present but not culturally valued. The emphasis she placed on family, community, duty, and deference has been identified as a cultural norm (Mac, 2006).

All participants explained who they were by telling or retelling a series of anecdotal stories in which they were the central character. As Wortham (2001) explained, "A self emerges as a person repeatedly adopts characteristic positions, with respect to others and within recognizable cultural patterns in everyday social action. Because the positioning that partly constitutes the self depends on social contexts that shift over time and on the unpredictable counterpositioning of others, the self is an ongoing, open-ended, and often heterogeneous construction"(p. 12).

So here we see another paradox, a self that feels constant that is nonetheless in a constant state of change. The self-stories of each participant were based on themes that evolved incrementally over time under social pressure. The resultant self-maps outlined what might be thought of as "super-narratives," but unlike the anecdotes used to develop them, the maps were not linear. There were many possible entry points or beginnings that may be selected on the basis of context, purpose or focus. Thus, the narratives were retrospective stories grounded in the self-structure at hand. Blackmore (2002) argued that the notion of a stream of consciousness is an illusion created as a retrospective story concocted when we focus our attention. With this perspective, the selves of participants were narratives concocted from memories once their attention was focused with the question "Who are you?" If the conscious self at any given moment is such a retrospective story, then the importance of memory in constructing and reconstructing such stories is paramount, and the need for a grounding to ensure that the self so constructed feels true is explained.

In each of these stories, positive new self-interpretations were coupled with what counted as objective evidence interpreted in such a way as to accommodate a sense of permanence or continuity. For example, those that excelled at sports interpreted their success as evidence supporting attributes of which they had previously been unaware. This retrospective attribution suggests a mechanism whereby the new (or amended) self might feel true, in contrast to a bad person pretending to be good or an incompetent person pretending to be competent.

Self-identifying memes related to both the objective and subjective may be mapped in the same manner used with the suicidal youth in chapter 1. The links between memes formed cognitive pathways that were modified in therapy. But while the mind involves organizing and interpreting sensory inputs based on templates framing understandings that are culturally learned, it cannot be divorced from the more primal emotive functions connecting it to the brain.

The Self as a Small-World Network

While psychotherapy is largely about the efficient internal regulation of emotion, studies into the self have tended to be cognitive exercises. Although affect and connotation formed part of the definition of the meme, the degree to which emotion factored into the participant's view of self in this research was unanticipated. Seven participants said the ability to feel a range of emotion was essential to being human, and the remaining four implied as much in their self-maps. Tina refused to take medication for anxiety disorder prior to this study because she wanted to feel a full range of emotions, and she placed a menu of emotions at the base of her self-map. Trevor agreed that the ability to experience a full range of emotions was essential to being human and suggested categories of people who failed to meet this criterion. He suggested that street prostitutes reduce their capacity to feel and in doing so suppress an element of their humanness. He supported a former girlfriend's attempts to "be human" by refusing antipsychotic medication. To be human, then, is to feel a normal range of emotions, and drug and alcohol abuse may turn one into something less. If a person is no longer fully human, then that person is no longer responsible in the same way predatory species are not responsible for acting on instinct. Taking a retributive stance, the objects of Pangloss's moral outrage were treated without civility, compassion or consideration. Since he had already declared that humans deserve to be treated in such ways, the objects of his rage were perceived as less than fully human.

Judy said being human involved experiencing a range of emotions, with humanness defined as having emotional, intellectual, and social components, and she placed a "Feeling of Me" at the base of her self. Fredelle said she learned, "being human is multidimensional and one can't put humanity into boxes." Although she had initially denied a place for emotions, she placed "menu of emotions" at the base of her self-map during her third interview, with the interpretation this represented an assertion of her feminine self following an orchidectomy. Nick agreed being human is a totality and suggested it is "a closed system … not divisible."

Four participants (Maomao, Magdelyn, Chantelle, and JohnB) did not discuss the quality of humanness, but three of these presented human feelings as the base of who they were on their self-maps. The remaining participant, Magdelyn, had an interpretive code "Feeling of Self" connected to her meme "rememberer." JohnB and Chantelle placed a range of emotions at the base of their maps. Brent identified an entire section of his self as his "feeling self."

While the hypothesized emotive element attached to individual memes forms a mechanism whereby memes may be said to bond with other memes, self-affirming and self-animating emotions play a more prominent role than had been previously depicted. Damasio's (1999) claim, "Consciousness may be separated from wakefulness and low-level attention but it cannot be separated from emotion" (pp. 15–16) is affirmed. We not only experience emotions as essential to our being, but these emotions are tied to a feeling self without which we would be unable to tell it is "us" having a given emotion. For people with modern selves, emotions are not simply additions to thoughts, but each emotional state presents as a distinctly different way to think (Minsky, 2003). For example, Pangloss's feeling of rage triggered by associations with his deceased aunt triggered a cognitive sequence involving retributive justice, whereas his feeling of compassion, associated with his deceased mother exhibiting similar behavioural traits, triggered a cognitive sequence involving understanding.

Epstein (1994) assumed people adapt to the world using two different systems—rational and experiential—and that they have constructs about the self and the world in both. The rational system consists of a set of beliefs, while the experiential system could be thought of as implicit beliefs or generalizations "derived from emotionally significant past experience" (p. 715). Such a dichotomization between thought and feeling would explain how an individual could reach widely different reactions to similar presenting conditions. An ontological problem with this model is determining who or what it is that chooses between the systems. If we grant evolutionary primacy to the "feeling brain," then at what point and under what conditions does the logical brain take over? The subjects in this study were aware that they were both cognitive and emotive beings, and their maps reflected both.

A directional arrow leads from Judy's "Feeling of Me" at the base of her self-map in figure 5.9 to empowered decision maker and animator themes. Directional line arrows from themes to clusters of memes are used to indicate that these themes can trigger cognitive pathways. Directional arrows from Tina's menu of emotions at the base of her self-map (figure 5.8) are used to indicate that context specific emotions may activate specific memetic clusters. In all, seven participants displayed a menu of emotions at the base of their self-maps, with diffuse directional arrows emerging from that base. Other participants had directional arrows from thematic centres such as "rememberer,""empowered," or "love." Whereas the self-map of the suicidal youth initiating this study consisted of a matrix of short-range connections between adjoining memes, the maps in this study included additional long-range connections signifying emotive or thematic triggering of more distant clusters. As we saw in chapter 2, such systems may be described as "small-world networks." In commending their use, Basssett and Bullmore (2006) said, "A small-world topology can support both segregated/specialized and distributed/integrated information processing. Moreover, small-world networks are economical, tending to minimize wiring costs while supporting high dynamical complexity" (p. 512).Small-world networks can be used conceptually to understand efficient design of service delivery with respect to mass transit, the delegation of power in systems of governance, the architecture of the internet, and gene networks as well as brain activity. The use of this design system in self-structure acknowledges its efficiency. A system consisting of only short connecting vertices between memes, while illustrating cognitive pathways, would be slow and methodical in contexts where quick and decisive action is required. A system of strictly long-range connections would result in random and chaotic behaviours.

Sequentially linked memes (memetic self-map paths) may be viewed as cognitive scripts leading to patterned behaviours within an overarching self-defining narrative. The self is both constituted by and is the protagonist in narratives based on the outlines provided by such scripts. As we have seen, edges representing simulated forces of attraction and repulsion create localized clusters. Missing from the maps of the youth discussed in chapter 1 were emotive mechanisms leading to the triggering of memetic clusters. The frequency of such triggers in her home community led the youth to change communities so that she could more easily practise the scripts associated with her new or revised self. The long-range triggering of local clustering is not necessarily dysfunctional.

Watts and Strogatz (1998) demonstrated that the existence of even a few longer-range connections reduced the minimum path length of networks of self-organizing systems without deleterious effects on local clustering. For example, such a mechanism allowed JohnB to switch quickly and efficiently between work, social, community, and private selves dependent on context and without the laborious and time-consuming task of tracing cognitive pathways from his initial focus to the one required by shifting circumstances. Similarly, Tina's emotional base could trigger a focus on specific clusters of her self-definition centred on themes such as "empowered," "family person," "love," or "anxious." Those triggering emotions could be stimulated by internal factors such as memories or by external contextual cues.

Mayer and Salovey (1997) proposed a model of emotional intelligence centred on a person's skill in recognizing emotional information and carrying out abstract reasoning using that information. Emotionally intelligent people are, in their estimation, aware of their emotions, regulate their emotions, and use those emotions to inform their thinking. Emotional intelligence from the memetic mapping perspective would similarly include recognizing the emotion, locating the triggered cluster, and vetoing the operation if the result has unwanted consequences. We are reminded of Libet's (1985, 1999) idea that actions can commence before conscious thought, but that consciousness still has time to reverse such actions.

While the focus of this section has been on the role of emotions in triggering memetic clusters in the self, other psychological characteristics are also in play. Figure 5.8 illustrated how Tina's depression and associated guilt acted to block feelings emanating from her menu of emotions. Both JohnB and Pangloss wanted the researcher to assess them, presumably to uncover unconscious psychological factors influencing their behaviours. JohnB suggested that he was more interested in the researcher's perspectives on who he was than his own. Pangloss said he was nervous and excited about his second interview, wanting to know how the researcher would assess him. Although it was explained that it was not the researcher's role to assess the selves of participants, Pangloss returned to the third interview with the same objective in mind. When such feedback was again not forthcoming, he became less interested in the project.

Clinical and counselling psychologists normally do assessments in their client-centred practices. A small-world network perspective of the self allows such psychologists to place assessed psychological characteristics in relation to the cognitively understood self so as to better illustrate the potential effects of such characteristics to the client.

Practically speaking, that which cannot be brought into consciousness through processes such as self-reflection cannot be properly thought of as part of one's self-definition; however, it would not be true to suppose that a person who refused to bring into awareness such information had no self or a self that is not influenced by those factors. Indeed, most people do not engage in a process of self-mapping, but, nonetheless, act on the basis of whom they believe themselves to be. An implicit self may be interpreted from behaviours, emotions and thoughts. For example, Tina believed she suffered from depression, but did not define herself as a "depressed person." The small-world network model allows for the mapping of the conscious self in the form of memes along and to acknowledge other factors influencing behaviour that are either beyond one's consciousness or are otherwise rejected as part of one's self-definition.

Teaching Self: Family and Community

Social feedback has been cited as necessary for self-construction and self-maintenance (Gergen, 1996; Ishiama, 1995; Kang, Mann, & Kawakami, 2006). Tina reported that her son's statement "I like it when you have breakfast with me, mom" led her to realize that she had been depressed, and that she should change that aspect of her self. Another interpretation would be the feedback from her son was an acknowledgement of worth that, in itself, began to lift the depression. With either interpretation, the feedback from her son had an impact on how she defined herself. We are conscious of the significant other even when they are not physically present, and we modify our presentations to some degree, by our perceptions of them.

Trevor's most powerful remembered feedback was from an uncle who gave him his Indian name, "Against the Wind," but he continued to report the importance of feedback from close friends. During the course of this study, Magdelyn accepted feedback from her boyfriend and her mother that she was not spending enough time with them, and this influenced her decision to reduce her athletic activities. Brent used feedback from a former girlfriend to find ways to reduce his "packrat" self and to become more flexible in understanding and accepting the values of others. Nick said feedback from Canadians, whom he described as from "a more relaxed culture," led him to become "more calm." Maomao said feedback from friends who had called her "selfish" led her to re-evaluate how she treats other people. This, in turn, connected to an emergent "self-changer" meme.

The feedback participants reported receiving was not necessarily accepted as presented but was subject to interpretive effect. For example, Judy's friends and colleagues had told her that she appeared harsh or "severe." This was not how she defined herself, and even with such feedback from multiple sources she refused to define herself in this way. Instead, she evaluated her behaviour and changed it to more closely match her self-image as caring, compassionate, and fun-loving. As a boy, Fredelle was taunted, physically assaulted and sexually abused by other boys who reacted to his femininity. This particularly harsh feedback led to a deep hatred for a part of herself she defined as male and to an ideology centred on the notion of male oppression.

Feedback is not always accepted as delivered and appears to be mediated by an already present self. The question that then stymies constructivism is, "From whence did that individual come?" There can be no other incubator for such an individual self than family and community. As Mischel and Morf (2003) explained, "As the person acquires strategies for dealing with different types of interpersonal situations during the life course, he or she develops a preferred theory of the self. The self-theory at first may be rudimentary, but it becomes elaborated and increasingly complex over time as the person seeks to test and validate it in the social world" (pp. 29–30).

The evolutionary account outlined in chapter 4 accords with what is known about the acquisition of the self in childhood, a developmental acquisition that must be taught (Harre, 1984; Harter, 2012; Waldron, 2007). We speak to infants as though they already have a fully developed self when we interpret their cries, gurgles, and smiles as though they have individual desires, thoughts, and wishes. Later we provide them with a language of the self replete with indexical pronouns. Such interventions are necessary but insufficient. Harter (2012) suggested that narcissism in childhood is developmentally normative, but she failed to consider that a person without a self would not be able to distinguish his emotions and desires from those of others. If there is no self, there can be no boundaries. Thus, what Harter observed in children was not narcissism at all; it was selflessness.

The problem of selflessness extends into adolescence with concern over the constitution of a "true self" in opposition to a variety of roles that the young adolescent may play. Indicative of selves that are still impoverished or incomplete, the adolescent explores various roles and characteristics in a process of self-definition. The incorporation of roles and characteristics to describe one's self is the "objective self" of James. The subjective self is inferred from that which is objectively verifiable. For example, the proposition that an individual is a good (or poor) learner implies the existence of a knower that can determine such things. Such a knower must have temporal constancy otherwise that which is known would be inconstant and unreliable. For boundaries to exist between the individual self and those of other persons, the knower must be unique to the individual described. Despite boundaries demarcating an individual, links between family and community remain.

The self-maps of ten participants contained memes associated with family, with six also indicating a connection to community. One person (Fredelle) failed to incorporate either family or community into her self-map, but her involvement with the Unitarian Church supported her self-definition as a worthy and transsexual person.

Two participants (Tina and Chantelle) credited their pregnancies, coupled with the values they placed on family, with their decisions to change their selves in some positive ways. Trevor and Judy saw themselves as "parentified" due to their childhood experiences of raising younger siblings, and they carried values they learned from the experience into their adult lives. Judy described herself as "the family connector." Despite an earlier unhappy marriage, JohnB maintained his family connection through his daughter, whom he continued to mentor in adulthood. Pangloss reported a desire to defend his sister even though they were not particularly close. Magdelynn resigned from a national team to spend more time with her family with the result that she felt "less fractured." Brent said he did not feel close to his parents, but he was making an effort to reconnect with them through "almost weekly" contact, and he reported a desire to raise a family himself. "Family person" was the second most recorded meme in Maomao's self-map, and it was closely linked to the most mentioned meme on her self-map: "deferent."

Families of origin were not always idyllic. Six participants said they were raised in families that were dysfunctional in some ways, with neglect, alcohol, drug abuse, physical abuse, and sexual abuse reported. Five of these six (Trevor, Judy, Pangloss, Brent, and Chantelle) felt the importance of family irrespective of their personal negative experiences with them.

Six participants said community was important despite the question not having been asked. After identifying himself as "a big Indian," Trevor began learning traditional Cree ways. JohnB identified with the aboriginal community where he resides, and he attempted to improve their lives through a process of community development. Judy attempted to find a "community of like-minded people" with whom she could communicate. Maomao reported a sense of community with a Chinese Christian church. Magdelynn said she favoured team sports because of the comradery involved, while Brent was active socially and in leadership positions with local environmentalist and cycling communities.

Fredelle was the only participant who failed to develop a meme related to being a family member in her self-map. Her bitterness toward her father was illustrated by her happiness that her father's germ line ended with her. Pangloss, who also reported a dysfunctional family of origin, showed an ambivalent connection to family by excusing the conduct of his parents while stating that he would be happy to be "a community of one." Conversely, he placed a moral responsibility on the individual to protect and nurture family and community.

A personal sense of constancy appeared to be connected to memory, community and family. Chantelle and Trevor viewed memory as the vehicle that builds constancy. Earlier core memories, including what Trevor called "the learnings," remain and provide a stable self in a life marked by change. Chantelle saw herself as central actor in her memories, concluding, "I don't think my personality, or the things that actually make me, me, those don't change."

Five participants in this study identified a meme in their self-maps labelled "reflective," by which they meant the quality of thinking about and ascribing meaning to their memories. Reflectivity could be present, like the act of remembering, as a skill without being part of one's self-definition. Even Tina, who did not identify "rememberer" as a meme in her self-map, reflected on aspects of herself such as her bisexuality, and these reflections informed her worldview. If the self evolved as a cultural adaptation permitting the objectification of oneself and others, then a capacity for self-reflective thought would flow from that evolution. If memory is necessary to build an objective self, then we would be subjectively "rememberers" and "reflective thinkers" without consciously identifying ourselves as such. As Leary and Tangney (2003) suggested, "Some phenomena—such as long-term planning, choking under pressure, self-conscious emotions (such as shame and guilt), self-verification, and deliberate self-presentation—simply cannot occur in animals that are unable to self-reflect" (p. 3).

Much of the self is in a shared social arena; but, just as we may keep parts of who we are hidden from those around us, there may be truths about ourselves that remain to be discovered. Our friends, relatives, and even acquaintances may be aware of self-attributes of which we are not yet conscious. In line with the social constructionist argument that the self is formed in negotiation with others, we become aware of such self-attributes from various forms of feedback. Typically, self characteristics are inferred from behaviour. While our understanding of self must allow for inferred qualities, those qualities, once presented, must resonate with the person whose self is being understood.

"Constancy" here is defined as a feeling that some essential or recognizable aspect of the self has temporal stability. As discussed earlier in this chapter, all of the participants reported feelings of constancy, and they relied on their memories of self in support of such feelings, but those memories were associated with communities of people. All reported involvement with formally or informally constituted communities, supporting the notion that culturally relevant community validation is necessary in the maintenance of a stable self.

Trevor located constancy within his memories: Regardless of future changes, his memories would remind him that he is the same person who grew up in an underprivileged neighbourhood of a small Saskatchewan city. Nine other participants also presented with the act of remembering developed into either a meme or theme, and all participants engaged in the act of remembering when explaining who they were. Two of these (Magdelynn and Nick) questioned whether their feelings of constancy were illusory, with Nick adding that if he became another person, he would have no way of knowing because his memories would necessarily change. Self-constancy was thus linked to memory and memory may be imperfect.

Each participant recalled childhood and adult transitions to which they were able to relate items on their self-maps, with the inference that those transitions helped make them who they became. All remembered transitions involved relationships with other people. This relationship between others and one's own self is not surprising if we view the self to be cultural creation. Such a cultural construct is necessarily linked to family, community, and societal networks, and a self so constructed would be dependent on those encompassing networks for self-validation.

The relationship between cultural levels of organization is pictured in figure 6.1, with arrows representing memes travelling between levels. While the individual is influenced by family, community, and societal cultures, he also influences each of the other levels of cultural influence in a process of negotiation and reconstruction. Thus, lines illustrating memetic influence are pictured as flowing both inward toward the individual and outward from the individual.

By themselves, self-maps may be taken to perpetuate an illusion of the self as distinct and autonomous. That some memes are rejected or repelled was shown in the example of Judy rejecting the notion that she was "severe" when presented with that suggestion by friends and colleagues. In support of the idea that memes exhibit attractive and repellent forces with respect to other memes, information supportive of existing memes within the mature self will tend to be retained

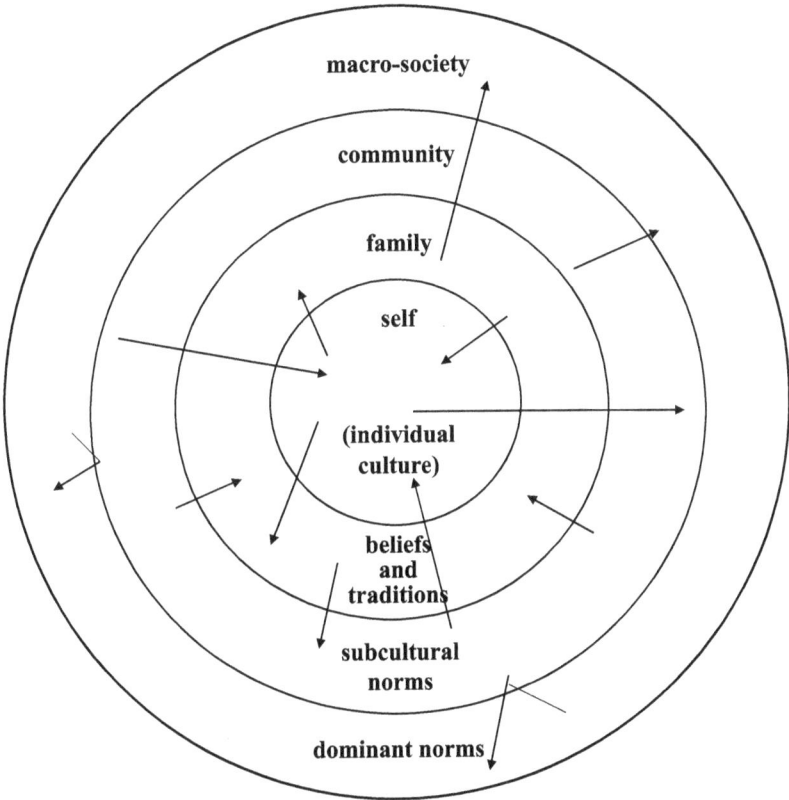

FIGURE **6.1.** *Four levels of cultural organization with hypothetical random memes flowing between each level with the potential for incorporation and repulsion.*

while information in opposition to one's self-definition will be rejected. If one's self contains a meme for "poor learner," the suggestion from family and friends that one is a capable learner may be discounted or minimized. Thus, the sense of constancy that is needed for self-maintenance is served, and memory selectivity maintains that sense of constancy.

As the example of Brent illustrated, a "poor learner" self-definition may be changed but such developmental change may require extraordinary intervention. Feedback from others can lead to changes, but such change is most often evolutionary, that is, consistent with existing elements within the self-structure. New evidence, if not rejected outright, must be filtered and interpreted in accordance with evidence stored in memory, and six participants reported that their memories served to preserve their sense of constancy amid change. Memories provide the self with a grounding that allows individuals to situate and accept change incrementally.

Six subjects said participation in sports resulted in positive developmental changes (Chantelle, Magdelyn, Brent, Trevor, JohnB, and Nick). Such participation implies involvement in a sporting community, and interactions between the self and such communities could be tracked using the model presented in figure 6.1. If our community supports the notion that we are capable and respected competitors, then self-evolution is supported along that direction. In similar fashion, the effects of family, churches, and researchers could also be understood using this model.

Put simply, the self may be viewed as a culture of one subject to change by processes similar to those affecting change in groups of people. The interdependence between self and family, community, and society goes beyond the dynamic of change. As Ishiama (1995) demonstrated, when immigrants to Canada were without a supportive cultural community, their self-stability weakened. My own examination of Indian Residential School Syndrome (Robertson, 2006) resulted in the suggestion that the removal of Amerindian children from their cultural communities led to similar problems of self-development and self-maintenance. Colonization led to a foreign-based "macro-society" resisted by aboriginal community and family cultures. In an attempt to overcome that resistance, the macro society removed aboriginal children from their communities and families in an attempt to re-engineer the selves of those children. This experience left those children without the supporting community needed to reinforce self-defining memes with resultant amplification of social and mental problems.

Community and memory form a complex system that both defines and maintains the self while allowing for change. The resultant sense of constancy may be a necessary condition supporting self stability, but it is illusory. Despite our best attempts to define what we are not, the felt boundary between our self and the other is also illusory. For example, was the meme "aboriginal spirituality" incorporated into Trevor's self-map him, or was it part of the community with whom he identified? If the answer is "both" then the boundary between the two is, at best, porous. Perhaps love is what we experience when we incorporate another being into our self. We put boundaries around our selves, our families and our communities so as to simplify that which we cannot otherwise cognitively understand. If we understand the concept of the self, not as a constant and distinctive formulation but as a locus of memetic gravity anchored to a physical being within a cultural milieu (with culture defined broadly to include all of the socially transmitted accumulated collective experience within which the individual has contact), then the question of clear self boundaries and constancy becomes provisional.

In summation, we know we exist because the community surrounding us supports that existence, and our memories, encoded in cultural units provided by community and society, translate our choices and experiences into an objectifiable record. Thus, both the subjective and objective self are interdependent in a way that confounds the dualism of Descartes with both supported, limited, and extended into the families and communities within which they formed. The demarcation between self and community is not at all clear.

Happiness, Transcendence, and the Evolution of Religion

Happiness has been considered a primary goal in fighting depression (Croezen, Avendano, Burdorf, & van Lenthe, 2015), relationship building (Gordon, 2001) and positive psychology (Seligman, et al., 2005). In their self-narratives, Tina and Trevor said happiness was one of a repertoire of essential emotions defining humanness. As with Trevor, Fredelle identified an inability to feel happiness with being male. Her tears of happiness at observing a young boy at a mall was attributed to her feminine self subsequent to the removal of her testes. Maomao said her experience of being deferent does not bring happiness, with the implication that happiness is a desirable condition. Nick described happiness as a "background goal," implicitly present in the development of all other goals. Brent sought happiness by becoming less rigid in his expectations of others. Others inferred happiness as a worthwhile goal. JohnB shared feelings of elation when successful in his roles as a community developer and activist. Judy said fun was important while possessions are not. Similarly, Chantelle inferred that reuniting with her son would make her happy, and the growth and satisfaction Magdelynn felt in her romantic relationship made her happy. Some participants related happiness to a feeling of transcendence.

Pangloss said acting to increase the world's level of happiness makes him happy: "The key to happiness is finding something greater than yourself and dedicating yourself to it." He found "something greater" in the common good and in moral purpose: "I have to be good, even if nobody else is; I have to be good because it's important to me. I understand the rightness of doing the right thing, doing the right thing for its own sake."

Fredelle implied transcendence in stating that interconnectedness with nature or a universal force provided her with meaning and purpose. JohnB also talked about interconnectedness with nature as a belief in something bigger than our selves. Trevor explained his political activism "was like igniting a fire that keeps me focused on something bigger than myself." For Magdelynn, as well as JohnB, that which was bigger than our selves was embodied in a creator-god who gave them assurance events would work out according to some benign plan.

All of the six participants (four theists and two atheists) who said some transcendental purpose or understanding informed their lives engaged in active behaviours to benefit the lives of others. Trevor strove to eliminate poverty and risky sexual behaviour contributing to AIDS. JohnB pursued a course of community development and interracial education. Pangloss attempted to increase human happiness by using his skills as a writer to give voice to those who do not have a voice in society. Fredelle sought to extend awareness of transsexual rights, while Magdelynn sought to have the strengths of people with disabilities recognized. Brent worked toward the greater good on environmental issues.

Three participants who did not mention a transcendental purpose also engaged in activities to help others. Tina defended students to teachers, cared for children not her own, and educated people about gays and lesbians. Judy mentored staff and educated others to challenge the root causes of poverty neglected by her profession. Chantelle decided to use her own experience as an ex-convict to help empower others in the prison system make changes in their lives.

The remaining two participants implied social interest. Although Maomao did not say she was actively engaged in activities to help others, she joined a Christian church motivated by a desire to do good. Nick said he could not be happy if his friends were not happy, implying that he would engage in activities to improve their conditions.

In a variation of the social interest theme, three of the five male participants said it was their role or duty to assess a situation, lay blame and take action against the person so blamed. Trevor reported feeling it was his duty to confront and intimidate the customers of prostitutes and parents who abuse their children. JohnB equated arrogant and forceful people with the mental abuse he had received from his parents, and he said he could be vengeful when confronting such people. He admitted, "That's one type of person that I will go out of my way to attack." The "wrongdoers" subject to Pangloss's wrath were those that used, manipulated, or humiliated others who could not defend themselves. In such instances, Pangloss said it was his duty to intervene not just in the defence of those so victimized, but to exact a kind of "rough justice." While admitting his assumption of vindictive power assumes a kind of arrogance, Pangloss said judging and acting on those judgments was a necessary part of the human condition.

This retributive approach may be contrasted with a softer approach used by Judy. She made negative judgments about immature people, stating, "They're selfish. They can be cruel. ... They can be bad family people; they can be bad employees; they can be bad employers. They can be self-destructive. They can be poor friends." Her response was not to punish the offenders, but to attempt to educate them and to change contextual environmental conditions so that good behaviour would be rewarded. Along with the three men who believed in retributive justice, her understanding implies superior knowledge in addition to a higher purpose.

Most participants in this study said increasing human happiness and engaging in social activism to help others were personal goals, with a majority connecting these goals to a transcendent purpose. The word "satisfaction" may be more appropriate than "happiness" with respect to meeting transcendent goals since life satisfaction and positive affect are separable constructs. One can imagine, for example, people living in trying times having the satisfaction of a life well lived despite difficulties. Lent (2004) suggested such a person would display autonomy, personal growth, self-acceptance, purpose in life, environmental mastery, and positive relations with others. If circumstances dictate that we cannot be happy, we can still attach deeper meaning to life experiences by relating those experiences to a transcendent purpose. That which is "bigger than we are" flows from our collective heritage.

Tension between individualism and collectivism, most clearly illustrated in Maomao's self-map, is inherent in the modern self. In every society groups of individuals, often in very large numbers, work together to accomplish collective goals provided by the culture in which they are immersed. Concomitantly, there is recognition that each person in these collective enterprises is an individual who is held accountable for making culturally approved choices. The capacity to make choices assumes belief as to outcomes and values. Belief is not possible without some conceptualization of objective truth supported by whatever counts as evidence in the mind of the individual. Such evidence must be present for a proposition to "ring true." The knower feels separate from that which is examined, with the sentence "I have a body" preferred to "I am a body." Thus, a disembodied self seeks happiness in something greater. It is a short hop from that proposition to a belief that reframes the self as a "soul" attaching itself to our bodies at birth or before.

In the Western tradition flowing from Plato, the consciousness seen as capable of examining itself is seen as evidence of such a separate self or soul (Descartes, 1643/1990; Doherty, 1999; Foucault, et al., 1983/1997). It was not until the eighteenth-century Enlightenment that the mind or its core representation, the self, was separated from the soul in scientific thought. We were then left with a soul, Buddhist-like, devoid of consciousness. While such a soul could be an animating principle in a schema of reincarnation, it would be incapable of appreciating the heavenly rewards of an afterlife.

We would probably find the mind of an individual in a pre-selved community incomprehensible. My language use betrays the problem. Could we call such a person an individual? Further, if we define the mind in terms of self-awareness, could we say that such a human had a mind? But such humans must have once existed. The incremental change of evolution makes the demarcation between "self" and "non-self" arbitrary. I have carefully used the term "modern self" to describe a manifestation of this evolution, with implications of individuality, volition, and causal reasoning. Earlier prototypical structures would have been built on sensory integration and relational functionality within community. Community members would be dependent on following preprogrammed responses to triggering stimuli with far fewer behavioural options than are currently available. Those cultural injunctions which could not be copied through direct imitation would have been learned through the use of myths and stories using the medium of language. Such cultures would have been incredibly complex to order the lives of entire communities. Assuming ontogeny recapitulates phylogeny and using our modern pre-selved children as a model, these humans engaged in magical thinking in their understanding of ordinary phenomena.

The Adam and Eve myth of the Judeo-Christian tradition illustrates a transition from self-less existence to consciousness and is compatible with modern selved humans nostalgically romanticizing an earlier stress-free time when they were one with the collectivity. With the eating of the fruit of the tree of knowledge of good and evil, mankind began to perceive reality in a more objective way with accompanying costs presented as a "fall from grace." They had to till the land, husband cattle and concern themselves with drought, pestilence, and potential enemies. They had to face the stress of knowing their decisions could lead to failure, and they became aware of their own mortality. While the biblical story is presented as a sudden transition, an evolutionary process requires slower incremental change.

The modern self represented an advance in the capacity of the individual to innovatively and creatively adapt to challenges. With this development, the myths and stories associated with the old cultures that ordered collective responses would have been seen through new eyes. From the perspective of the new individual, the ways of the past had brought survival without the stresses of having an individual self. For them there existed one known worldview with supernatural injunctions often ordering behaviour. The greater good, defined as good for the collectivity, would be assured through the codification of a set of beliefs in which the newly minted individualism implied by the existence of the modern self would be controlled.

An argument could be made that such a worldview, even when it contains supernatural entities, is not a religion but a storehouse of cultural knowledge, which Boyer and Barrett (2005) termed "a human-evolved intuitive ontology." For this argument to be sound the members of that culture would have to intuitively accept their knowledge as tentative—the contents of the storehouse of cultural knowledge would change as new knowledge is learned. If, on the other hand, elements of that storehouse are reified, as when a deity is said to have declared them to be sacred and beyond question, or when members of the cultural group are given a set of prescribed beliefs and practices to maintain their group membership, then we have a religion.

The evolution of a proto-religious worldview to formal religion may be accelerated by intercultural contact. The assumption of a universal consensus as evidence to support a particular worldview no longer works when large numbers of others do not share the same belief system. When overwhelmed in conquest, the old worldview may go the way of the Norse gods and cease to be a lived belief system, or it may mutate into a form that can better compete for souls. JohnB, a person with no North American aboriginal genetic heritage adopting Aboriginal Spirituality is evidence of this latter possibility. The newly embraced belief system was more attractive to the memes that made up JohnB's evolved self than the religion in which he was raised; however, it was sufficiently similar that he was able to declare it to be like what he understood was the original Christianity.

Once a proto-religious worldview encounters a more dominant religion or worldview, it must change. Paiute shaman Wovoka, who founded the Ghost Dance movement of nineteenth-century, illustrated the mechanics of such change. Wovoka taught that by living piously and by regularly performing a variation of a traditional round dance called the "ghost dance" the buffalo would return to the plains, the "white" settlers would be swallowed up, and the way of life of people to North America would be restored. Wovoka was orphaned and raised by devout Christians, and the Ghost Dance Movement parallels the messiah archetype he would have learned as a child. Wovoka performed magic at his gatherings, including levitation and bullet stopping. As a result of these performances, two of his Lakota Sioux disciples were convinced that with faith and the performance of prescribed rituals, ghost shirts would stop the bullets of the white men. The massacre at Wounded Knee in 1890 ended that notion.

As with genetics, memetic random mutations that are deleterious to the survival of the organism will normally not be copied.[1] In the example we have been discussing, the "organism" is a complex of memes identified as religious or proto-religious related to a traditional aboriginal culture. Although the Ghost Dance mutation failed, other changes have led to the survival of this developing memeplex. Trevor believed that he must learn and practise certain teachings identified with Aboriginal Spirituality. The application of a specific worldview, religiously held, to an identifiable people was successfully pioneered by the Jews approximately three millennia ago. If a worldview or religion is identified with a specific racial or ethnic group, then members of that group will be predisposed to adopt the requisite belief system.

Another mutation that assists systems of religious belief to survive is faith. The reason many followers of proto-religious formulations do not view their beliefs as religious is that their beliefs are not based on faith. They follow the practices of their ancestors based on evidence available to them at the time. Once other belief systems are available, what counts as evidence may change, and beliefs may change; however, the added element of faith in a particular worldview protects the accompanying system of belief from evidentiary examination. One way of instilling faith is to convince adherents that a creator-god has made a particular religious belief system sacred and transcendent beyond rational examination. Madelyn, for example, expressed a faith that everything will work out, or if not, it is all part of some master plan.

Although the faith mutation serves to protect the belief constellation's presence within a culture, it comes at a price. First, not everything within the primal culture can be effectively labelled sacred and that which falls outside is exposed to increasing pressures for change by a dominant culture. Second, the designation of sacredness implies constancy—that which is sacred must always have been so. Thus, while the proto-religious society is open to change the religious society resists change. For example, it was not until 1992 that the Roman Catholic Church admitted it was wrong in its seventeenth-century inquisition of Galileo for the heresy of promoting a heliocentric view of the solar system.

There are parallels between emergent religion and emergent selves. Both are assemblages of mutually supporting elements of culture. These elements or memes create identifiable structures within cultures, with albeit diffuse and permeable boundaries. A sense of uniqueness may be attributed to both. Both have a sense of constancy making them resistant to change. Changes that are compatible with existent memes or may be framed as non-changes are more easily adopted or incorporated into the overall structure and change. Changes to the self may be seen as reflecting a "true self" not initially recognized, while changes to religion may be interpreted as returning to earlier sacred truth that had been lost or distorted over time.

While complexes of interlocking self-memes are normally attached to one physical body, religions attempt to define a collectivity. As we have seen, our mapped subjects drew on emotions to authenticate and animate self-structures that were largely, but not totally, memetic, with the resultant conclusion that the self cannot be viewed solely as a cognitive structure. Emotional valence grounds the self to the individual entity, and successful religions have evolved ways to tap into the very same emotional centres. For example, a theme within Judaism is that those who keep to the Mosaic laws are happy, while a failure to do so creates an unhappiness associated with a lack of purpose or meaning. One of Judaism's descendants, Islam, equates happiness with obedience; indeed, the word "Islam" may be translated as "submission to Allah." A deeper happiness in Hinduism may be obtained through the practice of dharma (virtue). Buddhism promises a reduction of the obverse of happiness, suffering.

I displayed graphically how memes from the environment are added to the self in a process of self-construction. Memes that are already compatible with those present are more easily added, leading to a gradual evolution. Without precise boundaries, an amorphous self may expand into the reaches of surrounding culture some distance from the core of one's entity. Thus, if a meme identified with a particular religion becomes incorporated into one's self, then other memes associated with that religion, held in place by memetic attraction, will likely come to also occupy a place. An attack on that religion at any of its memetic points will then feel like an attack on that person's self. Religions that are felt to be essential to the self-definition of adherents have a competitive advantage over those that merely offer philosophical or moral grounding.

Religions that colonize minds for their own propagation have been compared to parasitic viruses that commandeer the resources of a cell (Dawkins, 2006; Dennett, 1996; Ray, 2009), but our memetic selves afford a level of consciousness that allows transcendence from purely biological imperatives, without which we would be driven solely by them. To the extent that religions or other complexes of memes within culture attempt to commandeer minds, the viral analogy holds.[2] On the other hand, religion has also served the adaptive function of collectivizing societies, allowing civilizations to emerge. Another adaptation proffered by various religions involves the regulation and control of immature adults.

Traditional societies failed to recognize an extension of childhood into what is now known as adolescence. While traditional societies typically began adulthood soon after puberty, the invention of adolescence allowed Western societies to extend the period of childhood dependency, facilitating the increased educational requirements of a modern industrial society. But the invention of adolescence is more than an artificial designation designed to conform to the needs of modern capitalism; it is a distinct developmental period when the brain is shedding neurons and reorganizing itself at a greater rate than at any time since infancy (Strauch, 2005). Hormonal balances swing widely, making mood and behaviour unpredictable. The frontal lobes responsible for predicting consequences, moral judgment, and other higher mental functions are not fully developed and are not fully connected with the structures of the limbic system, making impulse control difficult. Why would traditional societies universally ignore this developmental period?

The imperative to compress childhood and increase offspring has collective survival value in societies with high infant mortality and short life expectancy. On the other hand, the benefits of children or immature adults having children would be eroded if the behaviour of those young parents were unpredictable and if they exhibited poor anticipation with lapses in moral judgment. One way of resolving this problem would be to have the children of these children raised by their grandparents. A religious way of resolving this dilemma is to have post-puberty initiates experience mystical or sacred initiation rites coupled with strict role definitions that included an elevated status for elders, shaman and priests in providing practical and moral guidance. This effectively divides adults into decision makers with the followers mimicking adolescent dependency in the moral sphere.

Christianity made self-renunciation a condition of salvation, but it was not the total self that was being renounced. It was presumed that aspects of individuality such as volition and uniqueness could be renounced but that consciousness would continue into eternity. In his classic work on why people in pre-World War II Germany embraced fascism, social psychologist Eric Fromm (1969) noted that a central theme in Protestant Christianity is the individual's wickedness and powerlessness leading to a desire to subordinate one's self to an external higher power. He lamented, "The person who gives up his individual self and becomes an automaton, identical with millions of other automatons around him, need not feel alone and anxious any more. But the price he pays, however, is high; it is the loss of his self" (p. 209). The Nazi's message that the individual should accept personal insignificance while feeling pride in participating in the strength and glory of the higher power was in keeping with pre-existent religious traditions. The swearing-in ceremony for Hitler's government advised Germans, "It is the heart which is conscious of God, not the reason. Do not seek Adolph Hitler with your brains. All of you will find him with the strength of your hearts" (E. Hoffer, 1966/1951, p. 77). Daniel Goldhagan (1996) catalogued a historical connection between both anti-Semitism and the Nazi renunciation of the self within Christian teachings. It is no coincidence that many Protestants and Roman Catholics continued to support the Nazi agenda up until Hitler's eventual defeat.

Traditional Christian self-renunciation is related to the Muslim notion of submission to Allah. Suicide bombers who willingly give up their lives are biologically guided missiles who have already given up their selves to their higher power. As selfless or ego-less persons, their will is no longer their own, but their submission to their god is made possible through the intercession of human intermediaries who are presumed to have correctly interpreted divine will. Although the original Buddha, Siddhattha Gotama, was an atheist (Hutcheon, 2001; Kwee, 2012), Buddhism's "no-self" doctrine can lead to personal subjugation similar to that found in the theistic Western traditions. Tibetan Buddhist Sogyal Rinpoche (1993) advised initiates to see a master not as a human being but as the Buddha himself with the following account:

> Patral Rinpoche had been doing advanced practice of yoga and visualization, and had become stuck; none of the mandalas of the deities would appear clearly in his mind. One day he came upon Do Khyentse, who had made a fire out in the open and was sitting in front of it drinking tea. In Tibet when you see a master for whom you have deep devotion, traditionally you begin to prostrate your body on the ground as a mark of respect.
>
> As Patral Rinpoche started prostrating from a distance, Do Khyentse spotted him and growled menacingly, "Hey, you old dog! If you are brave, then come over here!" Do Khyentse was a very impressive master. He was like a samurai, with his long hair, his rakish clothes, and his passion for riding beautiful horses. As Patral Rinpoche continued doing prostrations and beginning to approach closer, Do Khyentse, cursing him all the time, started to hurl pebbles at him, and gradually larger rocks and stones, when he finally came within reach, Do Khyente started punching him and knocked him out altogether.
>
> When Patral Rinpoche came to, he was in an entirely different state of consciousness. The mandalas he had been trying hard to visualize spontaneously manifested in front of him. (p. 157)

If we make the decision to submit to the will of another, have we truly submitted? In our sample, Maomao concluded that "free will" was too much work and she preferred the life of a "robot awaiting the command"; however, when others issued commands she did not like she reserved for herself the ability to feel resentment. Similarly, Patral Rinpoche had previously made a decision to submit to the will of his master but as long as he maintained a self from which the "I" could observe, his submission was not absolute. This last vestige of independent will had to be removed to make the renunciation of his self total.

In what amounted to a social experiment of memetic self re-engineering during the nineteenth and twentieth centuries, the four leading Christian denominations in Canada attempted to forcibly assimilate young aboriginal children in institutions called Indian residential schools while minimizing parental contact (Barman, Hebra, & McCaskill, 1986; Woods, 2012). Children were seized by government agents when parents failed to voluntarily place their children in these schools. The students were made to wear uniforms, the hair of males was cut short, and expressions of individuality, such as speaking one's native language, were severely punished. Parental contact was minimized. Following World War II, children were allowed to visit their parents during the major religious holiday of Christmas, but in my work, I have found several residential school survivors who had been falsely told their parents were dead, thus removing that possibility. One woman, on unexpectedly encountering her very much alive mother at age seventeen, discovered they could not communicate because they spoke different languages! Effectively, the churches were attempting to re-engineer the selves of aboriginal children to assimilate them into a European collectivity; but as I reported in a previous study, "They did not have the knowledge to take into account the aboriginal memes already within the selves of the children, nor did they understand how their new Eurocentric memes would interact with those already in place. Further, they offered a caricature of a Euro-Canadian self from which these children could model" (Robertson, 2006, p. 14).

The resultant selves of numerous students who attended these schools displayed a set of symptoms similar to Post Traumatic Stress Disorder without the necessity of a triggering traumatizing incident. The symptoms included distressing dreams, intense distress at exposure to stimuli that symbolized residential schools, lack of spousal or familial attachment, a persistent tendency to abuse alcohol or other drugs, and anxiety or uncontrolled outbursts of anger. These symptoms were passed on to subsequent generations by the very mechanisms by which culture is transmitted. The attempted assimilation was at least partially successful. A majority of indigenous people in Canada continue to adhere to Christianity despite demanding, and receiving compensation for, having attended these residential schools.

Religious transcendence often involves self-renunciation. The evolved self made our ancestors into individuals. While this allowed a capacity for rational objective thought, it came at a cost. Individuality implies separateness from others and from nature. Worse, we became aware of our own mortality, and we became responsible for our own mistakes. Religions promise to relieve us of the terrible responsibility of individuality by submerging ourselves into the will of the collectivity from whence we originally emerged. This is presented as transcending limitations in human thought and reason. Once a complex of memes has evolved to represent beliefs religiously held, that complex necessarily represents that portion of the culture held to be sacred. Codification of selected cultural practices judged sacred preserves those practices from possible extinction. As we saw in chapter 3, it can also serve to preserve a sense of separateness between groups that would otherwise be susceptible to forces of integration and voluntary assimilation.

The ability of secular ideologies to repress individual will and volition may be limited. Nick was still a child when the Soviet Union collapsed, but he presented with aggressive individualism. If Communism had a lasting impact on the collectivist mentality of the population, one would not expect many such "Nicks" in Russian culture. Maomao was raised entirely in a Communist system, and she displayed a preference for a collectivist orientation. It is important to note that China had a collectivist culture before the triumph of Communism, and in Maomao's eyes, the state has less authority in espousing the collectivist values she embraced than the Christianity to which she converted. It is a reasonable inference that attempts to repress the self's individuality are more effective when made with appeals to a supernatural authority.

In chapter 3, we reviewed a study of verbal exchanges involving Chinese and Canadian students that showed the Chinese making more collectivist verbalizations when working with other Chinese as compared to Chinese-Canadian dyads, but that the Chinese students had no difficulty increasing their individualist responses when paired with a Canadian (Shi, et al., 2013). As demonstrated by these responses and the example of Maomao's self, while Chinese culture may value collectivism, the individualist aspects of self may still be invoked as needed. The difference is not in self-structure, but in judging when it is appropriate to use an individualist or collectivist response. There is a tension in all cultures between the collectivist need to produce a viable and cooperative society and the need to allow for creative and individual responses from the individuals in that society.

While the self, soul, and mind were once viewed as synonyms, Western religions came to identify the self with that which they were attempting to repress or control: individual will and volition. The weakening of religion during the Enlightenment in eighteenth-century Europe and America led to greater expression of inherent individualism. This left the soul as an undefined consciousness and the self as a subject of scientific investigation. Hindus have postulated a selved soul that is subject to reincarnation. Buddhists, on the other hand, have taken the position that the soul that is subject to reincarnation is nonconscious since consciousness cannot be split from the self. While this is a logical proposition, there is no point of postulating a soul without consciousness. A soul that is unaware has the same effect as no soul. A soul that is conscious would be self-aware, but since the only evidence for an entity such as the soul is the very same self which we have mapped, we have to conclude that the ancients were correct: the self and the soul are the same thing. The illusion, enforced by feeling, is that the resultant "I" has a body. In fact, I am my body plus those memes that contribute to my self-awareness. In becoming self-aware we transcend the matter of which we are composed.

We are potentially controlled by two sets of replicators: our genes and our memes. Religion represents a memetic way of enforcing collective conformity. Nonetheless, Dawkins (1976) optimistically stated, "We, alone on earth, can rebel against the tyranny of the self-ish replicators" (p. 215). All of the subjects who were mapped expressed awareness of the objective verses the subjective, and such awareness is the ultimate evolutionary payoff of selfhood. With this awareness we are able to deconstruct situations, posit possible alternatives, and predict consequences for each alternative. We can then test our predictions with the option of choosing alternative actions. The evolution of the modern self some three millennia past ushered in the beginning of scientific endeavour. But scientific thinking does not come easily even for those trained in the much more recent scientific method. Our behaviour (including the behaviour of scientists) most of the time conforms to the dictates of our genetic and memetic heritages. Usually those dictates serve us well. Our genetic inheritance evolved over hundreds of thousands of years and includes personality traits that allowed us to survive and thrive as social animals. Our memetic inheritance that evolved over considerably less time contains our accumulated collective cultural wisdom. While such cultural change could have only come through an algorithmic mutative process, we are left with the previously unimagined option of employing analytical thought and methodology to better objectively understand specific situations or problems. It does not feel like transcendence; it feels like hard work. We did not evolve genetically to do this kind of work, and although the practice of science is transmitted through culture, its use goes beyond the practice of memetic imitation. Once we have learned something new through a scientific process, broadly defined, we can with intention change the culture that created us.

Physical evolution did not have time to select for feelings of transcendence in scientific endeavour. It did have time to select for group identification, which was interpreted by our sample as believing "in something bigger than ourselves." That which is bigger has been variously represented as a tribe, a religion, a culture, a race, or mankind. With Fredelle, it was represented by the universe, understood as an organic but nonsentient being. In all cases, the self was felt to be interconnected with the larger encompassing entity. This feeling of transcendence associated with interconnectedness to a larger whole could be the basis of a secular spirituality common to the religious and nonreligious alike.

Affirming and Strengthening Our Understanding of Self

Nirvana's "Heart Shaped Box" likely inspired Suzie's meme of similar name. Similarly, Bob Seeger's "Against the Wind" was recorded about a decade before Trevor received this "Indian name." The concepts used in both songs were present in culture before the recordings were made. Trevor and Pangloss independently quoted SunTzu, indicating the presence of Asian memes in North American culture. Modern media have increased exposure to cultural memes with a corresponding increase in the possibilities available for self-definition.

Cognitive psychology places consciousness in a pre-eminent position based on what we can consciously know and state. Other approaches have suggested limitations to consciousness;

however, if we cannot know the parameters of that which is not understood then we cannot assess the extent of those limitations. While we cannot say hidden motivations or drives of which we are unaware constitute part of our self-definition, unconscious processes may be determinants of behaviour, but interpretations of such behaviour may be problematic. We intuitively recognize, however, that our conscious understandings of ourselves may be incomplete; therefore, the definition of the self, as developed in this study, is more than self-definition. The self is also constituted by emotions, motivations, and drives that may not be consciously understood.

Those participants (Pangloss and JohnB) who asked for feedback from the psychologist in extending their self-knowledge were expressing a desire to make the unconscious conscious. The process of self-exploration begins in infancy, when we begin to learn to define ourselves from the interactions we have with caregivers and others. We accept these initial interactions as proof of who we are, and we continue to exhibit a disquieting tendency to accept that which we first hear or understand on any given subject and discount subsequent evidence that conflicts with initially received information. As adolescents we try on new roles that confirm or disconfirm self-assumptions, building on the partial or proto-selves learned in childhood. While that which is already compatible with the existent self tends to be more readily accepted, as adults we evaluate the feedback we receive from others. We may accept suggestions from those with recognized authority, and apparently psychologists are an acceptable feedback source for some. Alternatively, we may engage in the hard work of defining, analyzing, and testing new propositions, which, if successfully incorporated, necessitate the rewriting of our self-narratives.

We may gain new understandings for our selves by recognizing and analyzing emotion-driven behaviours. For example, Fredelle was already an adult male before she decided on the basis of her emotions and accompanying behaviours and that she was not gay but transsexual. Our emotions are a link to primordial precognitive processes independent from memes, and those emotions may be used to infer aspects of the self of which the individual is not yet aware. We are not necessarily bound by our genes or our memes. There is no "true self" to which we must conform. That is our transcendence.

While the self is not purely a cognitive structure, that which is understood as known represents a theory of who we are that stands in constant revision as new information is consciously processed. The modern self is a relatively recent evolutionary adaptation allowing for conscious control over certain otherwise unconscious processes. Thus, we can choose to be monogamous when our procreative instincts may turn us in a different direction. We can even choose a life of celibacy and, with determination, live it. We can engage in altruism for strangers halfway around the globe. We can sacrifice ourselves for what we perceive to be the greater good. While we may have simply replaced genetic determinants of behaviour with memetic ones, the presence of a conscious self gives us the not often realized potential for independent thought and behaviour idealized as "free will." This potential flows from notions of volition and self-empowerment coupled with the idea of an objective reality outside of ourselves. As we have seen, all of our participants evidenced such memes, supporting a suggestion of universality.

Elements of self-constancy and uniqueness were inferred from the self-narratives examined and confirmed through questioning. These two aspects of the Jamesian subjective self may flow from the logic of having one. For example, JohnB worried he did not exist when reflecting on occasions in which he appeared to be a different person in different contexts. A self-definition must feel unique and constant in some ways to feel real.

The models of James (1890, 1892/1999) and Adler (1927/1957, 1967) examined in chapter 2 are not mutually exclusive. James's interest was in developing a theoretical model to encompass both objective and subjective aspects of the self while Adler's focus was on therapy. Adler postulated a self-actualizing "striving for perfection" drive that may, nonetheless, be thwarted by discouragement. Such a drive would be compatible with James's volition, as could Adler's "social interest," although the latter also implies embeddedness in community. James's quality of uniqueness or individuation has no direct counterpart in the Adlerian formulation, but Adler may have implied as much in discussing the totality of the individuum. Similarly, the Adlerian concepts of work (production) and love (intimacy) have no direct counterparts in the Jamesian formulation but could be interpretively included in the active, social, and psychological aspects of the objective self. Thus, the Jamesian and Adlerian models of the self could be viewed as different perspectives of an evolving social sciences model that may be extended to include reflectivity. The use of a memetic approach allows us to visualize how such a self is extended into family and community.

Although the self has long been considered a cultural construct, the technology of visualizing the self as units of culture was not well developed. The concept of the meme allows us to visualize the self as units of individualized culture within a framework of environmental and genetic forces. Self-maps prepared using this method displayed internal structure and relationships with memetic complexes found within surrounding familial, community, national, and religious cultures. Thus, a dynamic may be developed without firm boundaries between the inner and the outer while concomitantly maintaining a sense of stability. This memetic perspective is interactionalist, compatible with both those who emphasize the impact of the external environment in constituting the self (Lewin, 1931; Lock, 1981/1990; Mead, 1934) and those would extend the self into the social environment (Hermans, 2003; Shotter, 1997). With the Jamesian/Adlerian model of the self supplemented by a memetic perspective, we may examine how particular aspects of that social environment interact with aspects of the self.

Although Dawkins was not the first to give a name to elemental units of culture, he was the first to suggest these units exert attractive and repellent forces, and such forces would allow for stability sufficient to generate feelings of continuity and uniqueness without which there could be no feeling of self. This research demonstrated how the four dimensions assigned to memes (referent, connotative, affective, and behavioural) could serve to exert attractive force on other memes. For example, the memes for "wife," "daughter," and "cleaner" in Tina's self-map involved certain behaviours that were idiosyncratically linked providing support for each other's structural presence in Tina's self. The affect associated for both "wife" and "mother" was love, with "love" identified as a unifying theme. The two memes were thus united thematically. Both "intelligent" and "learner" memes in Nick's self-map included the connotation of empowerment; hence the two were linked to an empowerment theme in his self-map. Similarly, the referent meaning associated with both "daughter" and "only child" in Maomao's self-map involved being a child, thus providing a cognitive mechanism linking the two. Such attractive force neither resides completely within the individual nor externally in the "cultural soup" but is a felt experience resulting from the interaction of the internal and external. The memetic perspective allows for a rationale in linking units of culture within the self that was not available to earlier attempts at self-mapping.

Dawkins (1976) also said memes exhibit qualities of repulsion. Repulsion between memes was illustrated in this research by using lines of tension. As an example, Brent's self-map is drawn with a tension line between memes for "flexible" and "rigid," illustrating a conflict between these two cultural units. Given the tendency toward a stable self, we would expect the self would normally have few such lines of tension. Memes not compatible with an existing self would be expelled, ceasing to be part of the person's self-definition. Thus, Brent's self resisted the notion he was a learner for much of his adult life, and a developmental transition was required to change that understanding. Judy, Magdelynn, and Maomao made references to an authentic self, and Magdelynn said she experienced less dissonance when she succeeded in becoming the same person across contexts. Thus, both self stability and the ability to change over time is explained using a memetic perspective.

We found that change in the individual's self and worldview are related to a menu of possibilities provided by culture. Arthur (2003) found that international students may not be consciously aware of such changes while living in Canada even though the changes may become problematic upon their return to their culture of origin. The memetic perspective, presenting memes as being available in a surrounding "cultural soup" integrating with existent memes within a self compatible with one's worldview, provides explanatory power for this process of observed change. Mapping the self may also offer insights for predicting which changes would likely be assimilated from an adoptive culture and which memes would be repelled.

Memes as defined in this research have individualized as opposed to essentialist meanings. For example, the selves of four participants included a meme labelled "proud" in their maps. The narratives of all four of these participants included reference to accomplishments; however, their definitions of the proud meme varied with interpretation and experience. For Trevor, Pangloss, and Magdelynn, "proud" was either connected to "self-esteem" or it generated feelings of self-worth. In Chantelle, it connoted arrogance and was something to be tempered with humility. In Trevor, "proud" connoted potentialities for further accomplishment, while in Magdelynn it connoted being a good person in some ways. For her, "proud" included being "the most gimped" and being able to transcend her disability with tenacity. For Pangloss, being proud was connected to internal characteristics such as being open-minded and curious. It is possible no two memes with the same label were exactly the same for any of the participants.

If the content of most memes are uniquely tailored to the individual in some ways, then few, if any, memes will be copied exactly from one individual to the next. Existing memes may be modified during discourse either through a process of negotiation or through repeated exposure to alternate definitions presented in the form of differing perspectives. Do memes have sufficient copying fidelity to be considered replicators? Gabora (2004) compared them to primitive replicators like polymers whose self-assembly arises, not through coded instructions, but through chance molecular interactions that preserve a certain structure. Thus, the cultural unit of replication is not the meme but the associative pathway of ideas that create structured networks of memes. A similar structure of the self presented across a diverse sample of participants in this research, supporting Gabora's notion that it is the structure that is replicated. On the other hand, memes do not have the structural integrity of atoms, and they do not physically move from one location to another, with the resultant implication that some notion of replication is necessary to account for their dissemination. No analogy with the physical world can be exact, and we are creating new language to understand what happens in this nonmaterial universe.

It is not sufficient to suggest "the agent is constituted by language" (C. Charles, 1989a, p. 509). Unless we can understand from whence we have agency, then our models of self, including any culturally inclusive models of self, are incomplete. Using the technology of memetics, we have graphically illustrated how culturally mediated notions of animation and empowerment could come to inhabit the selves of individuals and how resultant notions of self-agency are then incorporated into the worldviews of those individuals.

The use of the concept of the meme also allowed us to represent a large amount of individualized data in nonlinear fashion. Numerous alternative linear narratives may flow from these selves while maintaining the integrity of the foundational structure. The selves so pictured exhibited a capacity for representing both stability and change. The memetically mapped selves in this research were holistic unitary structures that incorporated both objective and subjective dimensions. They were not pictured as discrete entities but were understood as extending into the cultures that surround them.

An implication of this research is that the self cannot be adequately represented by memes alone. Each participant self included non-memetic structures such as an emotive base and inferred Jamesian subjective themes. The self typically presents with the following structural elements: constancy, distinctness, volition, productivity/ activity, intimacy, social interest, psychological characteristics, remembering, thinking/reflecting, emotion, and community.

Every person in this study had a body with one self attached to that body. While acknowledging the possibility that people with multiple personality disorder may have multiple selves, the "one self to one body" rule is the norm. In fact, participants felt uncomfortable with the notion they may be different people in different contexts, and those who presented with this feeling sought a unity. Although the constructed self often referenced physical characteristics, it was defined as separate from the body it seemed to inhabit. As Nick noted, we speak of "my arms" and "my hands" as though they are objects owned by something or somebody. The original Buddhist notion of the self as an illusion fails to explain what or who is consciously making this assessment. Something else has indeed taken over our bodies and that something is no illusion: it is us. It feels as though we are nonmaterial and that feeling is partially accurate. We, that is, who we are now, evolved from units of culture which is, underlying any artefacts, nonmaterial concepts, ideas, memes. Through our "mind's eye" our physical body then appears to be like a possession, an artefact, of this evolved self, and even atheists act out this incipient dualism in their daily lives.

The self may be viewed as like a computer software program that boosts the power of the computer many fold without the necessity of increasing the size of the hardware. In this case the hardware is our physical brains, but it is through the software we have achieved consciousness. The very old notion that we might transfer our consciousness to new bodies is still in the realm of science fiction; indeed, such notions are themselves predicated on a mind-body dualism. If, however, the evolved self and the evolved body are two sides of one coin, then it is the dualism that is the illusion.

We are left with a conscious self that is dependent on the body to which it is tied for its existence. This conscious self then attempts to assert primacy over the body it calls its own; however, in some important respects it is not needed. For example, the body automatically reacts to perceived threats, before the conscious mind is even aware of those threats. So, as this conscious self peers out of eyes that do not always do its bidding, it realizes it is trapped. Since it cannot be loaded into a new body, it too will die. So it tries to make copies of itself.

We teach our children to have selves, and we like it when they display values, beliefs, and traits similar to our own. When our deeply held beliefs are attacked, we feel attacked because those beliefs have become part of who we are, and it becomes important to us that we replicate those aspects of our selves in the general culture. We write autobiographies to ensure our selves are properly understood and live on. No matter how successful we are in these efforts, the self that remains is still trapped. In our denial we turn to mental pyramids called religions, and we insist others respect these belief systems because their failure to do so increases the doubt and pain within our mortal souls.

Notes

1   An exception to this would occur where the deaths of the individuals in, for example, a suicide cult, serve to propagate the malevolent memes to other minds. For a full discussion of this phenomena as a "mind virus," see Roberson (2017b). This exception provides an example of how memetic and genetic replication differ.

2   Ray (2009) has argued that religions evolved to allow rational thought in most domains but disable it when referencing one's own religion. He uses the analogy of the rabies virus that "takes over the brain of the raccoon and reprograms it to bite other animals – even at the cost of its own life" (p. 28).

CHAPTER 7

Implications of Self-Mapping for Psychological Practice

The self, which is central to the practice of counselling and psychotherapy, was found in both collectivist and individualist cultures. The concept of the meme was used to map this self autobiographically, but initial representations were incomplete. The usefulness of these self-maps was enhanced with the inclusion of psychological characteristics that exist independently of conscious cognition but nonetheless shape behaviour. In the last chapter, the results of qualitative research were used to affirm and extend this understanding of the self. This final chapter explores the application of these findings to psychotherapy.

In keeping with the theory that the self is a linguistic construction, Harre (1998) provocatively said that certain pathologies could be treated by the teaching of locally valid grammars. While it is too early to consider replacing psychologists with English teachers, grammatical considerations are already used in mainline therapies (Ellis & Harper, 1997; Polkinghorn, 1995; Strong & Sutherland, 2006). Memetic self-maps serve as outlines of overarching grammatically based metanarratives. Psychotherapy can address missing elements in self-construction, and that will include teaching a locally valid incorporative grammar. From this we can surmise that grade-school teachers have a role in their student's self-construction.

Adlerians sometimes make a useful distinction between therapy and counselling: therapy happens when the objective is to change or develop the client's self; counselling assumes an intact self and proceeds with problem solving, communication skill development, and perspective taking. In practice, this distinction is blurred as all counselling reinforces an existent self or promotes self-change. In exploring potential applications of memetic self-mapping, I use the term "therapist" or "psychotherapist" to reference those professionals specifically engaged in a planned process of developmental self-change.

This chapter begins with a re-examination of the case study discussed in chapter 1. I then turn our attention to the theory of self as informed by the participants in chapter 5, with particular attention to issues of resonance, personal transition, self-change, and empowerment. The mapping procedure developed is then examined for application to stable-self, neurological, behavioural, constructivist, constructionist, and cross-cultural perspectives. It is suggested that memetic self-mapping serves to unite these diverse perspectives into a comprehensive whole. The chapter concludes with an understanding of the self as a unifying paradigm in applied psychology.

Extending the Example of the Suicidal Youth

After presenting the case of "Suzie" in chapter 1 to a doctoral graduate class, a cognitive behavioural therapist argued that I had simply been applying cognitive behavioural therapy (CBT) effectively. Suzie had been prompted to challenge some ineffective and obsessive cognitions using visual stimulation provided by a cognitive map, and she reinforced a more useful set of self-cognitions using behavioural "homework" assignments. A narrative therapist in the same class disagreed, suggesting that the youth changed her personal story to see herself as an activating agent capable of dealing with unfortunate circumstances in her life. In this interpretation, the self-map provided Suzie with an outline to understand how she had structured her previous self-narrative so she might change it. My own training in Adlerian psychotherapy led me to picture the self as core to a more encompassing "worldview," which admittedly is similar to CBT's "cognitive schema" or narrative therapy's "constructed reality."

Cognitive-behavioural methods to combat depression often emphasize hedonic pleasure, as when clients are encouraged to list and engage in activities that were perceived to have been enjoyable in the past, but life satisfaction and meaning may be related to meaning making separate from positive and negative affect. The development of a new human rights meme to replace Suzie's "depressed person" core was an example of such meaning making. If happiness is related to believing in something bigger than one's self, then linking transcendent purpose to a client's volitional ability will reduce depression. But "depressed person" was part of Suzie's self, so concomitant with building eudemonic purpose we needed to remove or reduce support for the "depressed person" meme.

The qualitative difference between having "depressed person" as part of one's self and merely being depressed was explored in De Man and Gutierrez's (2002) study into the stability of self-esteem. After factoring out the effects of depression, they found that unstable self-esteem correlated with suicide ideation in those with low self-esteem, but not in those with high self-esteem scores, concluding, "For those with low self-esteem, stable self-esteem may serve a protective function, whereas instability of self-esteem may be a good predictor of suicidal thinking" (p. 237). This accords with findings that the initial lifting of depression in youth, especially through the use of antidepressant medication, may increase suicidal behaviour (Fritz, 2007). If instability of self results in increased suicide risk among those with low self-esteem and suicidality increases when depression begins to lift, then Suzie's initial resistance to therapy can be seen as a self-protective measure. All eleven research participants reviewed in chapter 5 reported the need to maintain a sense of stability or continuity in their selves, and this would also be expected in those with dysfunctional selves.

Visualizing her self in memetic map form coincided with Suzie's determination to override defensive or protective measures and engage in a process of self-change. The exercise in visualizing her self gave her a sense of the totality that she would remain a unique entity with continuity while in the midst of change. Thus, the self-map, as opposed to the core meme within the map that we were seeking to change, served to preserve a sense of her continuity.

Suzie was also able to visualize the scripts she followed in her depressive cycle. Since memes are connected by emotive, connotative, and behavioural forces represented by vectors, thoughts will tend to follow routes traced by those vectors. Awareness of these thought patterns allowed Suzie to change them.

Situating "depressed person" within a cluster of related memes assisted in the co-construction of a treatment plan aimed at shifting it to a more peripheral location in her self. Although she had previously defined herself as a writer, Suzie had written from her depression thus reinforcing this dysfunctional core meme; however, she began to write from her new "human rights" centre following a graphic review of her self. The cognitive and behavioural plan developed to shift Suzie's writer self from supporting her depression to supporting her "human rights" meme also served to strengthen two structural components common to healthy functioning selves: community and volition.

In similar evolutionary fashion, Suzie was encouraged to redirect her anger externally in ways that would promote social interest. The energy provided by her anger was now directed toward her outspokenness and associated social causes with the immediate benefit of channelling self-defeating impotent anger to a growing sense of self-empowerment. Other memes, peripheral to but supportive of her depression, were eliminated entirely. For example, she saw herself as ugly, but "ugly" was not supported by a large cluster of memes, so it was possible to have her perform "homework" assignments designed to challenge that belief.

In general, the mapping activity allowed us to see which memes had less support and would be more easily removed from Suzie's self. Once removed, those memes no longer lent support to more ingrained dysfunctional aspects, and some memes were shifted to support structurally functional aspects. In chapter 5, we witnessed Tina spontaneously decide to become less of a "pleaser" and practise assertiveness skills following a review of her self-map. Similarly, Magdelynn decided to become "less fractured" and more consistent across contexts. The practice of visually examining a multifaceted self-representation invites reflection about possible self changes one may wish to make in both therapeutic and nontherapeutic settings.

With "depressed person" receiving less support from surrounding memes in Suzie's self, it became possible to reframe it, not as a self-defining meme, but as one emotion among many. If we view the self as purely a cognitive structure, then at this point we eliminated depression from the suicidal youth's self. The participants to our research, however, insisted on including emotion in their self-definitions beyond the affective dimension attributed to memes. Tina's self had an intricate representation of emotion, picturing depression and anxiety as serving to block other emotions. After reviewing this representation, she was able to take steps to reduce her depression levels so as to feel a full range of emotions, which was her original objective in refusing medication.

The suggestion that a core meme is somehow held in place by attractive forces generated by related memes may smack of environmental or cultural determinism incompatible with the notion of self-determined narratives. It is possible, however, to look at any phenomenon from different levels of abstraction. Just as it is possible to visualize Homo sapiens as a way for genes to propagate (Dawkins, 1976), it is also possible to visualize minds as vehicles of memetic propagation. None of this is in contradiction with another level of abstraction that allows us to see enselved human beings as volitional meaning-makers capable of exercising control over the elements of culture they use in their self-definitions, and both perspectives are useful in counselling and therapy.

The suicidal client shifted from feelings of impotent anger and sadness to action based on her core beliefs and values through a process of memetic map co-construction. With a cognitive-behavioural perspective, the visualization assisted her to reflectively develop those values empowering her to challenge the cognitive schemata that kept her in a self-destructive cycle. Therapists in the Adlerian tradition would replace the phrase "cognitive schemata" with "worldview." With this interpretation, the map-making exercise would be understood as a way of empowering the client to make changes to her worldview by coupling a psycho-educational approach with an appeal to social interest.

From the tradition of narrative therapy, the youth changed her personal story to picture herself as an activating agent capable of dealing with unfortunate life circumstances. With this interpretation, the self-map was an outline helping the client to understand how she had structured her previous self-narrative, giving her the opportunity to change the plot. The self-maps of all participants in this research exhibited memes suggestive of agency or volition and, arguably, Suzie had been deficient in these areas. She had pictured herself as a victim without the power to change her life circumstances in a way that would bring happiness. Her sense of empowerment did not begin to occur until after the creation of a human rights core, but this could be explained as a new empowering theme for her life-plot.

To summarize, the construction of the memetic self-map in this case study allowed both the client and therapist to visualize the client's self, agree on goals for change, and plan incremental changes leading to the realization of those goals. Since this process of self-map construction and concomitant treatment may be understood from a spectrum of theoretical approaches, the technique holds the promise of broad potential application.

Chapter 2 examined evidence in support of the stable, neuro-logical, constructed, socially constructed, and behaviourist perspectives on the self. The various schools of psychology may be said to operate from one or more of these perspectives. In Chapter 5 I found the following structural elements to the self: constancy, dis-tinctness, volition, productivity/activity, intimacy, social interest, psychological characteristics, remembering, thinking/reflecting, emotion, and community. The various schools of therapy may be thought of as emphasizing combinations of these structural elements. Cognitive behavioural therapy has stressed volition, activity, and thinking. Adlerian psychotherapy adds intimacy and social interest to the mix. Other therapies focus more specifically on emotion or remembered narratives. All therapies recognize the uniqueness of the individual, but most do not elevate this element to their central focus. Cognitivists may not specifically focus on emotion, but may, with some justification, assume that as thinking changes so does emoting. Similarly, a behaviourist might assume behavioural changes will lead to changes in thought patterns and emotion. Since changes to one part of a self will likely lead to changes elsewhere, diverse therapies may be seen as complementary.

There are a variety of potential starting points when initiating self-change. Each of our research participants had created a theory of who they were based on what they counted as evidence. Each meme is a proposition linked to other such propositions in logical and emo-tive ways. With new information it should be possible to construct better self-theories. We may have an impulse to seek evidence that will either confirm or extend our self-definitions. Participants vari-ously sought self-defining feedback from family, friends, and even (in two cases) the researcher. This may be a characteristic of healthy indi-viduals. Other individuals may harbour negative self-images and resist feedback because they fear confirmation of what they already fear is true. Still others may accept their selves to be a priori with only confirmatory feedback accepted as legitimate. The challenge of thera-pists is to provide insecure and overly rigid individuals the objectively defensible rationale for exploring self-enhancing change in a safe and nurturing place.

While the self may not be a purely cognitive structure, it is possi-ble to bring more of that structure into conscious awareness. The client may be relatively unaware of personal psychological characteristics such as intelligence, kindness, shyness, or other dispositional qualities that may be true but unacknowledged. Interestingly, three research participants added a meme labelled "self-esteem" to their self-maps indicating some recognition of such psychological characteristics.

Emotions may be a window to the unconscious. For example, in working with aboriginal clients exhibiting Residential School Syndrome (Robertson, 2006), I observed examples of rage in contexts where even anger would be unwarranted. Triggers to such episodes often reveal a connection to past events that counted as evidence in support of currently held dysfunctional worldviews. Self-mapping may be an aid in making these unconsciously held worldviews conscious. Since self-maps, as constructed here, are based on what is or may be consciously known, they allow us to explore deeper and heretofore unrecognized interpretations of selfhood. In all of the examples, the act of self-mapping led to reflective thought on the part of the client or participant exploring those deeper interpretations. Once we have fully explored the client's self, we can determine if any of the elemental components are missing. Such missing components may then be addressed.

We witnessed this process at work in the example of the suicidal youth. The new core meme suggested for her self focused on the missing element of social interest. Missing from Fredelle's self was identification with community, but she was endeavouring to create an active transsexual community in her home city. These efforts lend support to the notion, endorsed here, that individuals do not function well, for long, in splendid isolation.

All participants in this study recalled how significant others helped to determine who they became. On becoming a certain person, that person was maintained from selected memories supported by expectations of consistency and continuity from a surrounding community. Thus, an alcoholic who successfully completes a residential treatment program may still be considered an alcoholic by his community with a resultant increase in the probability of relapse. Therapists attempt to combat memetic pressure resisting self-change by temporarily occupying the role of significant other and by mobilizing resources, both internal and external, in support of the change process. The successful therapist acknowledges and buttresses those aspects of the individual's self-definition that tend to support the desired change and assists the client in redefining his surrounding community to give increased prominence to those supportive of the change effort.

The self needs a sense of stability along with a supportive community to reinforce it. Therefore, while supporting change, therapists also need to acknowledge aspects of the client's self not in need of change that support a sense of constancy. The client needs to feel that in some important sense the person coming out of therapy is still the same person who entered it. Seeing oneself in map form placing the desired change in perspective assists this sense of constancy.

Psychologists need to be aware of community and familial forces impacting on the self of the client, but as we saw in the discussion of constructivism, selves need not be supported by the dominant societal norms. Constructed selves may be maintained within minority communities. In this study, Fredelle found a community of people organized around the Unitarian Church supportive of her transsexual self-definition. Judy found a community of like-minded humanists. Tina found that lesbians and men were more accepting of her bisexuality than "straight" women, so she eliminated straight women from her inner circle. The model used here shows the self interconnected with and extended into familial, community, and societal cultures. Using this model, counsellors and clients may identify communities that reinforce beneficial memes within the structure of the self while avoiding identification with those detrimental to those memes. Interaction between the individual and the community is pictured as bidirectional. The selves of individuals extend into the communities of which they are apart, becoming part of the culture of those communities.

New memes can be constructed therapeutically supporting self-structures that include empowerment, uniqueness, constancy, productivity, intimacy, social interest, emotional competence, family, and community with recognition of attending psychological characteristics. Successful change requires support from memes already existent within the self, and such change may be viewed as part of an evolutionary process. For example, readers will recall I identified a meme labelled "aboriginal activist" before the participant Trevor consciously defined himself in this way. That meme, acting in concert with other memes already existent, produced yet another new meme, "artist," between interviews. This example suggests an evolutionary process of self-change is not unusual and may be used in generating developmental transitions.

Resonance, Transition, and Self-Change

To realize the benefits of seeing their selves mapped, clients need to identify personal qualities of continuity and uniqueness at a feeling level. I did not anticipate this would occur with drafts prepared after just one session; however, a majority of the research participants (7) echoed Trevor's initial comment, "This is an awesome picture … damn good in fact." Two participants said their initial self-maps did not resonate with who they felt themselves to be, and the remaining two did not indicate resonance or non-resonance. After refinements added during the second interview, ten of our eleven subjects reported experiencing such resonance.

The amended self-maps were reviewed again at a third interview, at which time six participants said the maps required no further revision. JohnB said his map "captures everything." Chantelle declared, "It's how I would describe myself, it's perfect." Two participants said their self-maps resonated with personal experience, but they proposed changes to the existing structure involving a shifting of meme placement. Magdelyn said a new interpretive code for transcendence (added after the second interview) "hit the nail on the head," but she said she had become more congruent with her "real self," so her self-map was amended to show fewer links to her relativistic cluster. Fredelle said that a wig is not the same thing as a hairpiece; therefore the meme labelled "wig wearer" was changed to "hairpiece wearer." Brent added a meme for "frugal" to his self-map, which was linked with both "Catholic" and "environmentalist" memes. Nick said he had gained the insight from his self-map to add a meme for "independent." These "tweaks" largely represented changes to the self between sessions inspired by self-reflection. The fact that these participants were able to see themselves in artfully prepared representational outlines speaks to a need to engage in self-reflective and self-affirming behaviour.

One participant failed to report resonance with his self-map. Pangloss questioned the accuracy of some information used following the second interview, advising, "I was determined to convince you that there were negatives in my personality, so I presented an inaccurate picture." During the third interview he admitted, "I can exaggerate things to the point of dishonesty." While our remembered narratives will almost always vary from actual events, when those remembrances are experienced as exaggerations, they ring hollow.

Although Pangloss was invited to correct his self-map during our third interview, he declined to do so, stating he pays attention to himself only to the extent of its utility, but that he came out of the process of this research as he thought he would: "complicated, contradictory, and confusing." Analysis of his emotional states puts structure on that confusion.

By the third interview Pangloss decided he wanted the researcher to like him, but with this he expressed a new dilemma. Anything he said to "correct" previous impressions would be reflective of this new emotion with a resultant "feel" of inauthenticity. While admitting he had "faked bad" during the second interview, even the information given in his initial interview was tainted emotionally. Aspects of his self-description as an avenging warrior may have reflected his ideal self as opposed to his real self, but his sexuality, his predilection to action, and his cognitive intellectualizing style were consistent across interviews. His demand for new insights into his self from the researcher was also consistently presented and may have reflected identity confusion resulting from not knowing which "Pangloss" he more closely resembled. Had he been an actual client, the material shared could have been the basis for more self-exploration and psychological assessment.

After stating that her initial self-map was a "good representation," Tina discussed her bisexuality and the complications this brought into her marriage. She admitted that she had not been comfortable discussing this aspect of her self during our initial meeting because she was not sure the researcher would accept or understand it. Her initial presentation was influenced by previous experiences of ridicule.

People may present a false self for fear of retribution. For example, clients whose participation in counselling is a condition for avoiding unwanted consequences with respect to employment or the justice system have an incentive to keep their "real" self hidden. The cost of such a strategy, in addition to the obvious stress of maintaining a deception, is to preclude self-growth. A second possibility is that people present false selves because, like prototypical adolescents, they have not yet developed a coherent self-identity. The activity of playing various roles and selves dependent on situation and inclination could become a lifelong habit precluding reflective self-examination. The cost of such a failure to ground oneself is inconsistency with attendant difficulty in establishing and maintaining long-term relationships. A third possible reason for presenting a false self may involve low self-esteem. If an individual suspects self-inadequacy, he may fear possible confirmation of that inadequacy. The cost of such a strategy is a felt (but undefined) fragile self with accompanying displays of anger whenever that fragile self is threatened. It is the role of the therapist to identify the reason for false self displays and allay the underlying emotional factors contributing to an unwillingness to engage in self-examination.

Three participants identified clusters of memes that were invoked in context-specific presentations. JohnB traced the developmental evolution of such "mini-selves" (numbered consecutively in figure 5.7) beginning with a "Challenger of Authority" theme, followed by a Worker/Social self, and concluding with a self based on empathy and spirituality. These mini-selves were united by an empowered "core" reminiscent of the Jamesian subjective self.

Similarly, Fredelle said her initial map accurately reflected tension between two mini-selves: the masculine "Fred" and the feminine "Fredelle," with her "empowered core" on the feminine side. Maomao reflected on the imbalance between her passive and active selves, with the passive self preferred. Paradoxically, a volitional core is needed to make that determination.

"Mini-selves" are not the "false selves" of our previous discussion, but are temporally evolved presentations that may be applied in different contexts while nonetheless comprising part of larger self connected to that self by shared memes. The existence of such mini-selves may challenge the requisite sense of stability and constancy. The challenge of the therapist is to show the internal logic of applying different aspects of self in alternative contexts while finding an underlying constancy that grounds the client.

This sense of constancy may assist clients in overcoming adversity. Nick said his sense of being empowered came from his childhood when he had pneumonia and refused to restrict his physical activity. When sent to Russia from Kazakhstan, he became involved in cross-country skiing and running, learning, "If you are good, you could do many things." As a student, he thought it would be good to see the world, and his academic chair suggested that he go to the United States. Although many people had difficulty obtaining visas after the 9/11 terrorist attack, his success led to the belief that if he "anticipates" something, it will happen. This sense of empowerment reportedly came from inside himself but was reinforced experientially.

The need for constancy is powerful. Maomao reported that in her formative years, even small decisions, such as what to wear, were made by her parents, particularly her mother. She attributed this parental influence with the development of her "passive self" that dominates the rest of her being. After experimenting with independent decision-making, she decided that the benefits of being passive outweighed the benefits an individualist volitional approach.

Feelings of resonance and constancy were enhanced by self-maps reflecting childhood and adult transitions. This recognition of prior transitional change suggests a fluidity that contrasts with a view of the self as unchanging. Each participant was able to recall such transitions, and those events, combined with their interpretations of them, were relayed to the researcher in the form of narratives or remembered self-defining stories. Often these transitions involved overcoming opposition or disadvantage. JohnB, who was born with a clubfoot, refused to accept this physical limitation: "I think that was quite critical in who I became to be because I wasn't supposed to play and I wasn't supposed to walk well, and I think there was the determination to do it. ... I'd come home from school and basically ... because you're not supposed to be doing that, how many times are you gonna hurt yourself, and I think it just gave me more determination to do it."

JohnB was able to trace the competitiveness found in his self-map to his childhood reaction to disability. He used this determination to overcome shyness and develop academic success. The parenting style in which he was raised also influenced his development. He described his parents as emotionally abusive with this emotional memory triggering negative, even vengeful, reaction toward people who are arrogant and authoritative. Cognitive change proved to be easier than emotional change. JohnB credited his experience of moving to northern Saskatchewan with changing from being a conservative Catholic to a more liberal and accepting individual. He noted that in his adopted community, "There are Aboriginal, Métis; extremes of wealth. ... One can play on a team with a cop, a drug dealer, aboriginals, executives—and they all get along." He was primed for cross-cultural change by the childhood experience of having a non-Christian, non-Caucasian friend who was, in his opinion, as entitled to go to Heaven as those in the congregation in which he was raised.

To the angst of counsellors since the beginning of the profession, the self in its striving for continuity resists change. Self-mapping aids in engaging the client's commitment to change by illustrating the structural integrity of the whole, thus satisfying the client's need for constancy. By referencing transitional events illustrating the ability to overcome early maladaptive self-definitions, we help empower further beneficial change. JohnB used the same determination that led him to overcome his childhood physical disability to change early self-defining memes of "extremely shy" and "social idiot." Judy credited a job as a carhop with the incidental effect of curing the extreme shyness she felt as a youth, although she continued to be cautious in her presentation style. Reflective self-analysis resulted in her understanding that this shyness led her to appear stern when she was not, and she was able to modify her presenting behaviours to better reflect the person she felt she was inside.

Self-change is facilitated by the opinions of significant others. Magdelynn credited her tendency toward overachievement, with accompanying self-criticism, to being the oldest in her sib-line, but she also reported that her motorcycle accident had resulted in more acceptance of environmental determinism. She described her subsequent acceptance of externally generated events over which she had little or no control as a "Forrest Gump life," and she was aided by a new-found curiosity leading her to explore where such a life would take her. This change, however, happened after the intervention of a valued friend:

> I was upset a lot and quite suicidal, I guess, until one of my friends, a new friend that I made, who was in a chair, he was like, "You were an athlete before; you can still be an athlete," and I was like, "What are you talking about? That don't make any sense to me." He said, "You have the heart and drive and determination to be as active as you were, and you still have that. You just have to find a different sport. You have to find a sport that works for you now."

A suggestion from a significant other also led Brent to experience a planned transitional change. He had believed himself to be someone who lacked academic ability due to a history of educational failure. Subsequent events were interpreted from that internalized frame, and he avoided academic challenges while maintaining a compensating interest in sports. With the encouragement of a swimming coach, he began to experiment with the "poor learner" meme contained in his theory of self. That experimentation led to successful experiences as a swimming instructor and as a cycling coach, which, in turn, led to a revised theory of self as a person of some intelligence. In memetic terms he replaced a "poor learner" meme with a "learner" meme. His subsequent academic success led to a mini-existential crisis in which his need for self-constancy was threatened. Instead of choosing the understanding that he developed academic acumen to become a competent learner, Brent chose to believe he had always been a competent learner, but external factors had interfered with previous attempts at academic success. Such an interpretation preserves constancy but invites externalized blame.

Brent's sense of self-constancy was also preserved through memories acknowledging parental influence. For example, he attributed both his frugality and his sense of empowerment to such influence. Brent used the ending of a relationship as the catalyst for change. A woman he had been dating said she did not feel comfortable at his house, which was cold and did not have a couch. He resolved, after the relationship, to reduce his packrat behaviours, to make his house more visitor-friendly and to become less rigid in his social interactions with other people. These are behavioural changes without the necessity of change to the self. While one might expect that sustained behavioural change will lead to changes in self-definition, the need for self-constancy can lead to the retention of old memes even after the behaviours supporting them have ceased. As with people who continue to define themselves as alcoholics years after they stopped abusing the drug, Brent's need for self-constancy led him to continue to define himself as a packrat after he had stopped exhibiting packrat behaviours.

Compulsive behaviours that became entrenched in one's self-definition were frequently traced to learned injunctions from childhood. Tina reported she compulsively cleans the homes of family and friends when visiting. She traced this behaviour to her desire to gain childhood approval from her mother: "When I was little I used to make my bed, and it would have no creases in it whatsoever, and I used to run over to my mom and show her. I was so proud of myself that I made my bed like that."

Although being a compulsive cleaner remained part of her self-definition, a process of individuation allowed her to engage in change that diverged from family norms. A particularly harsh event led Tina to question her family:

The first time that I had to ever deal with death was when my sister died, and that's a big thing that me and my family don't talk about very much 'cause it was an affair and they decided not to tell us about it. ... so we grew up in high school, a good two, three years she didn't say anything, and I was hearing impaired, and I seen her (another half-sister) at the fair, and she goes "Tina this is your sister," and I thought she said, "This is my sister," so I shook my own sister's hand and walked away from her the first time I met her, just hurt her completely, and my dad was freaking out 'cause he saw the whole thing from afar and he ended up telling me that night that was my actual sister. ... I got to know her for two years and she passed away.

The secrecy and pain Tina associated with her father's promiscuity was followed by several years of "partying" that included binge drinking and illicit drug use. She "sobered up" when she discovered she was pregnant, and she made a decision to raise this child "properly." Reflecting on her experiences, she proposed the idea of an open marriage with her husband providing he did not "sneak around." The crib death of her first-born led Tina to relapse into a pattern of binge drinking. Tina also credited this experience with the development of over protectiveness verging on paranoia with respect to the safety of her children. An unplanned pregnancy also led her away from binge drinking on this second occasion. On both occasions, powerful behavioural injunctions associated with motherhood resulted in her choosing a sober lifestyle.

The birth of a child prompted Chantelle to begin changing her self in some ways. Although she lost her son to foster care, she hoped to reunite with him when able to care for him properly. Chantelle stopped being a drug user, became less arrogant and overconfident, and added "intelligent," "determined," "serious," "responsible," "ex-con," and "counsellor" memes to her self. Both women were unable to voice why they would react to their unplanned pregnancies by changing their selves in positive ways in contrast with some women who maintain dysfunctional lifestyles throughout multiple pregnancies. Both shared a deeply held belief that their parents were deficient in some ways and that they had the ability to be different. From their descriptions, both had been lacking in social interest, and it is plausible that their pregnancies provided them with that interest. By becoming better parents than their parents, they were committed to making the world a better place for their progeny.

The general plot of inadequate parenting leading to emotional and behavioural difficulties with a subsequent decision to change in the direction of social interest is available to men as well as women. Trevor's self had a meme for "parent," even though he had no biological children at the time of the study. As a child, he was traumatized when abandoned by his father in a northern forest. His role as a protector also stemmed from his family of origin: "When my dad would drink or when anyone else would drink I would be the protector of the youngest ones, and that sort of shaped my role, sort of shaped how I became a man." He traced the anger he felt when people abuse children or women to this childhood protector role. While he no longer intimidates people by threatening physical violence, the anger at perceived injustice remains, leading to political activism. His personal quest included developing the ability to feel a full range of emotions and teaching others to become emotionally intelligent.

Pangloss also traced his anger over injustice to a dysfunctional family of origin, characterized by alcoholism and physical abuse. He recounted a series of stories involving violent or vengeful acts against a sister's spouse, a former employer, and an aunt. He bullied bullies and argued it is his duty to do so. He also engaged in a series of developmental transitions beginning with his decision to leave home, while still in high school, so he could pursue an education. In another transition, he left broadcasting to become a stagehand. His use of a SunTzu's quote from *The Art of War,* "No battle plan ever survived first contact with the enemy," suggests flexibility of approach coupled with an aggressive orientation within a dichotomous worldview. His self-map full of obvious contradictions may actually be related to a negation of self: the self is not important in comparison to the battles which must be fought.

Fredelle described a tormented childhood involving repeated degradation by other boys and her father. She recalled, "I was generally treated as someone who was a fag and lower than them and not respected." She was generally friendless, and she avoided situations of potential ridicule. This was complicated by a bad stutter:

> I also stuttered very badly; I mean so badly that it was a physical problem. I'd be shaking my head up and down; you would think I was having a seizure if you saw me. I'd be struggling so hard to

get that sound out that my jugular veins would be sticking out. I'd be shaking my head; it was a horrible thing. I recall sitting at the supper table trying to talk, and I was sitting against the wall. I'd be banging my head against the wall trying to get a sound out, and I felt like a freak.

Fredelle accepted the label "freak" with the interpretation that being born into a male body was the cause of her freakiness. She became intensely angry with her male side for uncaringly causing so much pain. Fredelle's "coming out" represented self-acceptance. In what has now become a recurrent theme, Fredelle found purpose or social interest in attempting to make the world a better place—in her case through political activism to advance the cause of trans-sexual persons.

At one level of perception, Fredelle's orchidectomy between our first and second interviews represented radical change; however, when viewed from the perspective of her self, the removal of her testes was a cosmetic change allowing her physical self to conform to her mental reality. In a very postmodernist way, we can become that to which we aspire, modifying the evidence provided by our environment to conform to our preferred reality. There is an important caveat on this ability: we are social animals defined by relationships and our ability to force our environment to conform to our preferred individual realities is dependent on their acceptance by significant others. Support for our narrative of reality is a form of legitimization without which our defined self rings hollow. As a child and youth, Fredelle could not construct her own viable narrative, nor was one provided to her wherein she could be positioned in a role where she had value or legitimacy. Her political activism may be viewed as an attempt to gain social acceptance for such a narrative, which, in turn, was therapeutic: "I think Fredelle is a wonderful person, and I am proud that I have liberated Fredelle, that she is completely free to roam within my, my beingness. I don't fight Fredelle, I don't try to, and I used to years ago when I was younger."

Fredelle reported that she was able to feel a range of emotions following the removal of her testes, having associated her former deficit in emotional functioning with maleness. The stereotype of male emotional retardation is readily available within North American culture, but while one other person (Trevor) referenced the same stereotype, he and other males in our sample (Brent, JohnB) incorporated a full range of emotional responses into their self-struc-tures.[1] An alternative explanation in Fredelle's case is that her testes came to represent emotional repression initially required for his own survival, and this led to a failure to develop and substantiate a self-narrative that could give her eudaemonic satisfaction when she began to identify as a woman. She concluded, in her emotional angst, that emotions were not properly part of the self. Her development of a self-enhancing narrative and its acceptance by supportive communities removed the necessity for tight restrictions on her ability to feel emo-tions. Since the self is an emotional as well as a cognitive structure, the removal of her testes may be seen as a symbolic action that trig-gered a personal transition toward completeness or wholeness.

Although I discussed just three participants in the section "Finding One's Self through Sports" in chapter 5, in fact, a majority of our sample participants (six) reported their participation in sports had resulted in increased self-esteem and empowerment. Trevor and Chantelle used their aggressive feelings to excel in martial arts and boxing. JohnB and Nick overcame physical limitations to excel at baseball, distance running, and skiing in childhood and learned that with determination they could meet their goals. Brent discovered that he had both leadership and teaching skills through his participation in swimming and cycling. Magdelynn did not define herself as an athlete until after a motorcycle accident, and her success in wheel-chair basketball was linked to her refusal to define herself as disabled. All six individuals generalized their success in sports to include a sense of empowerment in academics. While we cannot be certain how culturally specific participation in sports may be to building a posi-tive empowered self, it is clearly a vehicle for developmental transitioning in some individuals.

In these narratives, transitions are pictured as life-transforming events, akin to the religious notion of conversion: a woman gives birth to a baby and becomes a responsible person; a man encounters an insightful and authoritative swimming coach and comes away with sufficient academic self-esteem to enrol in university. If we view the self as an integrated complex structure with individuals presenting different sides of themselves in different contexts, the appearance of sudden change can be illusory. The fact that both times Tina became pregnant she modified her behaviour in identical ways suggests that the requisite parenting memes outlining a "pregnancy script" were already in place in her self waiting to be triggered. Although different presentations triggered by context does not imply self-change, incremental changes to the self are possible. While Brent's transition could be traced to his swimming coach, it was still a matter of years between this intervention and his ultimate enrolment in university. In the meantime, he experimented with coaching others first in one sport (swimming) and then another (cycling). He also experimented by taking responsible positions in his sporting associations and the environmental movement. Each success led to a slight revision of his self that in turn paved the way for further experimentation.

Up to this point, we have examined transitions retrospectively. Given the longitudinal component of the study (eight months), participants were asked if there had been any observed changes to their selves since their prior sessions. Four participants reported such changes.

Tina decided, between our first and second interviews, to become less paranoid and more assertive with her change effort following her decision to have breakfast with her children and subsequent comments from her eldest child. She decided to take medication for her depression, allow her children more freedom to play, and allow her husband to help her with housework. Before our second interview, Trevor reframed his "overweight" meme as the less pejorative "big." Prior to our third interview, he also created a new memetic centre for himself, "artist," from the convergent effects of other memes. Magdelynn said she had become less rigid and less of a role player between her first and second interviews with resultant improved familial and romantic relationships. She reported, by her third interview, that she now used the metaphor of a "mobile" instead of "fractured pie" to picture her self, and this permitted her to be more consistent across contexts.

Due to the incremental nature of self-change, it is not always possible to identify when a particular change occurred. Trevor reported he had become a political activist between his first and second interviews, and he was surprised to find that "political activist" already appeared on his initial self-map. That meme was constructed after our initial interview as a result of narratives in which he had taken direct action against a doctor who may have overprescribed medications and men seeking the services of prostitutes. More formal political action during the course of this study seemed to flow from this earlier orientation. While this result may be interpreted as a phenotypic manifestation of a meme that was already present, changes in expression may be precursors to a change in self-identification.

With this self-mapping technique, we can recognize conditions that lead to developmental change before any such change occurs. Brent had been shaken by the murder of a fellow cyclist immediately prior to the commencement of this study. He said he felt the deceased person's presence, and he awakened during the night afraid of seeing a ghost. He felt guilty after agreeing with another cyclist that the deceased "could be an asshole sometimes." He began thinking about what people might come to understand of him if he died. While this reflection could result in self-change, none had yet occurred. We might predict, however, that this increased awareness of his own mortality might lead to considerations of his potential legacy, and that he would become less aggressive or judgmental in asserting his strongly held beliefs. We might predict increased concerns about family—both with his family of origin and the development of a future family of his own. His self-map appeared to be laying the groundwork for such developments.

All of the transitions recounted in this study involved relationships with other people. Those relationships were remembered in narratives that included thematic interpretations of events. The storylines imputed cause and effect. JohnB's relationship with a high school classmate who was non-Christian led to his questioning of church doctrine and eventually to an acceptance of cultural diversity. Trevor's relationship with an uncle resulted in his thematic Indian name that gave direction to his life. Both Judy and Maomao said the criticisms of friends resulted in self-examination and behavioural change. We saw how encouragement Brent received from a swimming instructor eventually led to his teaching career. A friend encouraged Magdelynn to play wheelchair basketball, which eventually led to an invitation to play for the national women's team. Pangloss was coached through high school by a paternalistic Sikh who viewed his education to be of paramount importance. Two participants (Tina and Chantelle) experienced lifestyle changes prompted by the birth of children. Since all of these transitional events were based on relationships with other people, we need to consider the implication that therapy cannot be successful without consideration of such relationships and their effect on the self. Indeed, there are pivotal moments when the selves of others touch with our own.

In summation, both planned and unplanned changes occurred to the selves of some of the participants during the course of this study. All of the participants discussed transitions, both developmental and unplanned that led to who they became. Some of the changes were prompted by the comments of significant others. One change (Fredelle's emotive self) was the unforeseen consequence of a behavioural action thought to be consistent with a pre-existent self. One behavioural change (Trevor's political activism) was a new behaviour consistent with an already existent aspect of his self. One (Brent) reported conditions by which such change might be expected, but these changes had not yet become manifest. That these events happened over the course of about eight months supports the idea that incremental changes to the self are not infrequent.

If the objective of therapy is change, then self-maps may be thought of as snapshots at a particular point in time. To be effective, the client needs to identify with the snapshot taken with the realization that snapshots taken at different points of time would not be identical. Since the self cannot be viewed as static, it is important to bring into focus the notion of remembered transitions. Once clients can link previous developmental change to who they are in the present, they will be able to better visualize future planned change. Therapists can use the concept of incremental change in planning such developmental transitions.

Self-Map Co-Construction in Effecting Therapeutic Change

As we have seen, the utility of the meme, as a concept distinct from percept and idea, rests on the recognition of its referent, connotative, affective, and behavioural dimensions. These dimensions allow for a metaphoric attractive force to exist between memes, giving stability to resultant structures. While the use of the meme in this way was efficacious, it was insufficient as emotive factors not connected to specific memes also make up who we are, and these factors allude to unconscious drives and characteristics.

The proposition that the self consists of a complex of mutually attractive memes provides an elegant explanation as to why people retain negative or self-defeating aspects of their identities instead of simply constructing newer and better selves. For example, Suzie's initial attempts to change her self by removing "depressed person" from her identity resulted in feelings of instability coupled with suicide ideation and a reflexive retreat into depression. Visualizing her self in memetic map form coincided with her determination to override such protective measures and engage in a process of self-change. The act of situating "depressed person" within a cluster of related memes helped both therapist and client to develop a plan for building a more positive self-construction.

The therapist and client may use self-mapping to identify key structural elements that are weak or missing, and dysfunctional elements on which the client may rely for self-definition. Relying on the client's report of resonance with successive coauthored revisions will increase the likelihood that the representation is of sufficient quality. While no map represents a territory perfectly, they allow us to chart a course, and so it is with memetic self-maps. Planned incremental change can take into account groups of memes serving to keep dysfunctional core memes in place. Groups of such memes can be appropriated to support new desired alternatives. Peripheral memes are usually the easiest for the client to remove or replace. Since the map-building activity is necessarily a collaborative exercise between therapist and client, it commends itself to the joint planning of therapeutic alternatives.

The dynamic of co-constructing developmental transitions is a way of increasing client self-empowerment and commitment to change. Trevor and Brent said visualizing their selves in map form helped them to identify needed change and to make those self-changes at a faster rate than would otherwise have occurred. Judy said that her self-map both represented her and represented somebody she wants to be; the capacity for self-change is built into this conceptualization. Accepting the results of this research, volitional animation leads to a feeling of self-empowerment, and this core component to a healthy self is enhanced by controlling the direction of self-change.

Fredelle said the experience of self-map construction "empowered me to be physically free." This exuberant declaration should be judged in the context of her self-definition as a war between male and female archetypes. The self-map allowed Fredelle, like the gardener making plans to cultivate a yard, to see the terrain she wanted to prune while giving primacy to her feminine side, and that empowerment contributed to her mental health.

In contrast, having examined her volitional capacity in map form, Maomao consciously embraced her more passive collectivist self. Instead of invoking the notion that of parts of her constituent self were at war with each other, Maomao stated a preference for one while allowing that the unwanted volitional side could be invoked should circumstances so warrant. Empowerment in Maomao's case was evidenced through the capacity to make that choice.

Magdelynn said seeing her self represented on paper made it appear connected. In our initial interview, she had defined herself as "fractured," with different mini-selves operative in different contexts. Seeing her self in map form helped her to become the same person across contexts, which was how she wanted to be. Constancy is a fundamental structural characteristic of the self that in some ways sits in opposition to the empowerment implied by a capacity for self-change. Counsellors need to be aware of the need for a balance between the two, with the healthy individual displaying a capacity for both.

Brent said that his sense of self-empowerment was instilled in him by his mother, and the self-mapping project served to neither increase nor decrease that empowerment. JohnB identified his tendency to challenge authority as part of his drive for self-empowerment, but he was not positive that this is an innate characteristic, reporting that he had questioned it as such "as far back as I can remember." Conversely, Chantelle reported she was not empowered as a child. She had been a "shy foster kid," stopped going to school, and ended up with a series of criminal convictions. She said the process of "getting clean," going to jail, having her son, and then starting school all contributed to her growing self-empowerment aided by boxing and counselling. Once her sense of empowerment reached a certain threshold, it was not possible to become more empowered—either you have it or you do not. By the time of her participation in this research, Chantelle had demonstrated the ability to effect developmental self-change.

Ten of eleven participants in this research said that they had the ability to make changes to their selves while the remaining participant said he did not understand how he made such changes. Some participants (five) believed their participation in this research increased their capacity for self-change. Six participants said that an empowering drive that could effect self-change existed within them from an early age. It would be expected that therapeutic clients will feel less empowered than people who feel no need for therapy, and the effect of self-map co-construction on self-empowerment for those clients should be enhanced.

Two methods of memetic map construction have been described thus far. The method used in developing the self-map of the suicidal youth was directive: the youth was asked to prepare four lists consisting of self-defining roles, beliefs, negative attributes, and positive attributes. The method used with our qualitative sample consisted of open-ended questioning leading to self-descriptions in narrative form that were transcribed and coded for items meeting our definition of memes. With both methods, resultant memes were linked according to internal characteristics and displayed graphically. The second method allows for more possible variations and less therapist or researcher influence on self-depiction and is, therefore, preferred from a research perspective. The more directive method requires less of the therapist's time. Anecdotally, I have had good results using both methods. Whichever method is used, it is crucial to actively involve the client in co-construction and interpretation. If the directive method is used, it is important to supplement the information gathering by soliciting the client's perspectives on structural dimensions. For example, a failure to identify an emotive aspect to the self independent of affect attributed to individual memes should be explored to determine whether the client considers himself to be emotive or that emotion is to be avoided. It is possible that, using the "forty persons" method, the failure to identify such an emotional base is a methodological oversight. Similarly, a failure to identify a volitional centre using the directive method should not be interpreted as necessarily implying the client lacks volition; rather, the client's history and feelings with respect to self-empowerment should be explored further, leading to possible revisions. A comparison of the two methods of constructing memetic self-maps are shown in table 1.

Regardless of the method used, self-mapping appears to be compatible with a variety of therapeutic approaches. The mapping process used in this study resulted in the following potential psychotherapeutic benefits:

1. The process of preparing the maps recognized the participant as an expert in him or herself, and this helped establish a collaborative relationship with the therapist;
2. Rapport was developed quickly to the extent that by the second interview two participants (Tina and Magdelynn) shared sensitive details about their personal lives they had initially avoided;
3. The act of participating in the map-making exercise reminded participants of prior interpretive choices made in

TABLE 1.

A comparative outline of two methods of memetic self-map construction

	Self-Narrative Method	"Forty Persons" Method
1. **Data Collection**	The client or participant gives a detailed description of who they are. The researcher or therapist may give prompts to ensure a detailed description. The therapist asks about common self characteristics that may not be represented.	The client is asked to create four lists of who they are: ten persons that encompass roles, ten things they believe to be true, ten things they like about themselves, ten things they would change about themselves if they could.
2. **Manipulation of Data**	The therapist transcribes the narrative and then codes each segment using the "constant comparative" method common to grounded theory and transcendental realism.	The client is asked to rank each item on each list from the most important to least important. The therapist and client co-construct codenames representing each item.
3. **Identification of memes**	The therapist places coded segments into "bins" for each codename. Those codings, with connotative, behavioural, and affective characteristics, are declared to be memes.	The therapist explores connotative, affective, and behavioural characteristics associated with each named item with the client. Those items that have all three characteristics are declared to be memes.
4. **Arrangement of memes**	Those memes representing a larger number of segments are placed centrally. Those with similar connotation, affect, or implied behaviours are viewed as connected. If one meme leads to another behaviourally then those memes are also linked.	Memes that have been prioritized as more important by the client are placed more centrally on their self-map. Memes sharing the same characteristics (connotative, affective, or behavioural) are considered linked. Those that lead behaviourally to other memes are considered linked.
5. **Identification of clusters**	Groups of memes that may act in concert when triggered (as in a script), or may present as a "mini-self" in particular contexts, are identified.	Groups of memes that may act in concert when triggered (as in a script), or may present as a "mini-self" in particular contexts, are identified.
6. **Non-memetic factors**	The therapist and client explore personality characteristics, traumas, illnesses, and other predispositions that may trigger meme clusters. These are placed at the bottom of the self-map.	The therapist and client explore personality characteristics, traumas, illnesses, and other predispositions that may trigger meme clusters. These are placed at the bottom of the self-map.

response to transitional experiences, with the implication they could make other choices;

4. Memetic self-map co-construction increased the sense of empowerment in some participants;

5. The visual representation of the self allowed researcher and participant to place contemplated changes in perspective with respect to the entire self;

6. Absence of items identified as common to selves (continuity, volition, individuation, productivity, intimacy, social interest, feeling) may be "red-flagged" by the therapist for further examination; and,

7. Recognition of attractive forces existent between individual memes and the placement of memes with respect to other memes may generate new strategies for self-change.

In summation, the potential benefits of memetic self-mapping to the counselling process include enhanced development of collaborative counsellor-client relationships, increased rapport, added empowerment for self-change, a holistic perspective on the self-structure, and the generation of strategies for effecting change. With such mapping the client may be able to better understand the consistency of his or her actions, cognitions, and feelings with an underlying belief system so that a challenging of that belief system can begin.

Culturally Inclusive Counselling: Implications of Self

A conscious selved people cannot escape choice. Were we to follow a leader or a text with absolute faith, we still have to decide, as Maomao discovered, which leader or text to follow. We may long for an outside power greater than ourselves to lift us to imagined heights; however, to make the determination of which benign leader or cause to follow requires a decision, and that decision requires evidence. What constitutes evidence will vary between individuals and will be culturally informed.

Minority clients have responded to culturally responsive counsellors with increased willingness to return, more expressed satisfaction, and greater depth of disclosure (Ponterotto, Fuertes, & Chen, 2000). Cultural norms may vary with respect to defining behavioural strengths, benchmarks establishing counsellor or helper credibility, and preferences with respect to possible interventions.

The ability to perceive possible areas of cultural difference and to respond flexibly and positively to such differences is crucial when working with clients from disparate cultural groups (Robertson, et al., 2015). Cultures may be viewed as a series of probabilities based on the frequency of defining memes in a given population. Since no one individual will match perfectly a given cultural stereotype, the proficient counsellor will be open to exploring internal cultural variation within all clients. At its core, proficient multicultural counselling is simply good counselling practice recognizing individual difference.

Counselling and therapy predicated on respecting the uniqueness of the individual avoids many of the pitfalls attributed to ethnocentric practice. By learning the client's worldview, the counsellor comes to understand those cultural influences that have come to shape the client's self. Each client may be understood as having an internal culture of one. By mapping the self of the individual, we come to an understanding of his or her internal culture. Armed with such knowledge the counsellor is better able to identify those behavioural strengths, values, and practices that uniquely make up the individual. With such an approach, it is possible to effectively engage in therapeutic change while having little previous experience with the client's culture. For example, one of my previous clients was a Zoroastrian client originally from a Middle Eastern country—a rather select group that had heretofore not been part of my practice.[2] My previous knowledge of the religion was limited to a historical notation that the Judeo-Christian notion of Satan is descended from the ancient Zoroastrian god Ahriman (Ray, 2009).

The Zoroastrian client was in his thirties and presented with an inability to form meaningful relationships with women. Since age seventeen, whenever he had noticed an attractive young woman he would subsequently experience vivid misogynous dreams involving beatings, torture, and murder. He rarely ejaculated as a result of these dreams but reported a sense of satisfaction associated with the woman's pain while in his dream state. In an attempt to minimize the recurrence of such horrendous nightmares, he had avoided relationships with attractive women for almost two decades.

The client did not recall any instances of abuse during his upbringing, and he had not felt terrorized by the religious majority in his country of origin. Sex before marriage was a religious taboo, and he had not been allowed to have girlfriends as a youth. His mother said his violent dreams meant he needed a wife, and she had offered to arrange a marriage in accordance with their community's customs. The suggestion of marriage, even as arranged by his mother, terrorized him. He described himself as devout and had approached priests and elders for advice, but their prescription of increased prayer and meditation had little effect on this issue.

I asked the client to bring pictures, drawings, writing, or any other artefacts that would assist me to better understand his self narrative. He brought samples of his poetry. First, he would read a poem in his native language so I would get a feel for the melody, then he would provide a translation. In the poetry, women were placed on a pedestal of virtue with men pictured as admiring, cherishing, and protecting the feminine principle. This desire to protect was long-standing. He recalled that as a child an older sister and some of her friends had begun viewing an underground copy of Dracula, but he had unplugged the television when Dracula came to bite a female victim, and he insisted the movie be destroyed on the threat of informing the authorities.[3]

I asked the client to recount his nightmares describing himself and his victims in detail, including their physical characteristics. In these dreams he had no eyebrows. I asked him the significance of eyebrows in his culture. He replied he did not know, but that he would ask his mother. In our next session, he informed me eyebrows are a symbol of wisdom. I blurted out, "then it's your shadow!" I explained that the figure in his dreams was not him but a caricature of him lacking wisdom. I explained that according to Jung we construct an ideal self he called our "persona"—the good things we know we can be. The shadow consists of those parts of our selves that we have not included in our persona. I suggested that the dreams were saying that he has to come to terms with his sexual self. "But I am hurting them; I am not having sex with them," he declared. "And how would you feel if, in your dreams, you had sex with them?" I asked. "Terrible," he replied, "It would be sinful.""Exactly," I said, "Your subconscious is protecting you by hurting that which could cause you to sin."

Human beings are meaning makers; we need to situate our selves within a coherent worldview, and we need to feel as if our lives make sense. At this level of intervention, it is more important to provide a framework for self-understanding than attempt to find a mechanism that is objectively true. My insight in this case was not that representation of Jung represents objective reality, but that an aspect of his approach could be used to allow the client a new perspective for understanding his angst consistent with his prior cultural values. The new perspective allowed him to begin the task of uniting aspects of his sexuality with his already existent self. In subsequent sessions we explored aspects of his sexuality compatible with his goal of honouring women in culturally consistent ways. We began a behavioural experiment. He had been avoiding a young woman who had smiled at him in class. I encouraged him to invite her to have coffee with the provision that he had to explain that he just wanted friendship. To his surprise this did not result in the usual nightmares. They went for dinner. They spent an afternoon at a zoo. He concluded that he could relate to attractive women at a friendship level, and given his moral code this was preferred prior to marriage.

As noted in chapter 3, Korhonen (2002) was surprised to find fundamental commonalities between modern counselling theories. She expressed greater surprise at finding commonalities between those theories and the practices of traditional aboriginal Elders engaged in counselling. Western theorists and Inuit Elders alike believed in the interrelatedness of emotion, thought, and behaviour, and in the inseparability of the client from his social context. The individual was recognized as the locus of counselling change, with the intention for self-change formed within a unique worldview that includes context specific goals and predictions of consequence. The fact that the Inuit were effectively the last aboriginal people on the American continents to be colonized lends significance to these findings. Some of the Elders would have been children when first contact was made with people of European descent.

If fundamental cross-cultural commonalities to counselling practice exist, what can be said of cultural difference? Noting that aboriginal and international students often do not use university counselling services at the same rate as non-aboriginal Canadian students, I designed my doctoral practicum to offer alternative services in settings amenable to the targeted client populations: the university's Native and International Student Centres. Aboriginal students did not typically book appointments through the receptionist. Instead, they would "hang around" until my door was open and then politely introduce themselves, often engaging in idle chat, "feeling me out," before presenting an issue and making an appointment to discuss it. Often, they came with complete narratives that needed voice with the result that the "fifty-minute hour" became inoperative. Often, they were concerned with integrating the counselling practices with existent belief systems that were held to be traditional. Occasionally the client did not feel comfortable in an office setting, and we would move outside and sit under the trees. The program was effective in broadening counselling services to underserviced populations, and the university found funding to continue this specialized position in future years.

I have practised as a counsellor and therapist in largely aboriginal northern Saskatchewan, Canada, for more than a quarter of a century. Although I do not consider myself to be an Elder, I am sometimes given a gift of tobacco as a client's way of signifying the special relationship we are about to enter. Cultural differences with respect to the establishment of the counselling relationship, length of sessions, and their location need to be respected, but these differences are not fundamental to the counselling process. The following case vignette illustrates the use of self-mapping in therapy with a Cree woman from an isolated northern community.

"Olivia" presented with symptoms of Post Traumatic Stress Disorder after being raped during an episode of excessive alcohol consumption.[4] She reported that her spouse, parents, and employer had been supportive following the traumatizing event. Following six weeks of cognitive behavioural therapy, her anxiety attacks subsided, permitting a return to work; however, she requested continuing therapy for self-development. Her initial co-constructed self-map (figure 7.1) includes three clusters labelled "Spiritual/Fitness," "Social," and "Imperfect." The pattern of memes connecting these clusters suggests a potential for rumination, a suggestion that was confirmed by the client.

In keeping with a common aboriginal North American cultural norm (Berry, 1999), Olivia associated traditional outdoor activities with meditative and mystical processes, with the result that one cluster emerged combining spiritual and fitness themes. A second cluster, "Social Person" includes two groups, family and friends, connected by the meme "supportive," which Olivia defined as "doing for others." When she failed to do for others, she was told by her mother that she was "oversensitive" and self-centred. Self-defining memes for "depression" and "anxiety" form the core of the Imperfect cluster that also includes "drinker," "dependant," and "perfectionist." The latter meme was part of a pathway leading back to "Spiritual/Fitness." The bar at the bottom of the self-map represents context specific emotions, which, if triggered, could shift Olivia's focus to a particular cluster.

Clinical depression and anxiety were diagnosed and presented as psychological characteristics distinct from the memes of the same name and are pictured as triggers activating Olivia's Imperfect Self. Her family, spouse, and employer are presented as being supportive and are represented by broad arrows with external origins.

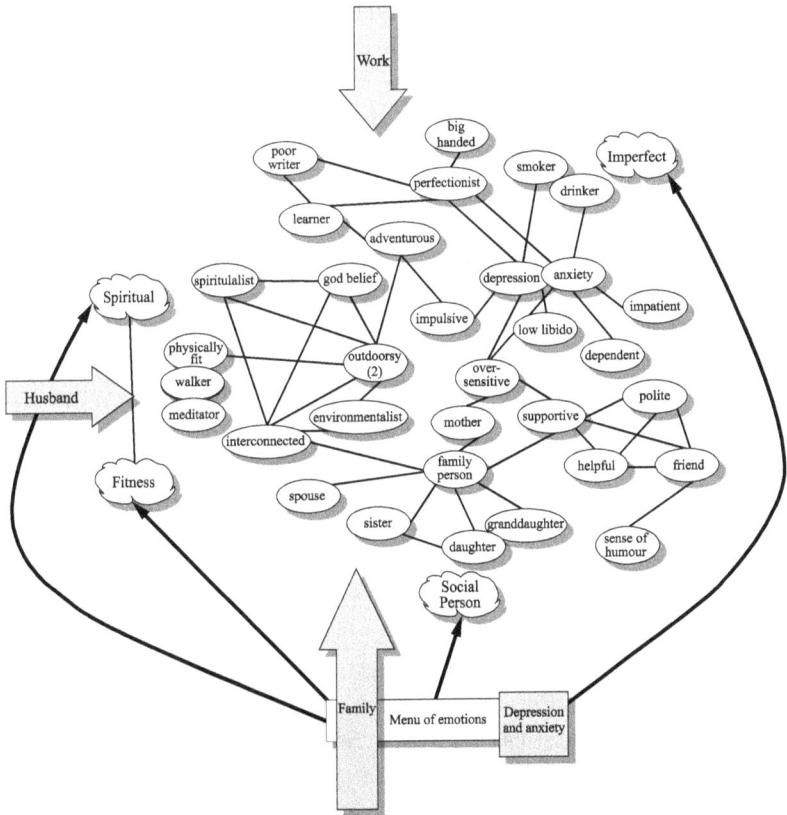

FIGURE 7.1. *Initial self-map of Olivia displaying memes, external influences, and emotions.*

Olivia's self-map was reviewed and revised throughout therapy. She observed that the negative transitions she had in her life involved alcohol abuse, and she decided to limit her consumption to two drinks per social occasion. With the successful application of this resolution, the meme "drinker" was changed to "social drinker." Unfortunately, her spouse, who continued a pattern of heavy drinking, began subjecting her to jealous accusatory behaviour. She left him and moved into a small unfinished cabin in the boreal forest and discovered that she liked herself more. She scored low on a standardized test for depression and this meme was removed from her self-map. Outdoor activities, represented by "outdoorsy" and "environmentalist," had been associated with drinking and she decided to replace that activity with photography. She also linked a new meme by this name to "sensitive," which was a reframe of the meme "oversensitive."

At this point in therapy, Olivia reported frustration that she was not given the information or latitude to do her job properly. She also found her family, particularly her mother, to be invasive and controlling. She came to realize that work and family were treating her as they always had, but actions that had been perceived to be supportive six months earlier were now felt to be restrictive. She moved to another community, found a new job, and began professional training in photography. She still had a loving relationship with her parents, but found their visits difficult and would contact me by telephone when she felt her new self to be threatened. During our final formal session, she offered the insight that being "sensitive" had led to her becoming "self-aware," and that, in turn, fuelled her newfound sense of independence and decision-making. This combination of independent decision-making and self-awareness led her to set boundaries with respect to her family, pursue her interests in photography and environmentalism, and to redefine her role as a mother. The empowerment implied by these activities was represented on a final self-map as a thematic or interpretive code. We explored those psychological qualities that helped her to revise who she was so effectively. We added introverted (which for her connoted self-reflection), self-assured, and intelligent to a list of psychological characteristics that was, in no sense, meant to be complete. She lived frugally, and with the money she saved by not drinking financed a two-month holiday in a foreign country. She used her time to explore and validate her new self, and to reflect on her relationship with her mother. She returned to her home community to find both her parents and former spouse related to her new self supportively.

Reflectivity is a volitional act. The process of self-examination contributed to a sense of self-continuity while engaging in selective self change. By focusing on her whole self instead of merely documenting inadequacies, Olivia was empowered to make profound transitional decisions sometimes, as was the case when leaving her spouse, informing her therapist after the fact.

All of the self-maps reproduced in chapter 5 had a structure that included empowerment, individuality, a sense of constancy, an emotional base, community, and a proclivity for production, intimacy, and social interest. The foundations of psychotherapy and counselling practice flow from this commonly held self-structure, and it can be hypothesized that clients lacking in one or more of these areas have a developmental need. Cultural differences may be found in the way that these foundational elements to the self are expressed and the value placed on these expressions. For example, Maomao acknowledged but did not value the animator/empowered aspect of her self. Although some schools of psychology place considerable emphasis on client empowerment with respect to making choices (Adler, 1967; Ellis & Harper, 1997), one could be consistent with these approaches and support a client's decision to not use her animator self, although that decision remains a personal choice. A client-centred therapist will have no difficulty accepting a plethora of worldviews from both individualist and collectivist perspectives.

The Inuit Elders in Korhonen's study viewed counselling as nondirective, and it is precisely this nondirectiveness that allows counselling to be multicultural. But traditional Elders commonly do more than counsel, and in some roles they may be quite directive. For example, they may be herbalists, shamans, and keepers of religiously held supernatural belief systems. In defining the role of counsellor or therapist, individuals from collectivist societies may use analogues, such as "Elder," in a directive role, thus miscasting the professional as an expert advice giver. Just as additional time may be required to learn the personal culture of the client, it may be necessary to spend additional time in cross-cultural situations explaining and negotiating the role of the counsellor. While that role may be nondirective, as a diagnostician the psychologist often assumes an expert stance, and in such cases, diagnoses should be made carefully. For example, a diagnosis of a Verbal Learning Disability might be inappropriate in an individual who is culturally predisposed to value nonverbal skills. A diagnosis of Attention Deficit Disorder might be inappropriate for an individual from a society where hyper-vigilance is required.

After reviewing nine studies showing low rates of diagnosed Post Traumatic Stress Disorder in US Amerindian populations, Waldram (2004) offered, "It is crucial to consider that aboriginal peoples may exhibit low rates of diagnosed PTSD because they have low rates of PTSD" (p. 221). Since humans share a similar biological platform, it is intuitive to think Waldram must be wrong: potentially trauma-producing incidents should produce similar rates of PTSD in divergent populations. It is possible that PTSD in Amerindian populations was under-diagnosed due to a failure to recognize culturally mediated symptoms. Working in British Columbia, Canada, Brasfield (2001) noted symptoms among some former students of Indian Residential Schools that varied from PTSD in some ways. While sleep disturbance, difficulties concentrating, anxiety reactions to triggering stimuli, and the emotional re-experiencing of past events were commonly experienced, these students also displayed extreme and irrational anger, aversion to aboriginal cultures, attachment difficulties, and a propensity toward drug abuse. This symptom complex was not restricted to students who had suffered physical and sexual abuse but included those who had no recollection of an initiating traumatic event. Further, their descendants also displayed the symptomatology. Brasfield (2001) argued this collection of symptoms was a form of PTSD that he labelled Residential School Syndrome (RSS); however, aspects of its etiology, such as the absence of a life threatening triggering event, aversion to symbols not representative of the stimulus, and the heritability of the condition, would mark RSS as a separate condition. I have previously argued that this phenomenon must be understood within the historical and cultural contexts in which it arose (Robertson, 2006).

During the final quarter of the nineteenth century, the government of Canada contracted with three Christian churches[5] to provide residential education to indigenous children and youth. While initially only three such schools were planned to service all of western Canada, in practice churches would build a school and demand funding for construction costs retroactively, and by 1931 eighty such schools were in existence. The church plan to pay for the maintenance of these schools through student labour using an industrial school model failed to generate anticipated revenue. Resultant cutbacks in nutrition and health care led to high mortality rates and in 1907 a commission of inquiry recommended their closure (Woods, 2012). A lobby of churches who viewed the schools as part of their proselytizing mission and indigenous leaders who viewed education to be essential succeeded in reversing this decision. Yet another parliamentary committee recommended their closure in 1948 and this was accomplished in most of Canada twenty years subsequent. The schools were maintained but transferred to Amerindian authorities in Saskatchewan and Canada's Northwest Territories.

To enforce attendance, students were apprehended when they were not delivered to the educational authorities voluntarily. Many students faced physical and sexual abuse. Such experiences could trigger PTSD, but the existence of additional non-PTSD symptoms requires explanation. Indian residential schools were developed to effect a mass forced change of a culture. Children were not allowed to speak their native languages and daily religious instruction, during which traditional aboriginal beliefs were characterized as heathen, was compulsory. Sexuality was repressed. With missionary zeal, the churches were attempting to replace aboriginal worldviews, and they had a captive audience relatively free from family or community influence. The churches did not have the knowledge to take into account the aboriginal memes already within the selves of the children, nor did they understand how their new Euro-centric memes would interact with those already in place. Further, they offered a caricature of a Euro-Canadian self from which these children could model. Given these conditions, we would expect many of the residential school students would develop structurally incomplete and conflicted selves even in the absence of overt sexual and physical abuse. Since the self both creates and is created by the surrounding culture, the self-structure and associated worldview would be transmitted intergenerationally by ordinary cultural mechanisms. If complete sequences of healthy memes are typically unavailable in the local culture, then unhealthy selves become normative. In such circumstances, individual treatment is less efficient than community development.

The experience of one northern community illustrates the tie between cultural history and community mental health. Stanley Mission is a Cree-speaking community established by Anglican missionaries in 1851,[6] but by the 1990s four to twelve suicide attempts were occurring in this community of 1,100 every month, with the majority involving youth between the ages of fourteen and twenty-five. In 1994, following the death of a twelve-year-old girl, I was invited to conduct a post traumatic stress debriefing with clinic health staff. I had conducted such debriefings before, but this time community members who were not employees came to the clinic visibly grieving. They were invited to join the debriefing. As more came, we moved the debriefing to a larger reception area. A "talking circle" format allowed everyone in attendance to speak their thoughts and feelings with group support. Grief turned into action. The community held a series of bereavement workshops, developed a volunteer crisis intervention team, and organized group counselling for people experiencing anger, depression, and self-esteem issues. Informal leaders organized a referendum banning alcohol from the community and worked with police to enforce that ban. They built a youth activity centre and equipped it with donations. They implemented workshops on sexual abuse prevention in both elementary and high schools.They organized elders to teach youth survival skills in the boreal forest. They agreed to store all firearms in lockers built for that purpose at a local cooperatively owned store. Parental patrols enforced a 10:00 p.m. curfew for all children under the age of sixteen. They did not have another completed suicide for a period of six years. But during that interval, divisions surfaced.

The band's health department, headquartered in another community 80 kilometres distant, threatened the community's elder support worker with disciplinary action for not sufficiently promoting Aboriginal Spirituality. The community elders said they recognized that historically their people had not always been Anglican, but their ancestors had voluntarily settled at the mission generations previously. They also noted that many of the forms of aboriginal spirituality being promoted had never been part of the northern Woodland Cree traditions.

The modern self described here is several thousand years old and combines the individual and the collective. There is no essentialist template for its structure. The elders in this community were Anglican and were satisfied that their selves and worldviews were healthy and meaningful. A major problem the community faced in the 1990s and prior had been insufficient transmission of those worldviews to younger generations. The community development initiative also re-established the community's volitional will to solve its own problems. The arrival of a new essentialist program questioning these elders' worldview disrupted their transmission of values and weakened the will of informal leaders in the community development enterprise. The local steering committee leading the community development effort stopped meeting. Increasing numbers of community members returned to being the recipients of services instead of actors solving their own problems. Alcohol and drug abuse became widespread again, and predictably, the community suffered a relapse of youth suicidality.

While it is important for those cross-cultural counsellors and therapists working with aboriginal people to have an understanding of the attending historical and socioeconomic issues, the lessons presented here are universal. There are probably people in every culture who carry with them a template of how people within that culture should be, and there are just as likely people, and communities of people, in those very same cultures who defy those templates. It is the business of the therapist to side with the interpretation of the client.

In an essentialist view, people of aboriginal descent without sufficient markers of aboriginality in their presentation might be deemed to be unhealthy. Therapists operating from such assumptions might destabilize people like Tina, who did not contain such markers, or Judy, who did not identify as Métis culturally. Even Trevor might be suspect because he incorporated both European and Asian memes into his self. In the end, it is the task of everyone to create self-centric worldviews with all the information available. This is more difficult for a colonized people, at least during the early stages of colonization, because many of the old worldviews are no long operative. From this perspective the term "Historic Trauma" might be understood not as a *psychological* condition but as an idiomatic *sociological* metaphor for the ethno-stress that came with colonization. After decades of work with aboriginal inmates in Canada's penitentiaries, Waldram (2014) was not sure whether this idiom was reducing distress or creating it.

Religions serve to position people into permissible roles based on status and attributed characteristics thereby governing acceptable relationships within a given society. Given that we interpret our selves into existence as a product of such relationships, it would be reasonable to assume that we are largely defined by dominant religions even in cases where the individual is not religious. For example, we saw how Pangloss viewed some people as intrinsically evil and deserving of punishment. There is a similar meme in the Judeo-Christian tradition, and even had he not been raised Christian, Pangloss would have still encountered that meme in the popular culture.

The last chapter examined complexes of memes that form religions and how those memeplexi attach to the selves of individuals by means of connotative and emotional valence given to such concepts as transcendence, community, and moral certitude. By means of such grafting, the religious belief system becomes part of the self. Given the head start afforded one's birth religion and the dependent relationship children have during their formative years, one would expect that people would tend to the religious belief system of their immediate families. It was surprising, therefore, to discover that a majority of our sample (eight of eleven), including three of four with minority backgrounds, recounted transitional narratives involving changes of religious belief.

While still a youth, Judy used a rational process to question the Roman Catholic values in which she was raised, recalling, "I think it (religion) gave me that sense that there was meaning; there was purpose. There was you know, a god that watches every sparrow fall which, I like that idea, but soon began to think that's not true. How come just me gets helped by this god and all these people in the rest of the world are on their own?"

The Métis in Canada traditionally defined themselves, in part, by their adherence to Roman Catholicism, but using a cultural definition of aboriginality (Robertson, 2014a), Judy concluded she was not Métis. JohnB also rejected his Catholic upbringing, but he replaced it with Aboriginal Spirituality. Trevor's self followed a similar evolution to that of JohnB, but his parents were Cree, not German. Defining himself as "a big Indian," he sought to attach a cultural meaning to this racial self-definition. Maomao was raised as nonreligious but converted to Christianity. By replacing her distant directive parents with a more immediate directive religion, she minimized the necessity of self-change.

Since participants from collectivist cultures reported transitional religious change, it cannot be considered strictly an individualist cultural phenomenon. Such change, however, requires alternate perspectives. A society that tightly controls media, education, and public discourse limits the memes available for such self-construction among its citizens. Opportunities for preferred jobs, housing, education, and travel may be limited to those who conform to a prescribed template, thereby enticing citizens to avoid self-reflection. Finally, in some countries, laws against blasphemy and apostasy have been used to imprison and even kill those who vary from the prescribed norm. It is not just collectivist societies that repress their citizens. Brent, for example, had to reaffirm his belief in Roman Catholicism (despite private misgivings), so that he could obtain work as a teacher in a publicly funded Canadian school.

Counsellors and therapists who make assumptions about the optimal religious or spiritual presentation of the client based on ethnic or racial preconceptions may be unwittingly acting as agents of oppression. Changes in religious belief may be developmentally transitional, even in clients who continue to maintain the religious label assigned to them in childhood. Ethically, the counsellor must understand the family, community, and societal contexts within which the client is embedded along with the client's drive for individuation so as to assist in making informed decisions.

In this counselling model, the mantle of expertise with respect to cultural and self-knowledge passes to the client. With this orientation, it is possible to construct a mental map of the self and plan developmental or therapeutic change without intimate knowledge of the client's culture, as I did with the Zoroastrian client. While knowledge of the client's culture may be an asset with respect to counselling efficiency, that very knowledge may lead to problematic generalizations and assumptions regarding identity and worldview of the individual as an individual.

It is not possible for the counsellor to become familiar with every representative group in a multicultural society. The role of the counselling psychologist is to assist the client in making their implicit theory of self explicit. Once voiced, the client takes agentive control over the very formulation that allows that control. The combination of the structural qualities of self—distinctness, continuity, individuality, community, even agency itself—becomes his or her own. Emphasis is placed on the understanding of meaning from the client's point of view, with attention paid to how group membership is negotiated and maintained. The concept of the meme allows for consideration of individual differences in linked cognitive, connotative, and emotive meaning, and it allows us to explore and develop new linkages with family and community. As social beings, we are cultural beings.

The Fourth Paradigm

Psychotherapy has balkanized into a plethora of competing schools, including cognitive, behavioural, cognitive-behavioural, rational-emotive, emotive, schema, neurolinguistic, gestalt, body-mind, body psychotherapy, person-centred, solution focused, psychodynamic, psychoanalytic, transpersonal, narrative, humanistic, existential, and so on. At one time students of psychology with eclectic impulses would be reminded by stern-faced college professors with evident seniority that it is necessary to build theoretically consistent intervention skills. In a remarkable display of relativism, generations of these students were told to pick a psychological "theory" to which their practice should conform. It did not matter so much which school of practice was selected as long as the resultant practice was "internally consistent" with the selected paradigm. Thomas Kuhn has been badly misapplied.

Kuhn (1970b) said scientific theories develop within a prevailing paradigm, and with the advent of a paradigm shift, previous theoretical understandings are rendered meaningless. Such a shift occurred when the Ptolemaic geocentric view of the universe was replaced with the Copernican view of a heliocentric solar system. With this new paradigm, previous observations recording erratic planetary movements from an Earth-centred perspective were reinterpreted. A theory is an explanatory model taking into account all observed data (or explaining away data that does not fit) within an existent paradigm governing assumptions about relationships. If no rational basis exists for choosing one over another, then paradigmatic choice would be based on one's personal values, beliefs, and desires. Thus, in chapter 2, we saw Gergen (1996) abandoning quantitative research into self-esteem in favour of a paradigm favouring communalism, interdependence, and participatory decision-making. Unfortunately for Gergen, there is no such paradigm to which he can retreat. According to Kuhn (1970a), psychology is a prescientific formulation, a protoscience that was yet to develop a disciplinary paradigm into which theoretical constructs may be placed. Preparadigmatic formulations are not mutually exclusive and may evolve, combine, and re-form in eclectic fashion before a central core of generally accepted principles becomes dominant. This would explain the multiplicity of formulations in the profession, really schools of thought that borrow from each other shamelessly while asserting their own uniqueness.

Using Kuhn's razor, that to be successful a paradigm must be compelling, efficient, and fruitful, Pat Duffy Hutcheon (1996) examined three preparadigmatic formulations in psychology: Freudianism (including Jung), genetic developmentalism (as represented by Piaget), and behaviourism. She declared that Freud failed on the grounds of economy and fruitfulness, genetic developmentalism lacked economy, and behaviourism was not believably compelling with respect to its implications of determinism "because it attacks the very roots of our cultural assumptions" (p. 461). She failed to consider a fourth formulation represented initially in the work of Alfred Adler with manifestations in cognitivist, humanistic, and neo-Freudian thought.

Chapter 2 demonstrated a convergence between the self-conceptualizations of James and Adler. The element of constancy that is part of the Jamesian subjective self is analogous to the Adlerian sense of self-stability. The Jamesian elements of volition and uniqueness are implied by the Adlerian supposition of the ability to self-change. The Adlerian suggestion that a functional self includes elements of pro-ductivity and intimacy could be reflected in the "activity" and "social" elements of the Jamesian objective self. Thus, the Adlerian and Jamesian models are not mutually exclusive, and may be viewed as the basis of an emergent understanding.

Adler, the therapist, sought to prove the internal unity of the individual to his clients. Once the client understood the consistency of his cognitions and feelings with an underlying belief system, then a challenging of that system could begin. This "indivisible totality" that is the individual led Adler to criticize his colleague Freud for being unduly reductionistic in the latter's formulation of id, ego, and super-ego. In the Adlerian perspective, the Freudian tripartite division of the self is, at best, a distraction from developing an understanding of the actual dynamic of a totality moving through time and space. Therapy, from this perspective, is more about assisting individuals to reach their potential than balancing unconscious forces and neurotic tendencies.

Adler viewed the self as a social construction beginning in childhood and accompanied by the development of a model of how the world operates. The self is a unified response within a constructed worldview. Dowd (1997) observed that the Adlerian concept of "world-view" is identical with the CBT concept of "core cognitive schemata" and the constructionist concept of "constructed reality." As Boeree (2006) noted, Adler's "striving for perfection" drive is similar to the modern concept of self-actualization common in humanistic thought. He suggested that neo-Freudians such as Rogers, Fromm, Sullivan, and Horney should have been called "neo-Adlerians" in that they adopted a teleological approach emphasizing personal choice. As we have seen, all of our participants reported developmental changes meant to improve themselves in some ways, supporting the notion of self-actualization. Some made reference to a "true self," which may be interpreted as a personal belief in a teleological drive.

The participants to this study displayed a tendency toward sta-bility in the self, with Magdelynn actively working to construct that stability during the course of the study. While a sense of constancy is necessary to be able to identify a self as one's own, that stability must be challenged in therapy. The case examples reported here showed how self-change may be promoted while assisting the client to

maintain an overall sense of continuity by picturing a mapped totality. What is sought is a dynamic stability capable of progressive
change as opposed to excessive fearful rigidity or its opposite, the
sense of not existing. Alder focused his change efforts on work, love
and, social interest; but my studies suggest a broader self-structure.

Humans have periodically subsumed their selves to the will of
religious or ideological collectivities. Maomao's rationale for such subjugation involved an avoidance of stress implied by the responsibility
for making good decisions. Others may be fundamentally unhappy
with who they are or with the limitations of selfhood. As previously
mentioned, the decision to subsume one's self could be taken to imply
the existence of sufficient free will to do so. If, however, the self is
socially constructed, then these "unwanted selves" were not the making of those who "possess" them, with the implication that any such
choice was predestined. Blackmore (1999) took an unequivocal stand:
"Each selfplex gives rise to ordinary human consciousness based on
the false idea that there is someone inside who is in charge. ... Free will,
like the self who 'has' it, is an illusion" (p. 236). Such a position supports
the behaviourist preparadigmatic formulation in psychology.

If genetics provides the hardware and memetics the software
governing our thoughts and perceptions according to heritable and
environmental programming, then we are but automata performing
our routines with after-the-fact rationalizations of personal choice.
Classical behaviourism failed to become the paradigm of psychology,
not because it was not effective, but because psychologists found the
notion of modifying the behaviours of automata distasteful. It is not
that cognitive psychology adds to the effectiveness of behavioural
therapy in dealing with clinically treatable conditions, but we value
our potential to exercise meaningful choice. The emergent dominant
thinking within the field values this human potential on both ethical
and selfish grounds. The denial of this potential in others is a denial
of the same potential in ourselves, with the result that psychologists
have a personal vested interest in the client authoring developmental
change. The paradigm presented here posits a recently evolved self-
understanding platformed on a biologically evolved organism capable
of contemplation. It is the reflective activity of contemplating the subjective that allows for meaningful choice.

A form of behaviourism is foundational to therapeutic practice.
Irrespective of the cognitions or emotions generated in session or perhaps because of them, the client is typically expected to exhibit new or

modified behaviours outside of therapy. Those behaviours that produce desired results will be reinforced by successful outcomes. The client may learn to create, with reflection, his own homework assignments, in effect self-reprogramming. In this paradigm, cognitions, emotions, behaviour, and even physiology are inseparably connected with change in one domain necessarily producing effects in others. Both Adlerians and cognitivists hold that beliefs driven by nonrational processes may be corrected through reflective thought coupled with new information. Constructivists believe that we create our selves while constructionists emphasize the social or societal role in self-creation, but the objective of both is to assist the client in this act of rational self-creation or re-creation. What emerges is a kind of Vygotskian duality: behavioural laws of cause, effect, and conditioned responses apply to ordinary, mundane material levels of existence, but we have the potential to become consciously aware of those effects and soar above them.

In chapter 4, I proposed an evolutionary process whereby the ability to contemplate the objective and subjective was a product of evolutionary change within a being that had already developed complex cultures through algorithmic processes. The ability to see oneself as an object is part of what we mean by the term "consciousness." Combining unconscious factors such as those that informed Freud and classical behaviourists with conscious factors emphasized in the cognitivist, positivist, and humanistic schools of psychotherapy results in a complex description of what it means to be human. As previously acknowledged, "If we take the view that human behaviour was, at least in the first instance, determined by biological and environmental forces, then the self that emerged subsequent to this materialist foundation would continue to reflect that foundation" (Robertson, 2017, pp. 4–5).

This explanation acknowledges that most of our behaviour is consistent with biological and environmental determinants, but it also allows for the practice of individual volitional choice. As with the practice of modern science, free will does not come naturally to humans and as Maomao discovered "it is hard work." We do not have free will as a given, but we can aspire to it as a potentiality to wit: We have the ability to recognize when we have begun a genetic or cultural script and to make a different choice. Without evidence demonstrating the impossibility of such a potentiality, the notion that there must have been some prior event causing each script change is a tautology and the secular equivalent to a statement of faith.

As we have seen, the concept of individual volition entails a being that is in some sense unique from others. Volitional planning requires an added feeling of constancy that the individual will be present in the planned-for future. Such planning requires making choices from possible behaviours while predicting results. It is precisely these qualities that therapists from all schools of psychotherapy attempt to teach their clients. The exercise of client free will in directing self-change is the primary goal of therapy, and this exercise is grounded in a vision of what it means to be human.

This conceptualization of free will explains both the success of classical behaviourism in therapy and psychology's overwhelming rejection of it. We remain, primarily, the determined beings that characterized most of our evolutionary history, but the idea of free will has become part of our self-definition as a species, and it has been the psychotherapist's project to help clients achieve this ideal.

Maomao illustrated a limitation of this conceptualization of free will: we are called upon to make decisions every day and do not have the time to adequately research and generate alternatives for each action. Yet, without such research, how is it possible to generate reasoned alternatives from which to decide? In Western societies, we may choose to be deferent to advertising, peer pressure, political or religious ideology, racial prejudice, or other heuristics that have the potential to limit our free will as much as deferring to our elders. A requirement that each decision be adequately researched for the purpose of generating alternatives is too strict a rule for determining the exercise of free will. The self, as it has evolved, is a reflective project. We have the capacity to review past patterns of behaviour and generate alternative scripts for implementation, in effect, reprogramming ourselves. This sounds like the project of psychotherapy.

The self was examined from five psychological perspectives: stable, neurological, behaviourist, constructivist, and constructionist. The subsequently prepared memetic self-maps are compatible with all five. Memes are tied to our neurological heritage but have an independent evolutionary dynamic. Units of culture, so created, formulate the selves of those within those cultures in a manner that is socially constructed, but the resultant entities have the capacity to recognize their own subjectivity. Such entities may then initiate developmental change, in accordance with the observations of social constructionists, but are concomitantly inhibited from doing so due to tendencies toward self-stability. Such stability may be explained as resulting from attractive forces between memes defined here as connotative, emotive, and behavioural associations. This introduces individual interpretive experience to memetic replication by allowing for individual expression of cognitive, connotative, and emotive meaning. In relating to past events and possible future change, clients situate their selves temporally with a fluidity that acknowledges process. This self-structure is compatible with a preparadigmatic formulation within psychology that recognizes the grounding of physical and environmental determinants while advancing our human potential as a conscious and cognitive species.

This volume began with the case study of a suicidal youth and a fortuitous intervention involving an ad hoc method of preparing a map of her self, and I returned to the theme of therapy in this final chapter. In the chapters between, the literature on the structure of the self, the nature of units of culture called memes, and a technique of mapping the self using a qualitative approach were discussed. I added a case study to the section on culturally inclusive counselling. The results confirmed and extended previous understandings of the self, and the trialed mapping technique proved to be compatible with a number of schools of psychology.

Although individuals from collectivist and individualist cultures participated in this research, it was not designed to study cross-cultural issues related to self-construction. While there may be a basic structure to the self, the importance placed on certain aspects of that structure and their relationship to other aspects of the self would be expected to vary between cultures. Memetic mapping may be used to further study how the selves in various cultures are constituted. As we have seen, the dichotomy between collectivist and individualist is simplistic as the self is constituted and maintained by social forces in all cultures. The study of cultural differences will include consideration of how such forces are accommodated, balanced, and interpreted.

Identification with a group or a cause affected some presentations. Fredelle admitted she wanted to use this study for the political purpose of bringing greater public understanding to the condition of transsexuality. While no other participant stated they wished to propagate a particular point of view, belief systems were presented. For example, Brent voiced a commitment to environmentalism and JohnB voiced support for Aboriginal Spirituality. We were not able to settle the question, in individual cases, whether actions to propagate what is perceived as knowledge or truths are an act of free will or the result of cultural programming, but our "fourth paradigmatic formulation" is compatible with either possibility. We should also consider the possibility that the propagation of strongly held beliefs may be necessary for self-validation and maintenance.

While all the participants to this study expressed an interest in making the world a better place for others, this result may be an example of selection bias. While not discounting evidence that altruism may be genetically programmed into our species, people who do not have this orientation would not be predisposed to volunteer for this kind of research. In any case, altruism and tendencies toward collectivism are linked.

We need to consider the variable of researcher effect. People have a need to build relationships. In ordinary discourse, the story-teller is building a relationship with the listener; therefore, the interaction between teller and listener needs to be assessed with the understanding that the story will necessarily change in some ways depending on the social objectives of the participants. When Maomao introduced me to her parents who were visiting from China, she was engaged in a social act. When Tina proudly showed off her newborn, she was extending a relationship. Pangloss admitted to attempting to convince the researcher of his negative qualities during our second interview but was motivated by wanting the researcher to like him during the third. If we tend to become the person we present to others, then we are the result of innumerable such negotiations since infancy. Yet, while most participants wanted to present an accurate picture of themselves, they were selectively using memories that are reconstructed routinely.

While researcher influence is a problem in theoretical research, relationship building is a necessary part of the therapeutic alliance. The act of self-map co-construction led to self-disclosure and decisions to engage in developmental change: important considerations for the practitioner. Practitioners may find it cumbersome to use the formal method of coding transcripts of nondirective interviews to create maps of the self as was done in chapter 5. In my practice, subsequent to this research, I have used the method first developed for work with the suicidal youth, modified to invite examples of common structural elements where those elements were not apparent in the initial exercise (see Robertson, 2016).

Participants from both collectivist and individualist cultures exhibited a similar structure of the self, and this included a feeling of constancy with antecedents dating back to childhood. Self-change occurred in histories of all of the participants, and they were able to detail environmental events that helped determine who they became. The initial proto-self was established in childhood and further change was evolutionary. Despite a feeling of constancy, different roles represented by memes or clusters of memes were enacted in differing contexts. Participants communicated their selves to others by means of a series of stories or narratives that, while linear in fashion, contained information about themselves which when assembled in map-form took on a nonlinear appearance.

A model of the self consistent with the approach used in this study suggests a cross-cultural construct grounded in genetic inheritance. The child is taught to have a self as part of the process of language acquisition by caregivers who initially interpretively supply the child with wishes, needs, intentions, and wants during their interactions. Thus, the self of the child begins as an other-determined construct. Later the child expands this self by incorporating cultural units from a menu of possibilities from his or her cultural environment, but since self-change is evolutionary, newly incorporated memes tend to be consistent with the previous self. The related need for a sense of self-constancy constrains self-determination even in adult selves. But we have the potential for more. Countering this conservative tendency is what Adler (1967) called a "striving for perfection," which involves becoming a recognized and competent person within one's cultural or sub-cultural group. Counsellors may appeal to that drive by inviting consideration of new possibilities.

Some of the properties of the self, such as the need for intimacy, are grounded in biology (Campbell & Ellis, 2005; Goleman, 2006), but other properties, such as the need for distinctness, may flow from the logic of having a self. If a person does not have a sense of being an individual, the locus signified by the indexical pronoun "I" will have been lost, and the person will be incapable of independent action. Which brings us full circle: The evolutionary advantage of having a self is to enhance human capacity to engage in purposive behaviour, and that is precisely the goal of counselling and therapy.

Notes

1 This stereotype of male emotional retardation can be connected memetically to stigmatization, as when Fredelle said in chapter 5 that

short-haired people are "mean and vicious." For a qualitative study into male stigmatization, see (Robertson, 2018).

2   This case was initially discussed in (Robertson, et al., 2015).

3   The client's county of origin maintained a list of Western films that were proscribed. This led to a "black market" for these films.

4   This case study was first discussed in (Robertson, 2016).

5   The list of churches approved to manage Indian Residential Schools was expanded to four in 1925 with the establishment of the United Church of Canada.

6   A more complete account of the history of this community and its community development can be found in (Robertson, 2015).

References

"Buddha." (1980). *The teachings of Buddha* (137th ed.). Tokyo: Bukkyo Dendo Kyokai.

Adler, A. (1927/1957). *Understanding human nature* (B. Wolfe, Trans.). New York: Fawcett.

———. (1967). *Superiority and social interest: A collection of later writings*. London: Roultlege and Keagan Paul.

Anderson, M. C., Ochsner, K. N., Kuhl, B., Cooper, J., Robertson, E., Gabrieli, S. W., Glover, G. H., & Gabrieli, J. D. (2004). Neural systems underlying the suppression of unwanted memories. *Science, 303*, 232–235.

Arthur, N. (2003). Preparing international students for re-entry transition. *Canadian Journal of Counselling Psychology, 37*(3), 173–185.

———. (2004). *Counselling international students*. New York: Plenum.

Arzy, S., Thut, G., Mohr, C., Michel, C. M., & Blanke, O. (2006). Neural basis of embodiment: Distinct contributions of temporoparietal junction and extrastriate body area. *Journal of Neuroscience, 26*(3), 8074–8081.

Atran, S. (2001). The trouble with memes: Inference versus imitation in cultural creation. *Human Nature, 12*(4), 351–381.

———. (2002). *In gods we trust: The evolutionary landscape of religion*. New York: Oxford University Press.

Bandura, A. (1999). A sociocognitive analysis of substance abuse: An agentic perspective. *Psychological Science, 10*(3), 214–217.

Bandura, A., Barbaranelli, C., Caprara, G. V., & Pastorelli, C. (2001). Self-efficacy beliefs as shapers of children's aspirations and career trajectories. *Child Psychology, 72*(1), 187–206.

Barman, J., Hebra, Y., & McCaskill, D. (1986). *Indian education in Canada: The legacy* (Vol. 1). Vancouver: University of British Columbia Press.

Bassett, D. S., & Bullmore, E. (2006). Small-world brain networks. *Neuroscience, 12*(6), 512–523.

Beike, D. R., & Crone, T. S. (2012). Autobiographical memory and personal meaning. In P. T. P. Wong (Ed.), *The human quest for meaning: Theories, research and applications* (2nd ed., pp. 315–334). New York: Routledge.

Bell, D. D. (2011). The bottomless pit becomes the arch-nemisis. *Ridged Valley Reflections*. Retrieved from http://justbetweentheridges.wordpress.com/2011/08/

Berry, J. W. (1999). Aboriginal cultural identity. *Canadian Journal of Native Studies, 19*(1), 1–36.

Bjorklund, D. F., & Blasi, C. H. (2005). Evolutionary developmental psychology. In D. M. Buss (Ed.), *The handbook of evolutionary psychology* (pp. 828–850). Hoboken, NJ: Wiley.

Blackmore, S. (1999). *The meme machine*. Oxford: Oxford University Press.

———. (2000). The power of memes. *Scientific American, 283*(4), 64–69.

———. (2002). There is no stream of consciousness. *Journal of Consciousness Studies, 9*(5/6), 17–28.

Bloomquist, M. L., & Schnell, S. V. (2002). Helping children with aggression and conduct problems: Best practices for intervention. New York: Guilford Press.

Blustein, D. L., & Noumair, A. (1996). Self and identity in career development: Implications for theory and practice. *Journal of Counseling & Development, 74*(5), 433–452.

Boeree, C. G. (2006). Personality theories. Retrieved from http://www.ship.edu/%7Ecgboeree/perscontents.html

Borghi, A. M., Scorolli, C., Calagiore, D., Baldassorre, G., & Tumolini, L. (2013). The embodied mind extended: Using words as social tools. *Frontiers in Psychology, 4*. doi: 10.3389/fpsyg.2013.00214

Boyd, R., & Richerson, P. J. (2000). Meme theory oversimplifies how culture changes. *Scientific American, 283*(4), 70–72.

Boyer, P., & Barrett, H. C. (2005). Domain specificity and intuitive ontology. In D. M. Buss (Ed.), *The handbook of evolutionary psychology* (pp. 96–118). Hoboken, NJ: Wiley.

Brasfield, C. R. (2001). Residential School Syndrome. *B.C. Medical Journal, 43*(2), 78–81.

Brave Heart, M. Y. H. (2003). The historical trauma response among natives and its relationship with substance abuse: A Lakota illustration. *Journal of Psychoactive Drugs, 35*(1), 7–13.

Bridges, W. (1980). *Transitions: Making sense of life's changes*. Reading, CA: Addison-Wesley.

———. (2001). *The way of transition: Embracing life's most difficult moments*. Cambridge, MA: Da Cappo.

Brodie, R. (1996). *Virus of the mind: The new science of the meme*. Carlsbad, CA: Hay House.

Buckman, R. (2000). *Can we be good without god? An exploration of behavior, belonging and the need to believe*. Toronto: Penguin Books.

Budd, J. W. (2004). Mind maps as classroom exercises. *Journal of Economic Education, 35*(1), 35–46.

Cahill, M., & Martland, S. (1996). Soft systems: Non-hierarchical evaluation of career counselling. *Guidance and Counselling, 2*(3), 15–19.

Campbell, L., & Ellis, B. J. (2005). Commitment, love, and mate retention. In D. M. Buss (Ed.), *The handbook of evolutionary psychology* (pp. 419–446). Hoboken, NJ: Wiley.

Caprara, G. V., Scabini, E., Barbaranelli, C., Pastorelli, C., Regalia, C., & Bandura, A. (1998). Impact of adolescents' perceived self-regulatory efficacy on familial communication and antisocial conduct. *European Psychologist, 3*(2), 125–132.

Cerqueira, C. T., Almeida, J. R. C., Sato, J. R., Gorenstein, C., Gentil, V., Leite, C. C., Busatto, G. F. (2010). Cognitive control associated with irritability induction: An autobiographical recall fMRI study. *Revista Brasileira de Psiquiatria, 32*(2), 109–118.

Chambless, D. L., & Goldstein, A. J. (1979). Behavioral Psychotherapy. In R. J. Corsini (Ed.), *Current Psychotherapies* (2nd ed., pp. 230–272). Itasca, IL: F. E. Peacock.

Charmaz, K. (1990). Discovering chronic illness: Using grounded theory. *Social Science and Medicine, 30*, 1161–1172.

Chiao, J. Y., Harada, T., Komeda, H., Li, Z., Mano, Y., Saito, D., Iidaka, T. (2009). Neural basis of individualistic and collectivistic views of self. *Human Brain Mapping, 30*(9), 2813–2820.

Chomsky, N. (2014). *The minimalist program.* Cambridge, MA: MIT Press.

Christopher, J. C., & Hickinbottom, S. (2008). Positive psychology, ethnocentrism, and the disguised ideology of individualism. *Theory & Psychology, 18*(5), 563–589.

Christopher, M. S., D'Souza, J. B., Peraza, J., & Dhaliwal, S. (2010). A test of the personality-culture clash hypothesis among college students in an individualistic and collectivistic culture. *International Journal of Culture and Mental Health, 3*(2), 107–116.

Connellan, J., Baron-Cohen, S., Wheelwright, S., Batki, A., & Ahluwalia, J. (2000). Sex differences in human neonatal social perception. *Infant Behavior and Development, 23*(1), 113–118.

Corey, M. S., & Corey, G. (2003). *Becoming a helper.* New York: Brooks/Cole.

Coyne, J. A. (1999, April). The self-centred meme. *Nature, 398*, 767–768.

Craik, F. I. M., Moroz, T. M., Moscovitch, M., Stuss, D. T., Winocur, G., Tulving, E., & Kapur, S., 1999, pp. 26–34. In search of the self: A positron emission tomography study. *Psychological Science, 10*(1).

Croezen, S., Avendano, M., Burdorf, A., & van Lenthe, F. J. (2015). Social Participation and Depression in Old Age: A Fixed-Effects Analysis in 10 European Countries. *American Journal of Epidemiology, 182*(2), 168–176.

Cross, S. E., & Gore, J. S. (2003). Cultural models of the self. In M. Leary & J. P. Tangney (Eds.), *Handbook of self and identity* (pp. 536–564). New York: Guilford Press.

Csikszentmihalyi, M. (1993). *The evolving self: A psychology for the third millennium*. New York: Harper Collins.

Cushman, P. (1995). *Constructing the self, constructing America: A cultural history of psychotherapy*. Cambridge, MA: Perseus.

Dahlsgaard, K., Peterson, C., & Seligman, M. E. (2005). Shared virtue: The convergence of valued human strengths across culture and history. *Review of general psychology, 9*(3), 203–213.

Damasio, A. (1999). *The feeling of what happens: Body and emotion in the making of consciousness*. New York: Harcourt.

Damon, W., & Hart, D. (1988). *Self-understanding in childhood and adolescence*. Cambridge: Cambridge University Press.

Davis, C. G., & Asliturk, E. (2011). Toward a positive psychology of coping with anticipated events. *Canadian Psychology, 52*(2), 101–110.

Dawkins, R. (1976). *The selfish gene*. Oxford: Oxford University Press.

———. (1982). *The extended phenotype: The gene as the unit of selection*. Oxford: W.H. Freeman.

———. (2006). *The god delusion*. New York: Houghton Mifflin.

De Man, A. F., & Gutierrez, B. I. (2002). The relationship between level of self-esteem and suicidal ideation with stability of self-esteem as moderator. *Canadian Journal of Behavioural Science, 34*(4), 235–238.

Denig, E. T. (1856/1961). *Five Indian Tribes of the Upper Missouri*. Norman: University of Oklahoma Press.

Dennett, D. C. (1991). *Consciousness explained*. Boston: Little, Brown.

———. (1995). *Darwin's dangerous idea: Evolution and the meanings of life*. New York: Simon and Schuster.

———. (1996). *Kinds of minds: Toward an understanding of consciousness*. New York: Harper Collins.

Descartes, R. (1643/1990). Meditations on the first philosophy and the principles of philosophy. In J. Pickering & M. Skinner (Eds.), *From sentience to symbols: Readings on consciousness* (pp. 10–20). Toronto: University of Toronto Press.

Devilly, G. J., & Spence, S. H. (1999). The relative efficacy and treatment distress of EMDR and a cognitive-behavior trauma treatment protocol in the amelioration of posttraumatic stress disorder. *Journal of Anxiety Disorders, 13*(1), 131–157.

DiCarlo, C. (2010). How problem solving and neurotransmission in the Upper Paleolithic led to the emergence and maintenance of memetic equilibrium in contemporary world religions. *Politics and Culture*. Retrieved from https://politicsandculture.org/2010/04/27/how-problem-solving-and-neurotransmission-in-the-upper-paleolithic-led-to-the-emergence-and-maintenance-of-memetic-equilibrium-in-contemporary-world-religions/

Doen, R. E. (1998). The king is dead; long live the king: Narrative therapy and practicing what we preach. *Journal of Family Process, 37*(3), 379–385.

Doherty, E. (1999). *The Jesus puzzle: Challenging the existence of an historical Jesus.* Ottawa, ON: Canadian Humanist Publications.

Dolan, C. A. (1995). A study of the mismatch between native students' counselling needs and available services. *Canadian Journal of Counselling, 29*(3), 234–243.

Donald, M. (2001). *A mind so rare: The evolution of human consciousness.* New York: Norton.

Dowd, E. T. (1997). A cognitive reaction: Adlerian psychology, cognitive (behavior) therapy, and constructivistic psychotherapy: Three approaches in search of a center. *Journal of Cognitive Psychotherapy, 11*(3), 215–219.

Duarte, C., Maurício, J., Pettitt, P. B., Souto, P., Trinkaus, E., van der Plicht, H., & Zilhão, J. (1999). The early Upper Paleolithic human skeleton from the Abrigo do Lagar Velho (Portugal) and modern human emergence in Iberia. *Proceedings of the National Academy of Sciences, 96*(13), 7604–7609.

Edwards, D. (1998). The relevant thing about her: Social identity categories in use. In C. Antaki & S. Widdicombe (Eds.), *Identities in talk* (pp. 15–33). London: Sage.

Ellis, A., & Harper, R. A. (1997). *A guide to rational living* (3rd ed.). Hollywood, CA: Wilshire.

Epstein, S. (1994). Integration of the cognitive and the psychodynamic unconscious. *American Psychologist, 49*(8), 709–724.

Fincham, F. D., & Beach, S. R. H. (2010). Of memes and marriage: Toward a positive relationship science Journal of Family Theory and Review, *2*(1), 4–24.

Foucault, M. (1982/1997). Technologies of the self (R. Hurley, Trans.). In P. Rabinow (Ed.), *Ethics: Subjectivity and truth* (Vol. 1, pp. 223–252). New York: New Press.

Foucault, M., Rabinow, P., & Dreyfus, H. (1983/1997). On the genealogy of ethics: An overview of work in progress. In P. Rabinow (Ed.), *Ethics: Subjectivity and truth* (Vol. 1, pp. 253–280). New York: New Press.

Freud, S. (1917). Mourning and melancholia. In J. Strachey (Ed.), *The standard edition of the complete psychological works of Sigmund Freud, volume XIV (1914–1916): On the history of the psycho-analytic movement, papers on metapsychology and other works* (pp. 237–258).

Fritz, G. K. (2007). Looking for evidence in evidenced-based medicine: Antidepressants and the risk of suicide. *Brown University Child & Adolescent Behavior Letter, 8.*

Fromm, E. (1969). *Escape from freedom* (24th ed.). New York: Avon Books.

Gabora, L. (2004). Ideas are not replicators but minds are. *Biology and Philosophy, 19*(1), 127–143.

Gazzaniga, M. S. (2000). Cerebral specialization and interhemispheric communication: Does the corpus callosum enable the human condition? *Brain, 137*(7), 1293–1326.

Gergen, K. J. (1996). Social psychology as social construction: The emerging vision. In C. McGerty & A. Haslam (Eds.), The message of social psychology: Perspectives on mind in society (pp. 113–128). Oxford: Blackwell.

Gerrity, E. T., & Solomon, S. D. (2002). The treatment of PTSD and related stress disorders: Current research and clinical knowledge. In A. J. Marsella, M. J. Friedman, E. T. Gerrity & R. M. Scurfield (Eds.), *Ethnocultural aspects of posttraumatic stress disorder: Issues, research, and cinical applications* (pp. 87–104). Washington, DC: American Psychological Association.

Gill, S. D. (1991). *Mother Earth: An American story.* Chicago: University of Chicago Press.

Gilley, B. (2017). The case for colonialism. *Third World Quarterly,* 1–17.

Godwin, D., Barry, R. L., & Marois, R. (2015). Breakdown of the brain's functional network modularity with awareness. *Proceedings of the National Academy of Sciences,112*(12), 3799–3804.

Goldhagen, D. J. (1996). *Hitler's willing executioners: Ordinary Germans and the holocaust.* New York: Alfred A. Knopf.

Goleman, D. (2006). *Social intelligence: The new science of human relationships.* New York: Bantam.

Gordon, S. (2001). *How can you tell if your really in love?* Avon, MA: Adams Media.

Gould, S. J. (1996). *The mismeasure of man* (Revised ed.). New York: Norton.

Greenfield, S. (1995). Journey to the centers of the mind. New York: W.H. Freeman.

Habermas, J. (2005). Habermas on Heidegger: Excerpts from Habermas' review from the Columbia University Press edition. *Heiddeger Reading Room.* Retrieved from http://evans-experientialism.freewebspace.com/habermasonheidy.htm

Harre, R. (1984). *Personal being: A theory for individual psychology.* Cambridge, MA: Harvard University Press.

———. (1991). The discursive production of selves. *Theory and Psychology, 1*(1), 51–63.

———. (1998). *The singular self: An introduction to the psychology of personhood.* London: Sage.

Hart, D., & Damon, W. (1985). Contrasts between understanding self and understanding others. In R. Leahy (Ed.), *The development of the self* (pp. 159–177). Orlando, FL US: Academic Press.

Hart, K. E., & Sasso, T. (2011). Mapping the contours of contemporary positive psychology. *Canadian Psychology, 52*(2), 82–92.

Harter, S. (2012). *The construction of the self: Developmental and sociocultural foundations.* New York: Guilford Press.

Hartman, A. (1995). Diagrammatic assessment of family relationships. *Families in Society: The Journal of Contemporary Social Services, 76*(2), 111–122.

Hawkins, S., Yudkin, D., Juan-Torres, M., & Dixon, T. (2018). Hidden tribes: A study of America's polarized landscape. New York: More in Common.

Heath, C., Bell, C., & Sternberg, E. (2001). Emotional selection in memes: The case of urban legends. Journal of Personality & Social Psychology, 81(6), 1028–1041.

Heaven, P. C. L., Simbayi, L., Stones, C., & Roux, A. L. (2000). Human values and social identities among samples of white and black South Africans. International Journal of Psychology, 35(1), 67–73.

Heidegger, M. (1962). Being and time (J. Macquarrie & E. Robinson, Trans. First English ed.). Malden, MA: Blackwell.

——. (2017). "Only a god can save us": The Spiegel interview (1966). in Heidegger (pp. 45–68). Abingdon, UK: Routledge.

Henson, H. K. (2002). Sex, drugs, and cults. An evolutionary psychology perspective on why and how cult memes get a drug-like hold on people, and what might be done to mitigate the effects. The Human Nature Review, 2, 343–355.

Hermans, H. J. M. (2003). The construction and reconstruction of dialogical self. Journal of Constructivist Psychology, 16(2), 89–130.

Hoffer, E. (1966/1951). True believer (First Perennial Library Edition ed.). New York: Harper & Row.

Hoffer, P. T. (1992). The concept of phylogenetic inheritance in Freud and Jung. Journal of the American Psychoanalytic Association, 40(2), 517–530.

Hofhuis, S., & Boudry, M. (2019). 'Viral'hunts? A cultural Darwinian analysis of witch persecutions. Cultural Science, 11(1), 13–29.

Hofstadter, D. (2007). I am a strange loop. New York: Basic Books.

Holland, J. L. (1997). Making vocational choices: A theory of vocational personalities and work environments (3rd ed.). Odessa, FL: Psychological Assessment Resources.

Holstein, J. A., & Gubrium, J. F. (2000). The self we live by: Narrative identity in a postmodern world. New York: Oxford University Press.

Hopper, J. (2003). The rhetoric of motives in divorce. In J. A. Holstein & J. F. Gubrium (Eds.), Inner lives and social worlds: Readings in social psychology (pp. 255–267). New York: Oxford University Press.

Howes, L., & Mazurk, K. (2006). Ethical Naturalism and Education: A Primer and Exploration. Gumanizacija Obrazovania 1, 81–100.

Hume, D. (1739/2010). A Treatise of Human Nature. Retrieved from http://www.gutenberg.org/files/4705/4705-h/4705-h.htm.

Hutcheon, P. D. (1996). Leaving the cave: Evolutionary naturalism in social-scientific thought. Waterloo, ON: Wilfred Laurier University Press.

——. (2001). The road to reason: Landmarks in the evolution of humanist thought. Ottawa, ON: Canadian Humanist Publications.

Ishiama, F. I. (1995). Culturally dislocated clients: Self-validation issues and cultural conflict issues and counselling implications. *Canadian Journal of Counselling, 29*(3), 262–275.

Jablonka, E., & Lamb, M. J. (2014). *Evolution in four dimensions: Genetic, epigenetic, behavioral, and symbolic variation in the history of life* (revised ed.). Cambridge, MA: MIT Press.

Jacob, E. J. (2001). Using counsellor training and collaborative programming strategies in working with international students. *Journal of Multicultural Counselling and Development, 29*(1), 73–91.

James, W. (1890). *The principles of psychology* (Vol. 1). London: Macmillan.

———. (1892/1999). The self. In R. F. Baumeister (Ed.), *The self in social psychology: Key readings in social psychology* (pp. 69–77). New York: Psychology Press.

———. (1892/2003). The me and the I. In J. A. Holstein & J. F. Gubrium (Eds.), *Inner lives and social worlds: Readings in social psychology* (pp. 121–122). New York: Oxford University Press.

Jaspers, K. (1951). *Way to Wisdom: An Introduction to Philosophy.* New Haven, CT: Yale University Press.

Jaynes, J. (1976). *The origins of consciousness in the breakdown of the bicameral mind.* Boston: Houghton Mifflin.

Johnson, D. M. (2003). *How history made mind: The cultural origins of objective thinking.* Chicago: Open Court Books.

Johnson, P. A. (2000). On Heidegger. Belmont, CA: Wadsworth Thomson Learning.

Johnson-Laird, P. N. (1988/1990). A computational analysis of consciousness. In J. Pickering & M. Skinner (Eds.), *From sentience to symbols: Readings in consciousness* (pp. 165–170). Toronto: University of Toronto Press.

Jopling, D. (2000). *Self knowledge and the self.* London: Routledge.

Joris, P. (1989). Heidegger, France, politics, the university. Pages Personelles de Michel Fingerhut. Retrieved from http://www.anti-rev.org/textes/Joris89a/

Jung, C. G. (1917/1972). Two essays on analytical psychology. In G. Adler & R. F. C. Hull (Eds.), *Collected works of C.G. Jung* (Bollington Series ed., Vol. 7). Princeton, NJ: Princeton University Press.

———. (1981). *The archetypes and the collective unconscious* (R. F. C. Hul, Trans., Vol. 9). Princeton, NJ: Princeton University Press.

Kabat-Zinn, J. (1994). *Wherever you go, there you are: Mindfulness meditation in everyday life.* New York: Hyperion.

Kamhi, A. G. (2008). A meme's-eye view of nonspeech oral-motor exercises. *Seminars in Speech and Language, 29*(4), 131–138.

Kang, S.-J., Mann, N., & Kawakami, K. (2006). *The effect of social inclusion and self-esteem on assimilation to social categories.* Paper presented at the Canadian Psychological Association Annual Conference, Calgary, AB.

Kariel, H. S. (1956). Democracy unlimited: Kurt Lewin's Field Theory. *The American Journal of Sociology, 62*(3), 280–289.

Keller, H. (1905). *The story of my life.* Boston: Houghton Mifflin.

Kim, H. S., Sherman, D. K., Sasaki, J. Y., Xu, J., Chu, T. Q., Ryu, C., Taylor, S. E. (2010). Culture, distress, and oxytocin receptor polymorphism (OXTR) interact to influence emotional support seeking. *Proceedings of the National Academy of Sciences, 107*(36), 15717–15721.

Koch, H. J. (1956). Sissiness and tomboyishness in relation to sibling characteristics. *Journal of Genetic Psychology, 88,* 231–244.

Koeda, M., Belin, P., Hama, T., Masuda, T., Matsuura, M., & Okubo, Y. (2013). Cross-cultural differences in the processing of non-verbal affective vocalizations by Japanese and Canadian listeners. *Frontiers in Psychology, 4.* doi: 10.3389/fpsyg.2013.00105

Korhonen, M.-L. (2002). *Inuit clients and the effective helper: An investigation of culturally sensitive counselling* (Doctoral thesis, University of Durham, Durham, UK).

Kuhn, T. S. (1970a). Reflections on my critics. In I. Lakatos & A. Musgrave (Eds.), *Criticism and the growth of knowledge* (pp. 231–278). London: Cambridge University Press.

———. (1970b). *The structure of scientific revolutions.* Chicago: University of Chicago Press.

Kulik, L. (2004). The impact of birth order on intergenerational transmission of attitudes from parents to adolescent sons: The Israeli case. *Journal of Youth & Adolescence, 33*(2), 149–157.

Kwee, M. G. T. (2012). Relational Buddhism: A psychological quest for meaning and sustainable happiness. In P. T. P. Wong (Ed.), *The human quest for meaning: Theories, research and applications* (2nd ed., pp. 249–273). New York: Routledge.

Kwiatkowska, A. (1990). Sense of personal continuity and distinctiveness from others in childhood. In L. Oppenheimer (Ed.), *The self-concept: European perspectives on its development, aspect, and applications* (pp. 63–74). Berlin: Springer-Verlag.

Leahy, R. L., & Shirk, S. R. (1985). Social cognition and the development of the self. In R. Leahy (Ed.), *The Development of the Self* (pp. 123–150). Orlando, FL: Academic Press.

Leary, M. (2004). *The curse of the self.* Oxford: Oxford University Press.

Leary, M., & Tangney, J. P. (2003). The self as an organizing construct in the behavioral and social sciences. In M. Leary & J. P. Tangney (Eds.), *Handbook of self and identity* (pp. 3–14). New York: Guilford Press.

Lent, R. W. (2004). Toward a unifying theoretical and practical perspective on well-being and psychosocial adjustment. *Journal of Counseling Psychology, 51*(4), 482–509.

LeVey, S., & Hamer, D. H. (1994). Evidence for a biological influence on male homosexuality. *Scientific American, 49,* 44–49.

Lewin, K. (1931). Environmental forces in child behavior and development. In C. Murchison (Ed.), *A handbook of child psychology* (pp. 94–127). Oxford: Clark University Press.

———. (1933). Vectors, cognitive processes, and Mr. Tolman's criticism. *Journal of General Psychology 8,* 319–345.

———. (1943). Defining the 'field at a given time.' *Psychological Review, 50*(3), 292–310.

Lewin, K., & Lippitt, R. (1938). An experimental approach to the study of autocracy and democracy: A preliminary note. *Sociometry, 1,* 292–300.

Li, C., Wang, S., Zhao, Y., Kong, F., & Li, J. (2016). The freedom to pursue happiness: Belief in free will predicts life satisfaction and positive affect among Chinese adolescents. *Frontiers in Psychology, 7.* doi: 10.3389/fpsyg.2016.02027

Libet, B. (1985). Unconscious cerebral initiative and the role of conscious will in voluntary action. *Behavioral & Brain Sciences, 8*(4), 529–566.

———. (1999). Do we have free will? *Journal of Consciousness Studies, 6*(8–9), 47–57.

Lock, A. (1981/1990). Universals in human conception. In J. Pickering & M. Skinner (Eds.), *From sentience to symbols: Readings on consciousness* (pp. 218–223). Toronto: University of Toronto Press.

Loftus, E., & Garry, M. (2004, May/June). I am Freud's brain. *Skeptical Inquirer, 28*(3), 16–18.

Loftus, E., & Ketcham, K. (1994). *The myth of repressed memory: False memories and allegations of sexual abuse.* New York: St. Martin's Press.

Logan, R. K. (2008). *The extended mind: The emergence of language, the human mind, and culture.* Toronto: University of Toronto Press.

Lycett, S. J. (2008). Acheulean variation and selection: does handaxe symmetry fit neutral expectations? *Journal of Archaeological Science, 35*(9), 2640–2648.

Mac, L. (2006). *A qualitative inquiry into the experiences of Chinese immigrant children in Canada: Adult reflections on childhoood experiences.* Paper presented at the Canadian Psychological Association Annual Conference, Calgary, AB.

Mahoney, M. J. (1991). *Human change processes: The scientific foundations of psychotherapy.* New York: Basic Books.

Marin, G., & Gamba, R. J. (2002). Acculturation and changes in cultural values. In K. M. Chun, P. B. Organista, & G. Marin (Eds.), *Acculturation: Advances in theory, measurement, and applied research* (pp. 83–94). Washington: American Psychological Association.

Marsden, P. (2001). Is suicide contagious? A case study in applied memetics. *Journal of Memetics.* Retrieved from http://cfpm.org/jom-emit/2001/vol5/marsden_p.html

Marx, K., & Engels, F. (1892/1975). *On religion*. Moscow: Progress Publishers.

Maslow, A. H. (1987). *Motivation and personality* (3rd ed.). New York: Harper & Row.

Mayer, J. D., & Salovey, P. (1997). What is emotional intelligence? In P. Salovey & D. J. Sluyter (Eds.), *Emotional development and emotional intelligence: Educational implications* (pp. 3–31). New York: Basic Books.

Mead, G. H. (1912/1990). The mechanisms of social consciousness. In J. Pickering & M. Skinner (Eds.), *From sentience to symbols: Readings on consciousness* (pp. 192–197). Toronto: University of Toronto Press.

———. (1934). *Mind, self and society*. Chicago: University of Chicago Press.

———. (1934/2003). The self. In J. A. Holstein & J. F. Gubrium (Eds.), *Inner lives and social worlds: Readings in social psychology* (pp. 125–130). New York: Oxford University Press.

Mehl-Madrona, L. (2003). *Coyote healing: Miracles in native medicine*. Rochester, VT: Bear & Co. .

Miles, M. B., & Huberman, A. M. (1994). *Qualitative data analysis: An expanded sourcebook* (2nd ed.). Thousand Oaks, CA: Sage.

Minsky, M. (2003). What comes after minds? In J. Brockman (Ed.), *The new humanists: Science at the edge* (pp. 197–213). New York: Sterling.

Miresco, M. J., & Kirmayer, L. J. (2006). The persistence of mind-brain dualism in psychiatric reasoning about clinical scenarios. *American Journal of Psychiatry, 163*(5), 913–918.

Mischel, W., & Morf, C. C. (2003). The self as a psycho-social dynamic processing system: A meta-perspective on a century of the self in psychology. In M. Leary & J. P. Tangney (Eds.), *Handbook of self and identity* (pp. 15–43). New York: Guilford Press.

Mitchum, N. T. (1989). Increasing self-esteem in Native-American children. *Elementary School Guidance and Counselling, 23*, 266–271.

Miyagawa, S., Berwick, R. C., & Okanoya, K. (2013). The emergence of hierarchical structure in human language. *Frontiers in Psychology, 4*. doi:10.3389/fpsyg.2013.00071

Montemayor, C., & Haladjian, H. H. (2017). Perception and cognition are largely independent, but still affect each other in systematic ways: Arguments from evolution and the consciousness-attention dissociation. *Frontiers in Psychology, 8*. doi:10.3389/fpsyg.2017.00040

Moody, R. (1999). Challenges and transformations: Counselling in a multicultural context. International Journal for the Advancement of Counselling, 21, 139–152.

Mueller, J. H. (2004). Research ethics: A tool for harassment in the academic workplace. In K. Westhues (Ed.), *Workplace mobbing in academe: Reports from 20 universities* (pp. 290–313). Lewiston, NY: Mellen Press.

Nishida, K. (1921/1990). *An inquiry into the good* (M. Abe & C. Ives, Trans.). New Haven, CT: Yale University Press.

Organista, P. B., Organista, K. C., & Kurasaki, K. (2002). The relationship between acculturation and ethnic minority mental health. In K. M. Chun, P. B. Organista, & G. Marin (Eds.), *Acculturation: Advances in theory, measurement, and applied research* (pp. 139–162). Washington, DC: American Psychological Association.

Oulanova, O., & Moodley, R. (2010). Navigating two worlds: Experiences of counsellors who integrate aboriginal traditional healing practices. *Canadian Journal of Counselling and Psychotherapy 44*(4), 346–362.

Packer, M. J. (1989). Tracing the hermeneutic circle: Articulating an ontical study of moral conflicts. In M. J. Packer & R. B. Addison (Eds.), *Entering the circle: Hermeneutic investigation in psychology* (pp. 95–117). New York: State University of New York.

Pagels, E. (1989). *The gnostic gospels.* New York: Vintage Books.

Patton, M. Q. (2002). *Qualitative research and evaluation methods* (3rd ed.). Thousand Oakes, CA: Sage.

Penfield, W. (1975/1990). The mystery of the mind. In J. Pickering & M. Skinner (Eds.), *From sentience to symbols: Readings on consciousness* (pp. 118–126). Toronto: University of Toronto Press.

Pickering, J., & Skinner, M. (1990). *From sentience to symbols: Readings in consciousness.* Toronto: University of Toronto Press.

Pinker, S. (1997). *How the mind works.* New York: Norton.

———. (2002). *The blank slate: The modern denial of human nature.* New York: Penguin.

Pluckrose, H., Lindsay, J. A., & Boghossian, P. (2018, October 2). Academic grievance studies and the corruption of scholarship. *Areo Magazine.*

Polkinghorn, D. E. (1995). Narrative configuration in qualitative analysis. *Qualitative Studies in Education, 8*(1), 5–23.

Ponterotto, J. G., Fuertes, J. N., & Chen, E. C. (2000). Models of multicultural counseling. In S. D. Brown & R. W. Lent (Eds.), *Handbook of counseling psychology* (3rd ed., pp. 639–669). New York: Wiley.

Poonwassie, A., & Charter, A. (2001). An aboriginal worldview of helping: Empowering approaches. *Canadian Journal of Counselling, 35*(1), 63–73.

Price, I. (1999). Steps toward the memetic self *Journal of Memetics—Evolutionary Models of Information Transmission, 3*(1), 75–80. Retrieved from http://cfpm.org/jom-emit/1999/vol3/price_if.html.

Racine, E. (2017). A proposal for a scientifically-informed and instrumentalist account of free will and voluntary action. *Frontiers in Psychology, 8.* doi: 10.3389/fpsyg.2017.00754

Radder, H., & Meynen, G. (2013). Does the brain"initiate" freely willed processes? A philosophy of science critique of Libet-type experiments and their interpretation. *Theory & Psychology, 23*(1), 3–21.

Ray, D. W. (2009). *The god virus: How religion infects our lives and culture.* Bonner Springs, US: IPC Press.

Rennie, D. L. (2000). Grounded theory methodology as methodical hermeneutics: Reconciling realism and relativism. *Theory and Personality, 10*(4), 481–502.

Richardson, F. C., & Fowers, B. J. (1997). Critical theory, postmodernism, and hermeneutics: Insights for critical psychology. In D. Fox & I. Prilleltenski (Eds.), Critical psychology: An introduction (pp. 265–283). London: Sage.

Richerson, P. J., & Boyd, R. (2005). *Not by genes alone: How culture transformed human evolution.* Chicago: University of Chicago Press.

Ridley, M. (2003). *Nature via nurture: Genes, experience, and what makes us human.* Toronto: Harper Collins.

Riel-Salvatore, J., Clark, G. A., Davidson, I., Noble, W., Derrico, F., Vanhaeren, M., Gargett, R. H., Hovers, E., Belfer Cohen, A., & Krantz, G. S.   (2001). Grave markers: Middle and Early Upper Paleolithic burials and the use of chronotypology in contemporary Paleolithic research. *Current Anthropology, 42*(4), 449–479.

Robertson, L. H. (2001). The new science of memes: Implications for counselling. *Guidelines: Journal of the Saskatchewan Guidance and Counselling Association, 35*(1), 16–20.

——. (2006). The residential school experience: Syndrome or historic trauma. Pimatisiwin: A Journal of Aboriginal and Indigenous Community Health, 4(1), 1–28.

——. (2007). Reflections on the use of spirituality to privilege religion in scientific discourse: Incorporating considerations of self. *Journal of Religion and Health, 46*(3), 449–461.

——. (2011a). An application of PLAR to the development of the aboriginal self: One college's experience. *International Review of Research in Open and Distance Learning, 12*(1), 96–108.

——. (2011b). Prior Learning Assessment and Recognition in aboriginal self (re) construction. *Pimatisiwin: A Journal of Aboriginal and Indigenous Community Health, 9*(2), 459–472.

——. (2011c). Self-mapping in treating suicide ideation: A case study. *Death Studies, 35*(3), 267–280.

——. (2014a). In search of the aboriginal self: Four individual perspectives. *Sage Open, 4*(2), 1–13.

——. (2014b). Native Spirituality: The making of a new religion. *Humanist Perspectives, 47*(1), 16–23.

——. 2015, pp. 317–332. The trauma of colonization: A psycho-historical analysis of one aboriginal community in the North American "North-West."*Interamerican Journal of Psychology, 49*(3), 317–332.

——. (2016). Self-mapping in counselling: Using memetic maps to enhance client reflectivity and therapeutic efficacy. *Canadian Journal of Counselling and Psychotherapy, 50*(3), 332–347.

———. (2017). Implications of a culturally evolved self for notions of free will. [Hypothesis and Theory]. *Frontiers in Psychology, 8.* doi: 10.3389/fpsyg.2017.01889

———. (2018). Male Stigma: Emotional and behavioral effects of a negative social identity on a group of Canadian men. *American Journal of Men's Health, 12*(4), 1118–1130.

Robertson, L. H., Holleran, K., & Samuels, M. (2015). Tailoring university counselling services to aboriginal and international students: Lessons from native and international student centres at a Canadian university. *Canadian Journal of Higher Education, 45*(1), 122–135.

Robertson, L. H., & McFadden, R. C. (2018). Graphing the Self: An application of graph theory to memetic self-mapping in psychotherapy. *International and Multidisciplinary Journal of Social Sciences, 7*(1), 34–58.

Robles-Diaz-de-Leon, L. F. (2003). *A memetic/participatory approach for changing social behavior and promoting environmental stewardship in Jalisco, Mexico.* (PhD dissertation, University of Maryland, College Park, MD).

Rodebaugh, T. L., & Chambless, D. L. (2004). Cognitive therapy for performance anxiety. *Journal of Clinical Psychology, 60*(8), 809–821.

Rosenberger, N. (1992). *Japanese sense of self.* New York: Cambridge University Press.

Rowe, B. (2012). Retrospective: Julian Jaynes and *The Origin of Consciousness in the Breakdown of the Bicameral Mind.* *The American Journal of Psychology, 125*(1), 95–112.

Rudestam, K. E., & Newton, R. R. (2001). *Surviving your dissertation: A comprehensive guide to content and process* (2nd ed.). Thousand Oakes, CA: Sage Publications.

Sanderson, J. (2010). Culture brings meaning to adult learning: A medicine wheel approach to program planning. *Pimatisiwin: A Journal of Aboriginal and Indigenous Community Health, 8*(1), 32–54.

Sasaki, J. Y., Kim, H. S., & Xu, J. (2011). Religion and well-being: The moderating role of culture and the oxytocin receptor (OXTR) gene. *Journal of Cross-Cultural Psychology, 42*(8), 1394–1405.

Savickas, M. L. (2001). Toward a comprehensive theory of career development: Dispositions, concerns, and narratives. In F. T. L. Leong & A. Barak (Eds.), *Contemporary models in vocational psychology: Volume in honor of Samuel H. Osipow* (pp. 295–320). Mahwah, NJ: Lawrence Erlbaum.

Schlossberg, N. K., Waters, E. B., & Goodman, J. (1995). *Counselling adults in transition: Linking practice with theory* (2nd ed.). New York: Springer.

Schurger, A., Sitt, J. D., & Dehaene, S. (2012). An accumulator model for spontaneous neural activity prior to self-initiated movement. *Proceedings of the National Academy of Sciences, 109*(42), 2904–2913.

Schwartz, J. M., & Begley, S. (2002). *The mind and the brain: Neuroplasticity and the power of mental force.* New York: Regan Books.

Seigel, J. (2005). *The idea of the self: Thought and experience in Western Europe since the seventeenth century.* Cambridge: Cambridge University Press.

Seligman, M. E., Steen, T. A., Park, N., & Peterson, C. (2005). Positive psychology progress: Empirical validation of interventions. *American Psychologist, 60*(5), 410–421.

Seta, C. E., Schmidt, S., & Bookhout, C. M. (2006). Social identity orientation and social role attributions: Explaining behavior through the lens of the self. *Self and Identity, 5*(4), 355–364.

Shepard, B., & Marshall, A. (1999). Possible selves mapping: Life-career exploration with young adolescents. *Canadian Journal of Counselling, 33*(1), 37–54.

Shi, Y., Frederiksen, C. H., & Muis, K. R. (2013). A cross-cultural study of self-regulated learning in a computer-supported collaborative learning environment. *Learning and Instruction, 23,* 52–59.

Shotter, J. (1997). The social construction of our inner selves. *Journal of Constructivist Psychology, 10*(1), 7–24.

Smollar, J., & Youniss, J. (1985). Adolescent self-concept development. In R. Leahy (Ed.), *The development of the self* (pp. 247–266). Orlando, FL: Academic Press.

Snow, D. A., & Anderson, L. (2003). Salvaging the self. In J. A. Holstein & J. F. Gubrium (Eds.), *Inner lives and social worlds: Readings in social psychology* (pp. 139–160). New York: Oxford University Press.

Sogyal-Rinpoche (1993). *The Tibetan book on living and dying.* New York: Harper Collins.

Stansbury, V. K., & Coll, K. M. (1998). Myers-Briggs attitude typology: The influence of birth order with other family variables. *Family Journal: Counseling & Therapy for Couples & Families, 6*(2), 116–122.

Strauch, B. (2005). *The primal teen: What the new discoveries about the teenage brain tell us about our kids.* New York: Doubleday.

Strong, T. (2000). Review of "The self we live by: Narrative identity in a postmodern world" by James A. Holstein & Jaber F. Gubrium. [Review]. *Gecko: The Journal of Deconstruction and Narrative Ideas in Therapeutic Practice, 3,* 81–85.

———. (2002). Collaborative 'expertise' after the discursive turn. *Journal of Psychotherapy Integration, 12*(2), 218–232.

Strong, T., & Sutherland, O. (2006). *Conversational ethics in therapeutic dialogue: Discursive considerations.* Paper presented at the Canadian Psychological Association Annual Conference, Calgary, AB.

Tang, M., Fouad, N. A., & Smith, P. L. (1999). Asian Americans' career choices: A path model to examine factors influencing their career choices. *Journal of Vocational Behavior, 54,* 142–157.

Tavakoli, M. (2013). Content and style of advice in Iran and Canada. *Canadian Journal of Counselling and Psychotherapy, 47*(2), 299–311. Retrieved from https://cjc-rcc.ucalgary.ca/article/download/60817/46157/

Taylor, C. (1989). *Sources of the self: The making of the modern identity.* Cambridge, MA: Harvard University Press.

Taylor, S. E. (1989). *Positive illusions: Creative self-deception and the healthy mind.* New York: Basic Books.

Torres, B. G. (1990). Development of self-descriptions in the context of play: A longitudinal study. In L. Oppenheimer (Ed.), *The self-concept: European perspectives on its development, aspects, and applications* (pp. 31–44). Berlin: Springer-Verlag.

Trimpey, J. (1996). *Rational recovery: The new cure for substance addiction.* New York: Pocket Books.

Uddin, L. Q., Davies, M. S., Scott, A. A., Zaidel, E., Bookheimer, S. Y., Iacoboni, M., & Dapretto, M. (2008). Neural Basis of Self and Other Representation in Autism: An fMRI Study of Self-Face Recognition. *PLoS One, 3*(10). doi:10.1371/journal.pone.0003526

van Uchelen, C. P., Davidson, S. F., Quressette, S., Brasfield, C. R., & Demarais, L. H. (1997). What makes us strong: Urban aboriginal perspectives on wellness and strength. *Canadian Journal of Community Mental Health, 16*(2), 37–50.

Vodde, R., & Giddings, M. M. (2000). The field system eco-map: A tool for conceptualizing practicum experiences. *Journal of Teaching in Social Work, 20*(3/4), 47–69.

Vygotsky, L. S. (1939). Thought and speech. *Psychiatry: Journal for the Study of Interpersonal Processes 2,* 29–54.

———. (1986). *Thought and Language* (A. Kozulin, Trans.). Cambridge, MA: MIT Press.

———. (2004). Imagination and creativity in childhood. *Journal of Russian & East European Psychology, 42*(1), 7–97.

Waldram, J. B. (2004). *Revenge of the Windigo: The construction of the mind and mental health of North American aboriginal peoples.* Toronto: University of Toronto Press.

———. (2014). Healing history? Aboriginal healing, historical trauma, and personal responsibility. *Transcultural psychiatry, 51*(3), 370–386.

Waldron, S. (2007). The significance of the emergence of language and symbol in the development of the young infant. *Journal of Religion and Health, 46*(1), 85–98.

Warwar, S., & Greenberg, L. S. (2000). Advances in theories of change and counselling. In S. D. Brown & R. W. Lent (Eds.), *Handbook of counselling psychology* (3rd ed., pp. 571–600). New York: Wiley.

Watkins, J. W. N. (1964). Hobbes. In M. Cranston (Ed.), *Western political philosophers* (pp. 45–52). London: The Bodley Head.

Watts, A. W. (1963). *The two hands of god: The myths of polarity.* New York: Braziller.

Watts, D. J., & Strogatz, S. H. (1998, June). Collective dynamics of 'small-world' networks. *Nature, 393,* 440–442.

Weeks, F. H. (2002). Behaviour problems in the classroom: A model for teachers to assist learners with unmet emotional needs. *Dissertation Abstracts International: Section A. Humanities & Social Sciences, 63*(1–A), 89.

Weng, L., Flammini, A., Vespignani, A., & Menczer, F. (2012). Competition among memes in a world with limited attention. *Scientific Reports, 2.* doi:10.1038/srep00335

Wertsch, J. V. (1988). *Vygotsky and the social formation of mind.* Cambridge, MA: Harvard University Press.

Whitam, F. L., Diamond, M., & Martin, J. (1993). Homosexual orientation in twins: A report on 61 pairs and three triplet sets. *Archives of Sexual Behavior, 21*(3), 187–206.

White, L. (1969/1990). Four stages in the evolution of minding. In J. Pickering & M. Skinner (Eds.), *From sentience to symbols: Readings on consciousness* (pp. 173–182). Toronto: University of Toronto Press.

Widdicombe, S. (1998). But you don't class yourself: The interactional management of category membership and non-membership. In C. Antaki & S. Widdicombe (Eds.), *Identities in talk* (pp. 52–70). London: Sage.

Wiedenfeld, S. A., Bandura, A., Levine, S., Oleary, A., Brown, S., & Raska, K. (1990). Impact of perceived self-efficacy in coping with stressors on components of the immune system. *Journal of Personality and Social Psychology, 59*(5), 1082–1094.

Wilcke, M. M. (2006). Reconstructing identity: The experience of women refugees from the former Yugoslavia. *Journal of Immigrant and Refugee Studies, 4*(2), 31–47.

Williams, C., Williams, S., & Appleton, K. (1997). Mind Maps: An aid to effective formulation. *Behavioural & Cognitive Psychotherapy, 25*(3), 261–267.

Wilson, E. O. (1999). *Consilience: The unity of knowledge.* New York: Vintage Books.

Witkiewitz, K., & Marlatt, G. A. (2004). Relapse prevention for alcohol and drug problems: That was Zen, this is Tao. *American Psychologist, 59*(4), 224–235.

Wolford, G., Miller, M. B., & Gazzaniga, M. S. (2000). The left hemisphere's role in hypothesis formation. *Journal of Neuroscience, 20*(RC 64), 1–4.

Woods, E. T. (2012). *The Anglican Church of Canada and the Indian residential schools: A meaning-centred analysis of the long road to apology.* (PhD thesis, London School of Economics and Political Science, London, UK).

Wortham, S. (2001). *Narratives in action: A strategy for research and analysis.* New York: Teachers College Press.

Wu, M. (2017). The process of self-cultivation and the mandala model of the self. [Hypothesis & Theory]. *Frontiers in Psychology, 8.* doi: 10.3389/fpsyg.2017.00024

Zimmerman, D. H. (1998). Identity, context and interaction. In C. Antaki & S. Widdicombe (Eds.), *Identities in talk* (pp. 87–106). London: Sage.

Index

Health and Society

Series editor: Sanni Yaya

Health occupies a central place in public debate, and the *Health and Society* series provides a space for dialogue on different fields of expertise (sociology, psychology, political science, biology, nutrition, medicine, nursing, human kinetics, and rehabilitation sciences), generating new insights into health matters from individual as well as global perspectives on population health. The principal domains explored in *Health and Society* are hospitals, communities, medicine, social policies, medico-sanitary institutions, and health systems.

Previous titles in the *Health and Society* collection

Sylvie Frigon, ed., *Dance: Confinement and Resilient Bodies/Danse : Enfermenent et corps résilients*, 2019.

Martin Rovers, Judith Malette, and Manal Guirguis-Younger, eds., *Touch in the Helping Professions: Research, Practice and Ethics*, 2018.

Serge Brochu, Natacha Brunelle, and Chantal Plourde, *Drugs and Crime: A Complex Relationship. Third revised and expanded edition*, 2018.

Marie Drolet, Pier Bouchard, and Jacinthe Savard, eds., *Accessibility and Active Offer: Health Care and Social Services in Linguistic Minority Communities*, 2017.

Marie Drolet, Pier Bouchard, and Jacinthe Savard, eds., *Accessibilité et offre active : Santé et services sociaux en contexte linguistique minoritaire*, 2017.

Isabelle Perreault and Marie Claude Thifault, eds., *Récits inachevés : Réflexions sur la recherche qualitative en sciences sociales*, 2016.

Mamadou Barry and Hachimi Sanni Yaya, *Financement de la santé et efficacité de l'aide international*, 2015.

For a complete list of the University of Ottawa Press titles, visit:
www.press.uOttawa.ca

Printed in August 2020
at Imprimerie Gauvin,
Gatineau (Quebec), Canada.

www.ingramcontent.com/pod-product-compliance
Lightning Source LLC
Chambersburg PA
CBHW051953270326
41929CB00015B/2638